Saving My Enemy is a true and profound story about war and the struggles of soldiers that follow. Bob Welch has unearthed history that transcends the battlefield and culminates in a story about peace, forgiveness, and humanity. Two soldiers—enemies in World War II—become friends late in life and, ultimately, pass their unlikely friendship on to future generations for safe-keeping. This is a rare story for our times—division becoming unity—and one so necessary in our deeply fractured America."

—**Tony Brooks**, author of *Leave No Man Behind*

"For those who wage war, armed conflict does not always vanish when the guns become silent. Veterans of World War II often concealed their emotional baggage of combat for decades. In *Saving My Enemy*, Bob Welch masterfully unveils a different battle fought by these aged warriors in their golden years: a reckoning with the past. Exploring the evocative themes of survival and guilt, Welch paints endearing portraits of two soldiers who mustered the inner strength to forgive their former foe. *Saving My Enemy* is a stirring tribute to the last of a generation."

—**Erik Dorr and Jared Frederick**, co-authors of *Hang Tough: The WWII Letters and Artifacts of Major Dick Winters* and *Fierce Valor: The True Story of Ronald Speirs and His Band of Brothers*

"This is an enthralling, epic book. Well-versed about war-triggered PTSD—having experienced it myself—I've never read a story about combat and its personal aftermath quite like *Saving My Enemy*. We veterans shoulder and suffer the war alone—with or without our families. But *Saving My Enemy* defines in living color how two soldiers overcame their moral injuries by connecting with each other. Reading this book will help veterans and their families suffer less, knowing there is a path of healing to follow—a trail broken by an American soldier and a German soldier, one-time enemies who became friends. As one who has seen the carnage of combat, I was inspired to read the rare war story with a happy ending."

—**Diane Carlson Evans**, Vietnam War combat nurse and author of *Healing Wounds*

"*Saving My Enemy* is a true and profound story about war and the struggles of soldiers that follow. Bob Welch has unearthed history that transcends the battlefield and culminates in a story about peace, forgiveness, and humanity. Two soldiers—enemies in World War II—become friends late in life and, ultimately, pass their unlikely friendship on to future generations for safekeeping. This is a rare story for our times—division becoming unity—and one so necessary in our deeply fractured America."

—**Tony Brooks**, author of *Leave No Man Behind*

"For those who wage war, armed conflict does not always vanish when the guns become silent. Veterans of World War II often concealed their emotional baggage of combat for decades. In *Saving My Enemy*, Bob Welch masterfully unveils a different battle fought by these aged warriors in their golden years: a reckoning with the past. Exploring the evocative themes of survival and guilt, Welch paints endearing portraits of two soldiers who mustered the inner strength to forgive their former foe. *Saving My Enemy* is a stirring tribute to the last of a generation."

—**Erik Dorr and Jared Frederick**, co-authors of *Hang Tough: The WWII Letters and Artifacts of Major Dick Winters* and *Fierce Valor: The True Story of Ronald Speirs and His Band of Brothers*

"This is an enthralling, epic book. Well-versed about war-triggered PTSD—having experienced it myself—I've never read a story about combat and its personal aftermath quite like *Saving My Enemy*. We veterans shoulder and suffer the war alone—with or without our families. But *Saving My Enemy* defines in living color how two soldiers overcame their moral injuries by connecting with each other. Reading this book will help veterans and their families suffer less, knowing there is a path of healing to follow—a trail broken by an American soldier and a German soldier, one-time enemies who became friends. As one who has seen the carnage of combat, I was inspired to read the rare war story with a happy ending."

—**Diane Carlson Evans**, Vietnam War combat nurse and author of *Healing Wounds*

Saving My Enemy

A TRUE "BAND OF BROTHERS" STORY

SAVING MY ENEMY

How Two WWII Soldiers Fought Against Each Other and Later Forged a Friendship That Saved Their Lives

BOB WELCH

Bestselling Co-Author with SGT. DON MALARKEY of *Easy Company Soldier*

REGNERY
HISTORY
Washington, D.C.

Regnery History™ is a trademark of Salem Communications Holding Corporation
Regnery® is a registered trademark of Salem Communications Holding Corporation

ISBN: 978-1-68451-033-7
eISBN: 978-1-68451-074-0
Library of Congress Control Number: 2020953034

Published in the United States by
Regnery History, an Imprint of
Regnery Publishing
A Division of Salem Media Group
Washington, D.C.
www.RegneryHistory.com

Manufactured in the United States of America

10 9 8 7 6 5 4 3 2 1

Books are available in quantity for promotional or premium use. For information on discounts and terms, please visit our website: www.Regnery.com.

In memory of my mother, Marolyn Welch Tarrant, who stood for peace and reconciliation and who thoroughly enjoyed getting to know Fritz's sons, Matthias and Volker, and Don's daughter, Marianne, during our back-deck interviews

The will of God, to which the law gives expression, is that men should defeat their enemies by loving them.

—Dietrich Bonhoeffer, *The Cost of Discipleship*[1]

Author's Note

I n 2007, in Salem, Oregon, I did more than a dozen interviews with Band of Brothers hero Don Malarkey, a paratrooper in the 101st Airborne's 506th Parachute Infantry Regiment, E Company. Then, together, we wrote his World War II memoir, *Easy Company Soldier*.

Not, of course, that Malarkey hadn't already enjoyed some notoriety. His unit had been richly chronicled in Stephen Ambrose's 1992 book *Band of Brothers* and in the Tom Hanks and Steven Spielberg–produced HBO series of the same name in 2001.

Malarkey was an extraordinary soldier, having served more consecutive time on the front lines—177 days—than any other member of Easy Company. At some point amid my interviewing him in a basement cluttered with World War II and 1940s Big Band memorabilia, Don mentioned befriending a German soldier after the war. Intent on making our fast-approaching deadline, I offered only a, "Huh, interesting," and nudged him back to the task at hand: his story during the war.

The book came out in 2008. Time passed. At ninety-six, Don became the oldest surviving member of Easy Company and then died on September 30, 2017.

Sixteen months later I got an email from his youngest daughter, Marianne McNally. Was I interested in writing a second book involving her father, a story about—wait for it—Don befriending a German soldier late in his life? And about how, afterward, she and her husband Dan had become close friends with the soldier's two sons?

I met with Marianne and Dan not expecting to say yes. I had enough on my literary plate. And, though the story was interesting, I wasn't convinced the subject could sustain an entire book.

I was wrong. Really wrong. The more I heard, the more I realized I should have listened to Don the first time around. As the author of a handful of books about men and women in war, I had never come across anything like this. I eagerly said yes to my second chance.

The story is true. It's based on interviews, eyewitness accounts, letters, documents, historical records, photos, film footage, books, and, above all, the spoken and written words of the two men who lived it: Don Malarkey and Fritz Engelbert. In the interest of giving as detailed and full an account as possible, some scenes and gaps in dialogue have been filled in based on what we know about the time, place, and circumstances—but always strictly maintaining the real-life context of the moment.

This, then, is Don and Fritz's true-life adventure: the rare war story with a happy ending. All because of a couple of former enemies who made the most of their own second chance.

Bob Welch
Eugene, Oregon
April 2020

CONTENTS

Prologue

It was three days before Christmas 1944, though most soldiers were too weary to notice the approaching holiday. World War II in Europe, now in its sixth year, clanked relentlessly on with the resolve of a German Panzer, grinding through whatever got in its way: Soldiers. Civilians. Christmas. Whatever it took to feed the beast.

U.S. Army nurses would be preparing wounded soldiers for surgery and realize they were back for seconds or thirds. American GIs chiseled foxholes from the iron-hard earth, sometimes using helmets for shovels and frozen enemy corpses for roofs. In Belgian villages beyond, Nazi soldiers huddled around Esbit stoves in hopes of reviving the feeling in their fingers.

"Surgical tents sagged under accumulations of snow, and the bellies of the wounded steamed when surgeons cut them open," Albert Cowdrey wrote in *Fighting for Life*.

That winter was one of Europe's coldest on record. The chill bored through the burlap bags in which some GIs had wrapped their boots. Nurses warmed plasma on the radiators of idling jeeps. In houses whose terrified occupants had fled, German *Landsers*—foot soldiers—chipped ice from frozen canteens and rifled through cupboards in search of any morsel of food.

Beyond the Ardennes Forest, evergreen trees to the east gave way to farmland, both blanketed in deep snow that, to the eyes of fighter pilots, softened the scene with Christmas-card serenity. Up close, however, the illusion was shattered like a mortar-shredded pine.

Machine gun fire chattered from village to village. Heavy-artillery shells flashed and thudded. Flames crackled from recently shelled houses, barns, and churches.

"The clouds turned red with the flames of burning farm buildings," wrote German general Heinz Kokott.

"Mama, Mama," a dying American soldier would cry, writhing in the snow.

"Mutter, Mutter," a dying German soldier would cry, entombed in a burning tank.

Desperate Belgian parents—faces iced with tears, fingers red with blood—clawed through rubble in search of missing children who would be found only in memories. Across whitened landscapes pocked with bodies and stained with blood, refugees pushed wooden carts of their belongings toward whatever future they could reach for with hands chilled by the cold of winter and souls numbed by the callousness of war.

Past such scenes on December 22, a German soldier brought his *Kettenkrad*—a motorcycle with tank-like tracks on the back—to a stop on a snow-packed road in Marvie. His name was Fritz Engelbert, and he was a messenger in the Panzer Lehr Division, Regiment 901, 5th Company.

Engelbert was nineteen years old and from the town of Hilchenbach, where his parents ran an inn, the Gasthaus Engelbert. The Gestapo was chagrined that the inn's guesthouse rooms did not feature pictures of Adolf Hitler, the Nazi Party leader and chancellor of Germany. Frankly, so was Engelbert. Nearly a decade in the Hitler Youth had fueled a hunger in him to become one of Hitler's elite Waffen-SS soldiers, but his father had refused to give his permission, so Fritz had had to settle for being part of the Wehrmacht—the regular army. In other words, he was an ordinary soldier—though an ordinary soldier who had just been invited into an extraordinary moment.

Engelbert headed to a dilapidated command post carved out of an abandoned farmhouse on the eastern fringe of Marvie, two miles southeast of Bastogne. As a *Gefreiter*—the lowest rank in the German army, equal to a U.S. Army private—Engelbert would not normally be privy to high-level information about Germany's war tactics. But he knew something that many German soldiers—even a few German officers—did not: English, or at least some. He had learned it, along with Spanish, at Höhere Handelsschule in Siegen, near his hometown.

Engelbert greeted the battalion commander, a major, with his most fervent "Heil, Hitler!"

Beyond a makeshift desk, the Wehrmacht major squinted, as if he was doubtful of Engelbert's capabilities or wanted to remind the boy that he was a servant in the king's palace.

"Stimmt es, dass Sie Englisch sprechen?"

"Jawohl, Herr Major!"

The commander handed Engelbert what appeared to be a letter, written in English. At the bottom it said, "The German Commander." No name. No signature.

There was, the major told Fritz, disagreement about whether one particular line of the document was correct English. He pointed to a sentence midway through the short letter: "There is only one possibility to save the encircled U.S.A. troops from total annihilation: that is the honorable surrender of the encircled town."

Bastogne, thought Engelbert. *We're demanding that the Americans surrender Bas—.*

"Ist das richtig?" asked the commander with urgency.

Was it correct? Engelbert felt his face flush. He tugged at his collar. Beyond the redundancy of "total annihilation," yes, it seemed correct to Engelbert. And he timidly told the major as much, thinking it would be splitting hairs to suggest that an army couldn't be partially annihilated. Like being pregnant, either the army was annihilated or it wasn't; no middle ground.

"Sind Sie sicher?"

Yes, he was sure, Engelbert said, a bit flustered by the major's impatience. The major nodded. Fritz was dismissed.

Seventy-five years hence, a classmate of Engelbert's from his *Volksschule* (elementary school) days said that his interaction with the major accurately reflected the boy she'd once known. He was reserved but smart. "Fritz never raised his hand to come forward during lessons," said Waltraud Menn, who, in 2020, at age ninety-six, still lived down the street from Gasthaus Engelbert. "But when the teacher asked him a question, he always had the correct answer. *Always.*"

Now, as the December day deepened, Engelbert crunched his knee-high boots through the snow and felt the oddest temptation to smile, something that had never come easily to him. *The Americans might surrender Bastogne? If so, could that lead to a German victory on the Western Front?* He remained stone-faced. He was, after all, a soldier—even if, as the war dragged on, he had begun wondering why he'd been so eager to become one. Less than a mile away, the snow was still a deep crimson where his company commander, Lieutenant Karl Neupert, had been killed the day before, his body shredded by shell splinters in an American mortar attack. Fritz's closest friend had died earlier in the month in France. Both men were right beside Fritz when they fell.

But the message now arriving at the front from General Heinrich von Lüttwitz—"the German commander"—suggested that such defeats were small aberrations in what would soon be a big victory. In less than a week of fighting, the Germans' Ardennes counteroffensive, the general believed, was on the verge of bringing the Americans to their knees. The *Vaterland* would be saved. And Germany, after winning what historians would remember as the "Battle of the Bulge," would continue its return to greatness.

German troops had the Americans virtually surrounded at Bastogne, with the 101st Airborne Division the proverbial "hole in the middle of the doughnut." In the 101st, in E Company of the 506th Parachute Infantry Regiment, was one Staff Sergeant Don Malarkey. Age twenty-three, he was from Astoria, Oregon, where his father had run an insurance agency before going belly-up—or, in Don's eyes, before the man had given up.

Malarkey was hunkered down in the snowy Bois Jacques—Jack's Woods—about five miles north of Fritz Engelbert's location in Marvie, bracing for the inevitable battles to come. And, meanwhile, shivering Don was quietly reciting the lines of his favorite poem, "Invictus," by William Ernest Henley: *It matters not how strait the gate, / How charged with punishments the scroll, / I am the master of my fate, / I am the captain of my soul.*

In Marvie, Fritz Engelbert watched as a group of four German soldiers climbed into a half-track, a hybrid vehicle that was part tank and part truck. The party consisted of two officers, a Major Wagner of the 47th Panzer Corps and Lieutenant Hellmuth Henke of the Panzer Lehr Operations Section, and two enlisted men from the same 901st Panzer Grenadier Regiment of which Fritz was part. Henke carried a briefcase.

Unlike the other *Landsers* who were watching, Engelbert knew the men's destination and their purpose.

"Er geht jetzt nach Bastogne, um ihre Kapitulation zu fordern," Engelbert whispered to a comrade.

Weary from war—Germany had been fighting since September 1939—the soldier's eyes widened. *Are you speaking the truth? Our commander is seeking the surrender of Bastogne from the Americans?*

"Ja."

The rumor spread through the 901st like a forest fire. The half-track headed for Bastogne. When the entourage returned later that day, however, Engelbert concluded from the dour looks on the men's faces that their mission had not been successful. And he was right. That evening, with a rare sliver of time on his hands, he wrote home to his folks, Fritz and Anna.

"Bastogne," he wrote, "is encircled. Today our negotiators went over there. Surrender has been declined. Tonight, Bastogne will be softened by heavy shelling. Tomorrow it will be taken.

"We are going through hard, hard days and are sustaining many casualties. The day before yesterday our company was hit during an attack in our vehicles. This morning the rest of our company got into a mortar attack. . . . Now there's just a handful of us left. . . . Believe me, all these days I've been invoking God, asking for help many times. . . . I'd like to come to an end now. I'm not in the mood for writing any more. The situation here is too turbulent."

On Christmas Eve, Fritz Engelbert and the rest of the men in 5th Company passed around a few bottles of wine in the cellar of a two-story stone house in Marvie that had otherwise been decapitated by mortars. The Germans had won back part of the village, but for the second straight day the Americans had attacked with everything they had; for the second straight day, the Germans had held them off. But the battle had taken its toll. Men were either dead, wounded, or completely exhausted.

Engelbert sat on the floor, his back against a wall upon which a Belgian family's photo listed badly at an angle. The cellar smelled of wet concrete, damp wool, cigarette smoke, sweaty men, and the gaseous remains of their dinnertime pea soup, atop which fat had been swimming.

"Engelbert!"

The voice was that of his new commander, Lieutenant Johannes Jähningen, who had replaced the now-dead Neupert.

"Bringen Sie diese nach Nachricht nach Lutrebois!"

An urgent message needed to get to Lutrebois, where another part of the 901st was hunkered down, about a mile to the south. Given the cellar's stench, Engelbert was more than happy to oblige. Any cold beat this. He took the dispatch case from the field officer, grabbed his rifle—a Karabiner 98 bolt-action—and walked outside. A *Kettenkrad* would have been faster with its linked metal tracks, but the Americans were only a few hundred meters to the west. *Stay quiet. Stay safe.*

Outside, the air was crisp, the temperature below zero degrees Celsius, though feeling even colder to Engelbert because of a slight wind. He caught a whiff of dead bodies that were piling up, the frozen earth only grudgingly giving way to the unit's gravediggers. A half-moon peeked from behind scattered clouds, illuminating fields of white and the occasional burned-out hulk of an abandoned tank. The skies had finally cleared enough for the German air force, the Luftwaffe, to fly, and Engelbert could hear the buzz of planes and the occasional thud of bombs being dropped on Bastogne. Otherwise, all was quiet.

He was enjoying the walk, enjoying the silence, enjoying the peace. Near Lutrebois, in a grove of spruce trees cloaked in white, he crossed a small stone bridge, the water beneath it hardened like stone. That's when he saw it: the body.

It was that of an American GI. It was glazed in ice and lying in the snow. A shiver shot down Engelbert's spine.

"I still remember this feeling, this trepidation in the chest, seeing this human being lying there, outstretched in the snow," he would say decades later.

He had seen men die right beside him; what made this different was the context, the quiet, the serenity of the moment. No ear-splitting mortars. No mad scramble to avoid becoming a victim. No responsibility to return fire or drag a man to safety or race from this house to that with a message. In battle, nobody had time to look at death. But now Engelbert had all the time in the world; it was just him and a dead American soldier.

He knelt and looked at the soldier more closely in the moonlight. The dead GI looked almost like a mannequin, though he was twisted in the snow, eyes barely visible beneath eyelashes and eyebrows veiled in frost. The scene filled Fritz with *Beklemmung*—a tightness in the chest, a constriction in the heart. Later, Fritz would remember two distinct thoughts from the incident: *First, that soldier could be me. It could be my parents who get the letter telling them that their son is dead. Would they miss me? Mother, yes. Father, perhaps, especially when he realized I wouldn't be taking over the inn so he could rest. And, second, this soldier, too, had a family who will miss him no less than my family would miss me. The color of the uniform did not matter.*

Alas, he reminded himself, he mustn't grow soft and sentimental. Even amid the quiet of Christmas Eve, it was his job—in a sense, his honor—to revel in the man's death.

He was, after all, the enemy.

On January 13, 1945, Don Malarkey crouched behind an outbuilding on the edge of the village of Foy, about five miles north from where Engelbert had been walking on Christmas Eve. After weeks of waiting, the Americans were forcing the issue. They attacked. After crossing a snow-covered field, Easy Company took cover on the edge of a farm. Malarkey tucked behind an outbuilding.

Ch-ch-ch-ch-ch-ch-ch-ch-ch-ch-ch-ch-ch-ch-ch-ch-ch-ch-ch-ch.

The German machine-gunner fired at the structure as if reminding them that Malarkey and his E Company buddies had been spotted and soon would be dead. Single shots pinged here and there from a flanked position, apparently from a sniper in a barn. Exhausted, Malarkey breathed heavily, the air fogging with each exhale. He and the corporal next to him had seen a German soldier in a hayloft opening, a prime position from which to pluck advancing GIs.

"He's mine," whispered Malarkey.

"Sarge, you're in charge of this outfit," the corporal said. "I'll take the shot."

Reluctantly, Malarkey nodded yes; it wasn't his preference, but—by the book—it was protocol. The corporal inched his head around the corner.

Pffft. A bullet pierced the man's throat, a mist of blood turning to crimson crystals in the sub-zero air. The corporal crumpled to the snow, dead before he landed. Blood pooled in his mouth.

Enough. Malarkey was at a breaking point, angry, cold, and tired. He'd been fighting for eight months since parachuting into Normandy on D-Day; the blackberries on the Nehalem River back in Oregon were slipping further and further away into whatever memory of home he still had left.

His weariness triggered a flash of nothing-to-lose bravado. He spun around the corner, spotted the German soldier partially shielded by the hayloft door, and opened fire with his Tommy gun. The sniper fell from his perch and splayed to the snow below. Malarkey moved forward, now shielded by the barn from other enemy fire.

There, at his feet, lay the body of the German soldier who'd died from Malarkey's marksmanship, sprawled awkwardly, belly up, torso twisted so his face was half-buried in the snow. Malarkey inched into the barn sideways.

"Anybody else in here need killing?" he yelled.

Except for the distant burst of machine-gun fire and scattered solo shots, all was quiet. For now, Malarkey was safe, hidden behind the barn. And until the other platoon took out the machine-gun nest, he couldn't advance. All he could do was wait out the skirmish. He took one last look around to make sure he was alone, then bent over the body of the soldier he'd just killed. Two or three bullets had bloodied the man's chest.

Malarkey had never touched an enemy soldier—until now. He gently pulled on a shoulder, which untwisted the torso and turned the head so that it was visible. Malarkey recoiled in shock. *Holy mother of God!* The face was not that of a man, but of a boy whose eyes stared beyond Malarkey to everywhere and nowhere.

Malarkey's stomach lurched. The kid couldn't have been more than seventeen years old, eighteen tops. Maybe Hitler Youth. Malarkey took a knee and fished out the young man's "soldier's record" from a pocket. *Oh, my God.* The kid was only sixteen, seven years younger than Don. He swallowed hard and, once again, looked around. All was still.

With the reverence of a priest celebrating Mass, Malarkey took his gloved hand and wiped away a splotch of snow clinging to the soldier's face. The boy's skin was smooth; he looked as if he hadn't even begun to shave. Malarkey carefully folded the boy's records and placed them back in the pocket from which he had taken them. He stepped back and rubbed his tired eyes with a hand. He remembered the time when, as a kid back in Astoria, quail-hunting with a BB gun, he had accidentally killed a robin—and how the guilt had burned in him like acid.

It sounded to Malarkey as if someone had silenced the machine-gunner outside the barn. The sound of small-arms fire snapped Malarkey back to the present, to the war, to the purpose he had embraced at Airborne camp in Georgia.

"All clear!" someone yelled.

Malarkey couldn't beat himself up over the incident, he realized. If he hadn't killed the kid, the kid could have killed him or one of Don's own buddies—or the whole blasted platoon. It was his job to kill the soldier, whether he was sixteen or sixty-five.

He was, after all, the enemy.

An American, Don Malarkey.

A German, Fritz Engelbert.

Two soldiers. One war. And neither of them with any idea that sixty years later, during a commemoration of what would become known as the Battle of the Bulge, they would meet each other in this same place. Only this time they wouldn't be trying to kill each other. They would be trying to save each other's lives.

PART I

YOUTH

Older men declare war. But it is youth that must fight and die.

—Herbert Hoover, 1944 Republican Convention speech

CHAPTER 1

Hitler Youth and Huckleberry Finn

Fritz

Fritz Engelbert was thirteen years old on the night when the family's butcher, Seligmann Hony, was dragged from his shop and nearly beaten to death for being a Jew. It was November 9, 1938. The incident happened less than two hundred yards from Gasthaus Engelbert, the inn that was frowned upon by Nazi party members because, among other things, its owner flew the old German flag, not the swastika, on national holidays.

At the sound of breaking glass, Fritz awakened in his bed, above which hung a poster of a blond-haired boy superimposed over a headshot of Adolf Hitler, the placard punctuated with large, bold words: *Jugend dient dem Führer* (Youth serves the Führer). He rushed to the window.

Though at sixty-five he was growing hard of hearing, Seligmann, too, was awakened by the sound, which came from his shop directly below the apartment in which he lived alone, his wife having died four years before. He cautiously crept downstairs to investigate. What he saw sent shards of fear through him: three Nazi stormtroopers, guns drawn, eyed him like rabid dogs, having stepped into his shop from the window they had obviously just shattered.

The trio stood in jackboots, brown shirts, and peaked caps stitched with an eagle above a skull, their left biceps wrapped in swastika armbands. Seligmann knew who they were: members of Hitler's paramilitary wing, the Sturmabteilung, men whose job was to suppress and terrorize Nazi opposition—and a major reason why his son, Kurt, his son's wife, Hilde, and the couple's four-year-old daughter, Alice, had already fled to America.

The Brownshirts smelled of liquor and looked pleased; the power and age imbalance were to their liking.

"Wir haben gehört, dass es Filet im Sonderangebot gab," said the leader while the other two muffled laughter.

No, Seligmann told them, there was no special tonight on tenderloin.

Apparently, they didn't appreciate his earnestness.

"Dann kommst du vielleicht besser mit uns!" the leader shouted.

What was going on here? Why must he go with them? What had he done wrong?

"Du wurdest als Jude geboren!" the leader said. It was as simple as that—because he had been born a Jew. The other two grabbed

Seligmann's arms and flung him forward through a jagged fin of glass that had survived the window's breaking. He stumbled onto the sidewalk and fell, his head bloodied by glass and cobblestones. The three spit on him, cursed and kicked him.

"Stinkender Jude!"

The lead stormtrooper put the barrel of his rifle to Seligmann's head to frighten him and remind him who was in charge. Then he twirled the rifle and rammed the butt plate into the man's nose for emphasis. Blood gushed.

At the sound of Seligmann's screams, Fritz opened his bedroom window. He could hear more than he could see: the laughter of soldiers, a man's groans, more glass breaking. Beyond Seligmann's place, he saw flames. Smelled smoke. Heard screams. *It was happening. It was actually happening!* He had heard the rumors a few days ago at his Home Meeting. But now it was obviously taking place.

Fritz Engelbert smiled ever so slightly.

Hilchenbach was home to only four other Jewish families at the time: the Honys, Sterns, Schäfers, and Holländers. All were paid similar visits during the pogrom that would become known as Kristallnacht ("Night of Broken Glass"). Seligmann would be one of thousands of Jews whose blood would be spilled in the streets that night.

Soldiers shouted. Civilians screamed. Windows shattered. Dogs barked. The bedlam seemed only to embolden the soldiers, fueled by hate, alcohol, and a license to destroy whomever or whatever got in their way. *Blam!* A dog barked no more.

Jewish men were crammed into the backs of trucks and taken to concentration camps. Synagogues were burned, homes vandalized, shops looted, schools ransacked, family fortunes stolen, women raped, and children traumatized.

Compared to some others, Seligmann was fortunate. He was being led to the back of a truck when Constable Schramm—not a Nazi—intervened.

"As Hilchenbach's constable, I am well aware of this man's misdeeds," he said, shooting Seligmann a knowing glance. "I will arrest him and see to it that this menace finds a home elsewhere."

The three Nazis looked at Schramm, then at each other. "Good riddance," the leader said. "For us, one less rat to dispose of." Soon after the Nazis left, the constable let Seligmann free; he knew and respected the butcher as a reputable part of the community.

Across Germany, in two days of rioting, more than 30,000 Jews were arrested and 236 killed—shot, beaten, or burned to death by Brownshirts carrying rocks, rifles, and grudges. Killed for the same reason the stormtroopers had given Seligmann: *Because you were born a Jew.*

The *New York Times* later editorialized that the nationwide riot had produced "scenes which no man can look upon without shame for the degradation of his species."

Fritz's reaction was different. When he was younger, Mr. Hony would often wink at him and slip him bite-size pieces of sausage. He had liked the man. But he was a child no more. He was now in his fourth year of Hitler Youth. Why would the Brownshirts—the very men whom

Fritz had been taught to honor, to emulate, to aspire to be—attack without justification?

In the last few years, as Fritz replaced his childish thinking with a growing understanding of the "new Germany," he had become a tad suspicious of the butcher and those like him. He had begun wondering if Seligmann was more foe than friend. Perhaps the scales in the meat shop had been rigged to Seligmann's advantage. Perhaps he was overcharging his customers. If Fritz's Hitler Youth leaders had said it once they had said it a million times: "Die Juden sind unser Unglück!"

And the teenaged Fritz Engelbert had begun to believe it. *The Jews were our misfortune.*

He had not always been so suspicious of others, but he had been born into a world—a place, a movement, a fear—that fed on suspicion. Just as a raging river sweeps away anything along its banks, so did this movement take the innocent and unsuspecting. As a little boy, Fritz Engelbert—like millions of others—was among those swept away by the Third Reich.

He had been born in Hilchenbach, a village of about six thousand people, seventy miles north of Frankfurt in central Germany. It sat on high rolling plains in the most heavily forested county in Germany. The town's roots dated to 1292; a thirteenth-century stone castle's keep—a refuge of last resort should the rest of the castle fall to an enemy—was still standing on the town's fringe. Over the centuries Hilchenbach had survived numerous wars, two major fires, and economic collapses, the latest a fallout from World War I. The biggest employer in town was the *Lederwerke*, which turned hides of cows and other animals into leather goods.

Through a child's eyes, the world in Hilchenbach was not so dark. Fritz kicked soccer balls, cross-country skied, and ate ice cream. But the culture of his home was stained by the past, which portended a storm for the future. World War I had ended only seven years before Fritz was born on May 10, 1925. Disabled veterans still wandered the streets regularly seeking handouts from Gasthaus Engelbert. More than a million orphans cried for dead or missing mothers and fathers. Half a million women had become widows. Such pain was twisted in a twine of shame; the world blamed Germany for starting World War I, and the Treaty of Versailles was making the country pay for its aggression.

Amid such darkness, people clung desperately to any sliver of hope—and many began finding it in an upstart Austrian-born leader named Adolf Hitler. When Anna Engelbert went into labor in May 1925, editors at the Franz Eher Nachfolger publishing company in Munich were preparing the final galleys for a book the house would release in two months. It was to be called *Mein Kampf* (My Struggle), and it had been dictated to Rudolf Hess in the Landsberg Prison by Hitler, who at the time was a fledgling political leader clawing his way to prominence in the far-right National Socialist German Workers' Party, or the Nazi Party.

Hitler had been imprisoned for high treason for his role in a Nazi Party uprising that came to be known as "the Beer Hall Putsch." In reaction to the German government's resuming payment of World War I reparations to Britain and France—an unwarranted burden on Germany, in the Nazis' view—the party was trying to seize the government by force.

Hitler hoped that a national uprising would mobilize the German army to bring down the government in Berlin.

The plan failed, and Hitler was jailed. When he was released 264 days later, the *New York Times* predicted that he would return to Austria and "retreat into private life." History remembers otherwise. *Mein Kampf*, in which Hitler blatantly said that Jews and "Bolsheviks" were inferior and threatening while "Aryans" and National Socialists were superior, would serve as his national calling card. The book sold poorly at first, but in 1933, by the time Fritz Engelbert was eight, it was a national bestseller. And Hitler had not retreated to Austria. Instead, despite losing the 1932 presidential election, he had bullied his way into power—President Paul von Hindenburg was so burdened by political pressure that, in January 1933, he had little choice but to appoint Hitler as chancellor of Germany.

Even before his rise to the top, he had launched Hitler Youth (Hitlerjugend, or HJ) in 1926, a year after Fritz had been born. The organization was similar to the United States' Boy Scouts and Girl Scouts, though with a decided twist of jingoism, Nazi indoctrination, racism, and, as the years passed, military fervor. Not, of course, that it was sold to children as such; it was promoted as an invitation to excitement, adventure, and personal and collective power.

"It gave [youth] hope, power, and the chance to make their voices heard," wrote Susan Campbell Bartoletti in her book *Hitler Youth*. "And for some, it provided the opportunity to rebel against parents, teachers, clergy, and other authority figures."

Fritz was all but predestined to be part of the organization, regardless of how his parents felt about it. He grew up as the only child of a loving mother and distant father—both much older than most first-time parents in 1920s Germany. When Fritz was born, his father, also "Fritz," was forty-four, and his mother, Anna, thirty-nine.

Fritz at age six with his father, Fritz Sr., and mother, Anna.
Courtesy of the Engelbert Family Collection

He was baptized and confirmed at St. Veit, a Protestant church—most Germans in the area were Protestants—less than a hundred yards from his house. He played games with buddies Heinrich Solms, Hans-Hermann Otto, and Günther Busch; tussled with Putz, the family cocker spaniel; and charmed guests at the family's inn with his sweet smile and blond hair. But Fritz's was a sheltered childhood, his imagination not taking him much beyond his tin soldiers.

Anna mothered him; Fritz disciplined him. The man, though not abusive, was strict, serious, and among the few wary of Hitler. His parents' expectations were high. Among those expectations? Fritz was to be seen and not heard. And he was to think for himself, an honorable notion at the time but, when the Nazis took power, one with a dark side his father had not anticipated.

From dawn to dusk, Gasthaus Engelbert pulled Fritz and Anna numerous ways; beyond guest rooms, their business included a restaurant, a grocery store, a petrol station, a scale for weighing trucks, and even supplies for farmers. As his parents served customers this way and that, Fritz essentially raised himself.

In the 1930s, most Hilchenbach residents were poor. World War I had splintered Germany's economy; only a steady flow of American dollars was keeping the country afloat. But when the U.S. stock market crashed on October 29, 1929, a wave of devastation swept across Germany like an aftershock. In 1933, poverty and unemployment in Germany reached all-time highs.

The Engelberts fared better than most. Fritz Engelbert Sr.'s decision to offer an array of services and products meant that despite small profits on each, the end-of-the-day receipts were substantial. The three-story Tudor inn had been built in 1689 and purchased by Fritz's father around 1880. Fritz Sr. had been born there, and so had his son.

Like virtually all of the structures in Hilchenbach, it featured steep roofs to more easily shed snow. Its white base was accented with brown decorative half-timbering, giving it a Bavarian look. The ground floor was the lobby, restaurant, and kitchen; the second floor—called the first floor in Europe—was where the guests stayed; and the third floor where the Engelberts lived.

The inn was located in the center of the village, its front door opening to a cobbled commons that was popular for makeshift markets and fairs.

In spring and fall, oak, beech, and birch trees added inviting dashes of color to the town; in the spring, snowmelt raised the level of Ferndorf Creek, a tributary to the river Sieg that ran through the town of Siegen and into the Rhine.

Fritz took his studies seriously, did well in school, and tried—with limited success—to learn the violin. He was quiet. Well-behaved. Organized. Easy-going. Lovable. In a forest of animals, a relative once said, he'd be the koala bear. Not particularly threatening. And yet as he grew, the Hitler Youth toughened his soft nature, twisting his more innocent bent.

Some saw Fritz as one of those children who was just "born old." Not that he didn't embrace the innocence of youth when the opportunity arose. In particular, he loved to run, loved what was known then as "athletics." When Fritz was seven, Germany beat only one of ten nations competing in the 1932 Olympics in Los Angeles, winning three gold medals to the United States' forty-one. Hitler seethed.

Still smarting from the defeat of World War I and from what the Nazis saw as unnecessarily harsh reparations demanded of the country after the war, many Germans had grown bitter about the country's falling from a world power to a world laughingstock; Hitler saw that as an opportunity.

He plotted how he could gain power, how the Nazis could gain power, and how together they could *Deutschland wieder großartig machen* ("make Germany great again"). He reached out to a Germany battered first by war and then by the Great Depression, a Germany only too eager to follow someone somewhere for some illusive gain. He promised turnaround and triumph. He connived and lied. He blackmailed men who were above him and who obstructed his rise to the top. At times, he even killed—or at least had his henchmen kill for him. And within a decade of being released from prison, in 1933 Adolf Hitler became Germany's new chancellor. The Third Reich had arrived, its new beginning soon announced by the sound of soldiers' hobnailed boots as they goose-stepped—*click, click, click*—in vast courtyards for newsreels to be seen around the world.

To further his cause, the new German leader turned to unlikely allies: millions of young people. "I am beginning with the young," Hitler said in 1933. "We older ones are used up. . . . We are rotten to the marrow. We have no unrestrained instincts left. We are cowardly and sentimental. We are bearing the burden of a humiliating past and have in our blood the dull recollection of serfdom and servility. But my magnificent youngsters! Are there finer ones anywhere in the world? Look at these young men and boys! What material! With them I can make a new world."

Fritz Engelbert Jr. was among those "magnificent youngsters." Initiation ceremonies for Hitler Youth were always held on the Führer's birthday. On April 20, 1935, Fritz was sworn into the Jungvolk (Junior Hitler Youth). "In the presence of this blood banner which represents our Führer, I swear to devote all my energies and my strength to the savior of our country, Adolf Hitler," he pledged. "I am willing and ready to give up my life for him, so help me God."

Before the weekly meetings, Fritz would stand proudly in front of the mirror making sure he looked sharp: brown shirt, dark shorts, black swastika arm band. He took his involvement seriously; from day one he had been told that he could help Germany rise from the ashes.

"As kids we were raised to believe that, since the end of World War I in 1918, Germany was surrounded by enemies, all of which were more powerful than us," said Fritz, looking back on his childhood. "Under this impression, the rearmament after 1933 was not only accepted, but also welcomed throughout the country."

Hitler Youth joined SA stormtroopers in a night of book-burning, a warning to the population that a new world order was in place. (Disney movies would be banned in 1941.) One's allegiance could no longer be to those who promoted inane ideas; one must be loyal only to Hitler and the New Germany. Not to God. Not to family. And certainly not to freedom.

By now, half of all German children ages ten to eighteen were part of Hitler Youth or the female equivalent, Bund Deutscher Mädels (the League of German Girls, or BDM). In July 1935, *Time* magazine reported that nine million "apple-cheeked, wondering children" had participated in summer solstice festivals through Hitler Youth, at which they were told by Hermann Göring that Adolf Hitler was performing God's miracles. Later, students in Germany would be required to read material such as the essay "Comradeship" by Hans Wolf, which described Hitler Youth campouts as a time of "wonderfully thrilling stories" and "communing with nature."

"Our youth shall learn nothing but to think German and to act German," Hitler said in 1938, the year Fritz was inspired by the sound of broken glass on Kristallnacht. "A young boy or girl enters in our organizations at age ten, then they move from the Jungvolk to Hitler Youth four years later, and we will keep them there for another four years . . . and then put them into the party or the Labor Front, the Assault Division, or the SS. . . . And if there is still a bit of class consciousness and elitist thinking left in them, they will receive further treatment from the armed forces."

Don

Donnie Malarkey was thirteen years old on the night when he and his buddies decided it would be fun to roll an old tire from the lower reaches of Coxcomb Hill right through downtown Astoria, Oregon, and into the Columbia River. Seven blocks.

It was 1934, Halloween night, which in Malarkey's mischievous mind imbued the undertaking with a sense of boys-will-be-boys privilege, as if the expectation of juvenile mayhem lent a certain license to the deed.

"I wasn't a hell-raiser," he said, looking back decades after the incident. "I just did the Halloween-kid stuff."

And, frankly, he had grown tired of such juvenile pranks as tipping over garbage cans and smashing pumpkins. The tire roll was a prank for the ages. It was late; the streets were virtually empty. Of the three boys, one was stationed up top, at the intersection of Fourteenth Street and Jerome Avenue, only a few blocks from where Donnie's family lived. Donnie and the other boy were down below, between Astor Street and the wharf, near the ferry terminal.

The plan was set: to alert the tire-roller up top, Donnie would give five quick blinks from his flashlight to signal the coast was clear—no trains, no cars, no people. A steady light meant wait.

Below, Donnie and his pal gave a final visual sweep. It was time. Donnie clicked the five-flash signal. In a few moments they heard the tire. *Closer. Closer. Closer.* As it neared Astor Street, Donnie watched the tire rolling gloriously down Fourteenth beneath the streetlamps, like a bowling ball splitting the lane. Toward the end it veered off the road slightly, slammed into the Astoria & Columbia River Railway tracks, bounded high, and bounced like a basketball toward the pier. Then, as Donnie's eyes widened, it hit a railroad tie on the dock, soared into the air like a Nordic ski-jumper, and made a scintillating splash into an empty slip. *Puh-chooooo!*

He thrust a fist in the air and whooped. "Hip-hip hooray," he yelled, "for the Coxcomb Hooligans!"

Some neighbors of the Malarkeys were keeping a watchful eye on "the little troublemaker." But Michael Noland, the bewhiskered maritime pilot who lived next door, found him harmless enough; he believed Donnie just had a "sense of adventure." Flask at his side, Noland would sit on his front porch with the boy and regale him with stories of guiding ships in from the Pacific Ocean across the Columbia River sandbar, one of the world's most dangerous.

"Donnie, at times them waves'd be three stories high," he would say. "See that telephone pole? Them white horses'd snap that like a toothpick." Eyes wide, Donnie glanced at the pole. "There's a reason," said Noland, "they call it the 'Graveyard of the Pacific.'"

"Sounds scary," said Donnie. "Why do you do that, Mr. Noland?"

"It's the adventure, lad. It's wondering what's behind the next wave— and the one beyond that, and on and on."

Don, right, at age eleven with his
father, Leo, in the back and his
brothers John, left, and Bob, middle.
*Courtesy of the Malarkey Family
Collection*

In contrast to Michael Noland, some people regarded Donnie with
a touch of suspicion. The issues? Mischief in general and marbles in particular. Donnie was such a good player that the kids in the neighborhood
would routinely lose most of their marbles—and their allowances—to
the kid who lived on Kensington Avenue.

"You, Malarkey boy, come here!" one of their mothers demanded
one Saturday morning. He just laughed and gave back the marbles he
had won from the woman's little boy. Born July 31, 1921, Donnie was
just a kid living large in a town where everything was large: timber,
bodies of water, raindrops—even its history bulged with significance.
Within view of the Malarkey house near the top of Coxcomb Hill, the

largest river in the Western Hemisphere, the Columbia, separating Oregon from Washington State, emptied into the largest ocean in the world, the Pacific.

In the wet Pacific Northwest, Astoria was among the wettest places; years with seventy inches of rain weren't uncommon. Donnie endured nearly a dozen ear infections as a boy, something his mother blamed on Astoria's dank winters. Astoria had been the last stop on Lewis and Clark's exploratory trip west in 1804–1806, and it wasn't Indians they complained about, but the incessant rain. "Some rain all day at intervals," reads one journal entry. "We are all wet and disagreeable."

As the first American settlement west of the Rockies, Astoria had its pockets of wealthy residents who lived in the Victorian houses on Coxcomb Hill's higher perches: the timber barons, the owners of the fish canneries, the doctors and lawyers and their families. But for the most part it was a blue-collar town, a fish-and-timber place that smelled of canneries and lumber mills. A place where, above the wharf, the town's ambiance was as brackish as the salty air: bars, brothels, and brawls. From the river, an occasional blast from an incoming or outgoing ship punctuated the usual sounds of jitterbug music from the bars, seagull cries from the sky, and, of course, rain from the clouds pattering on roofs— and, when the wind was howling, on windows.

The west part of town was home to Finns, the east to Danes, Swedes, and Norwegians. The area in between was thick with Irish, including the Malarkeys. For most of the year the family lived in a mid-sized bungalow whose chimney—in the center, not at one side of the house—vaguely resembled a lighthouse. During the summer, however, they spent a lot of time in a ramshackle cabin on the Nehalem River, about thirty-five miles southeast of Astoria in the Coast Range.

The Nehalem was Donnie's dream world. He lived a sort of Huckleberry Finn life, particularly in the summer on the river. He loved the land, loved the water, loved the freedom that came with both. The Northwest was rich in Indian lore, and when Louie Jacobson—half Native American—took Donnie under his wing, the boy relished the lessons he learned. Jacobson taught him to shoot a yew-wood bow and arrow, to trap small animals, and to catch crawdads. People joked that Louie was half-Indian—and Donnie full-blooded.

He explored the river in an old rowboat, fished for sea-run cutthroats, picked wild blackberries, and camped on the riverbanks. No schedule. No responsibilities. Nobody to answer to—least of all his father, whose insurance business capsized in the Depression and who, if not lost at sea, was beaten and battered trying to stay afloat. His father was "never the same," Don Malarkey remembered as an adult. "Just went numb."

Books deepened Donnie's sense of adventure; like Mr. Noland, he began wondering what was beyond the next wave. When the rains came in November, he would curl up with Roy Rockwood's Bomba the Jungle Boy series. Inspired by Bomba's living-off-the-land spirit, he adopted a swath of alder saplings at Fifteenth and Madison as his own private jungle. He would climb to a treetop, grab a branch, start swinging it, then use the "whip" to send him to the next tree, where he repeated the process. He could go an entire block without touching the ground.

If Bomba inspired Donnie to climb up, his own imagination inspired him to jump down. In the early 1930s, when the U.S. Army was only

beginning to experiment with the idea of parachuting men out of airplanes, Donnie climbed to the roof of the Malarkeys' two-story house.
He popped open a beach umbrella and eased himself to the roof's edge.
As if he were the Statue of Liberty holding her torch, he thrust the
umbrella skyward.

    And jumped.

CHAPTER 2

Dueling Loyalties

Fritz

As Fritz Engelbert segued from boy to man, he imagined himself as an attorney. Fritz idolized his Uncle Fritz Pinkerneil, who was a lawyer, and he deemed the legal profession—or any other profession—preferable to taking over the family inn. Alas, there was little encouragement for such a dream in 1930s Germany. His father made it known that his son was to grow up and run the family business. On a broader scale, the country, the *Volk*, the national pride—these were the things that young boys were to hold dear; individual dreams were selfish distractions from a greater cause: Germany. The *Vaterland*.

"He alone who owns the youth gains the future," Hitler said at the annual Nazi Party rally in 1935.

Though some refused to follow, the Nazi Party became enmeshed in German culture, initially gaining popularity by positioning itself against Communists, churches, labor unions, and the press. (Anti-Semitism would become a point of emphasis later.) One German elementary school primer from the 1930s shows a drawing of snowball-throwing children. In the background, as if gleefully watching, is a snowman wearing a tin hat—flanked by a fort from which proudly flies a Nazi flag.

Children would make construction-paper cutouts of the Führer in honor of his birthday. They swapped Hitler Youth trading cards and listened to the radio on Sundays as he offered inspiration.

Despite his father's distaste for Hitler, Fritz, like most boys his age, responded with gusto. He was officially part of the Jungvolk and would be eligible for the Hitler Youth at age fourteen. His father, a member of the Social Democratic Party, was wary of Hitler and worried that his son—and the sons of parents all across Germany—was being indoctrinated with racism and groomed for war. Not that he could do much about it; refusing to allow your child to join would invite all sorts of pushback, from neighbors who might shun you to potential customers who might find other places to spend the night, eat their goulash, or buy their petrol. The pressure on parents to conform to Nazi standards was intense; failure to register a ten-year-old child for Hitler Youth could result in a fine or imprisonment.

But Fritz wasn't motivated by fear. He was an enthusiastic participant; his father's resistance to Hitler Youth seemed to him typical of a generation mired in the defeatism of World War I. What's more, peer pressure was intense; virtually all Fritz's friends attended the weekly meetings, the regional leadership rallies, and even the annual Nazi Party rally in Nuremberg. Why would he want to be any different?

"You should serve a community," stressed the Hitler Youth appeals, "live a life of comradeship, be harder and ready to fight, carry the will within to greater deeds."

To that end the young people distributed leaflets promoting the Nazi Party, campaigned for Nazis running for office, harassed Jews, disrupted teachers' meetings at schools that weren't flying the Nazi flag, and played trumpets loudly outside churches to disrupt services. Some even gave their lives for the cause. Between 1926 and 1932, fourteen Hitler Youths, including a seventeen-year-old girl, were killed in street fights, most incidents involving Communist youth who saw them as a threat.

Germans, particularly the young, were drawn to Hitler in a powerful and mysterious way. In January 1933, along the route of Hitler's inaugural parade after he'd been appointed German chancellor, Berlin police struggled to hold back crowds that had bulged to two-dozen deep. Radios broadcast the parade to nearly every German city. Parents held small children in the air gleefully waving Nazi flags.

"I longed to hurl myself into this current," Melita Maschmann, who was a teenager at the time, would say. "I wanted to belong to these people for whom it was a matter of life and death."

Germany hosted the Summer Olympic Games in 1936, and its unimpressive performance in Los Angeles four years earlier was quickly forgotten when the host nation won eighty-nine medals—thirty-three more than the runner-up, the United States. Germans ignored the unprecedented four individual gold medals won by the United States' Jesse Owens, saying Germany's victories proved the superiority of the Aryan race and National Socialist ideology. "We thanked our Führer that we had achieved this fantastic triumph," said Henry Metelmann, who was three years younger than Fritz.

Fritz Engelbert and literally millions of others bought into Hitler, but not all German youth did. Heinrich Himmler, head of the SS, was disturbed at the growing number of teenagers who resisted Hitler Youth. He referred to them as "Swing Youth" because of their taste in music. He had heard that instead of "Heil, Hitler" they mockingly said, "Swing Heil." He issued a memorandum instructing police to arrest Swing Youth ringleaders, male and female, along with teachers who supported them—and have them sent to concentration camps.

Although anti-Hitler youth gangs existed, they were glaring exceptions to the rule. As pro-Hitler momentum strengthened, parents worried about speaking frankly about Hitler even in the privacy of their homes. So powerful was the pull of Hitler Youth that some boys and girls denounced their families in the same way a religious zealot might denounce the devil. Karl-Heinz Schnibbe, a year older than Fritz and also a member of Hitler Youth, would remember it well. "Many parents got picked up by the Gestapo because their children turned them in," Schnibbe said. "It reached the point where children could not trust their parents and parents could not trust their children."[1]

The German Mother and Her First Child, a book by Dr. Johanna Haarer, only built the wall between parents and children higher. Published in 1934, the year Fritz turned nine, the hugely popular book "urged mothers to ignore their babies' emotional needs," according to

Smithsonian magazine. It sold millions and led to parenting classes based on its premise of creating distance between parent and child. "The Nazis wanted children who were tough, unemotional, and unempathetic and who had weak attachments to others, and they understood that withholding affection would support that goal."[2]

In other words, Dr. Haarer was attacking the idea of parents connecting emotionally to their children. And without such connections, parents with doubts about Hitler would have all the less opportunity, and reason, to try to broaden their children's perspectives on the Führer.

At school children greeted each other with "Heil Hitler!" Each day began with a pledge of allegiance, the children raising their right arms in honor of the Nazi leader: "I promise to do my duty in love and loyalty to the Führer and our flag." The Nazis pushed propaganda with unabashed zeal. The back of Fritz's Spanish books listed red-letter dates for the Nazi Party, including Hitler's birthday, April 20. At night before bed, hundreds of thousands of Hitler Youth members bowed their heads and prayed a prayer modeled after the Lord's Prayer in scripture: "Adolf Hitler, you are our great Führer. Thy name makes the enemy tremble. Thy Third Reich comes, thy will alone is law upon the earth. Let us hear daily thy voice and order us by thy leadership, for we will obey to the end and even with our lives. We praise thee! Heil Hitler!"

Waltraud Menn, a female classmate and neighbor of Fritz's, remembered it as a confusing time of "light and shadow," when the truth could be elusive. Her father was a member of the Nazi Party, and, not incidentally, Fritz's teacher; he showed up for class each day in his full Nazi uniform.

She asked her father about Arthur Holländer, a Jewish boy in her and Fritz's class who had disappeared. She has never forgotten his response: "Waltraud, you see, what the Nazis started was a revolutionary movement. And as in all revolutions, things are turned upside down, maybe like the French Revolution in 1789. Bad things happen. So, with all the light shed by the Nazi movement, you will also find dark spots, where things go wrong." (All seven members of the Holländer family would die in concentration camps, Arthur and his parents among others with Hilchenbach connections.)

Teachers not willing to go along with the Nazis had a hard time of it. Fritz's uncle Hermann was a teacher and wrote something in the school newspaper that the Nazis did not like. Brownshirts burst through the door of his classroom and beat and arrested him—right in front of his students.

In 1937, the year Fritz turned twelve, Hitler withdrew Germany's signature from the World War I Treaty of Versailles and stepped up paramilitary training for Hitler Youth. He had already stationed troops in the Rhineland, the buffer zone between Germany and France. It was no secret what this was leading to: war.

In 1938, eighty thousand youth gathered in Nuremburg to pay homage to Hitler. They marched in streets draped with swastikas; felt the pride when, unable to restrain their emotions, girls from the crowd would scurry out to plant kisses on their faces; and played war games. At week's end, for their grand finale, they marched in formation to spell out A-D-O-L-F—H-I-T-L-E-R.

Hitler came to the microphone. "You, my youth, never forget that one day you will rule the world!"

Alfons Heck, three years younger than Fritz, would never forget it. "From that moment on," he said, "I belonged to Adolf Hitler, body and soul."

Members of the Hitler Youth learned how to shoot weapons, throw hand grenades, and physically attack an enemy soldier. Boys were expected to build their military skills in the organization, serve in compulsory Labour Service, and then join the Wehrmacht, Germany's armed forces.

"Germany must live" was one motto hammered into the youths, "even if you must die."

The political indoctrination was pronounced, and the anti-Semitism became ever more intense. "These people," the boys were repeatedly told, "are filthy swine." After Kristallnacht, Hitler Youth went double-time on its message to boycott businesses run by Jews. Why would Germans want to help the very people who were hurting the German cause? It was the Jews, Fritz had come to believe, who had caused Germany to lose World War I and who had undermined the entire world by forcing the stock market crash of 1929. Though Jews comprised less than 1 percent of Germany's population—just over half a million people—they were somehow keeping Germany from being great again—or so said the Nazi party line.

"You cannot, with the same hand, offer 'Heil Hitler!' to the Führer and reach out to the Jews!" the young people were told. "And if you know people who are reaching out to the Jews, it is your patriotic duty to report them to the authorities—immediately!"

By connecting with boys at camps, rallies, and meetings—places where parents weren't allowed—Nazi organizers could more easily push their agenda on the youth. (Hitler Youth meetings were called "Home Meetings," but were held anywhere but in homes: barns, empty buildings, cellars—always led by youth, and away from adults.)

Young people who refused to join the organization were shamed at school by their fellow students and by teachers who might assign them to explain "Why I'm Not in the Hitler Youth." Employers wouldn't offer apprenticeships to young men and women who hadn't been part of the organization.

Hitler Youth had a monopoly on all youth athletic facilities and organizations. Its members were commanded to undermine churches in general and break up church youth groups in particular.

For German boys who had known nothing else and who had little perspective on political or social issues, the organization was the normal routine of life, spiced with adventure. The younger boys were particularly smitten with the knives members were given, the older boys with their leaders' encouragement to engage in premarital sex. After all, it was an all-Aryan organization, a self-selected precursor to what leaders hoped would become the new, purified Germany. The more the merrier, provided that the "more" came with the proper bloodlines.

As 1939 dawned, Fritz Engelbert, now fourteen, was on the cusp of transitioning from knives to girls. For three years he had been been part of German Youngsters in the Hitler Youth, and in six months he would step up to Hitler Youth proper, a virtual minor league system for the German army. He was becoming more assertive with his parents, his father in particular, and more impatient with the Jews his Hitler Youth leaders incessantly painted in dark shades of distrust.

If his parents lamented that their friend Seligmann was struggling to stay afloat amid the post-Kristallnacht boycott against Jewish businesess, Fritz did not. He looked at the world with a more jaundiced eye, believing that his parents' friendship with their neighbor blinded them to the insidious threat Seligmann posed as a Jew. When Fritz discovered an offense going on right beneath his eyes—his very own mother and father were sneaking cigarettes and food to Seligmann—he was stunned by their naiveté. "The Jew" would even occasionally show up at the Engelberts' inn, something that sent Fritz's head swiveling in search of the Gestapo. If the transgression were found out, Fritz could be demoted in Hitler Youth, perhaps punished.

How could his parents be working against the country they purported to love, the country that was preparing for a chance to regain its position of prominence in the world? His parents' betrayal was the very thing his leaders had warned him and the other boys about.

His father, thought Fritz, dreamed too small. The man would prattle on about how proud he would be to have his only child take over the family inn, shop, and petrol station. That wasn't Fritz's dream. His dream was big and bold—to be an elite soldier and fight for his *Vaterland*—then settle down and become an attorney. Over the past four years Fritz had been taught to love his country. And when you love your country, you need to stand up and defend that country.

Even if it might mean reporting your parents to the authorities for helping the Jews.

Don

As Don Malarkey segued from boy to man—he had survived that plunge from the roof with only a sprained ankle and a scolding from his mother—he too imagined himself as an attorney someday. But as the 1930s passed it became clear that that dream was neither a soul-born passion nor a particularly practical hope. The Malarkey family, which had once been financially comfortable, was now struggling. Law school was virtually impossible. Don's father, Leo, was now disappearing for weeks on end, forcing Don to go to work to support the family. The Depression lingered, clouding his future all the more.

The Great Depression hadn't hit Oregon as hard as it had a lot of other states; at the end of 1934, 14 percent of the state's eligible workers were receiving unemployment relief, compared with thirteen states that were at 20 percent or higher. People still needed to eat, and fish—Astoria's main cash crop—were plentiful. And because Astoria was tucked in the corner of the state, en route to nowhere, it hadn't drawn a glut of "railroad bums" like more mainline cities. Most Dust Bowl emigrants from the Midwest headed for sunny California, not rainy Oregon. That said, times were still hard. Jobs scarce. Pay low. In 1932, twenty thousand World War I veterans marched on Washington, D.C., demanding immediate payment of their military service bonuses.

Don was no stranger to physical work; at twelve, he had joined a bucket brigade to save Ben Gronnell's farm from the largest forest fire in Oregon history, the Tillamook Burn. Later that night, the fire swallowed the Malarkeys' cabin on the Nehalem River. In some ways, the incident was his coming-of-age moment. He had arrived at the farm as a boy but rolled into a sleeping bag that night as a man: hands bloodied, clothes wet, body whipped to a weariness he had never felt. At the same time, with the cabin gone, Don had lost his link to the river; his Huck Finn days were over.

Don's carefree life as a teenager in Astoria was in stark contrast to Fritz's Hitler Youth years. *Courtesy of the Malarkey Family Collection*

Another thing that marked the young man's shift from Halloween pranks to adult responsibility was going to work as a seiner on the Columbia River at the age of sixteen. People joked at the time that salmon in the Columbia were so thick you could walk from Oregon to Washington on their backs. A seiner's job was to help corral the fish—some the length of a man—in nets stretched out by a couple of tugboats. Once the nets were full, they were dragged to the riverbank, where teams of horses on shore took over, pulling the nets in so the fish were trapped in a tidy half-moon configuration. From there, Don and the crew scooped the wriggling fish into wooden boats, called "slimes," where they were chugged down river to the canneries in Astoria.

The seiners were housed fifteen miles upriver in a logging camp setting. Chow lines. Bunks. And three bucks a day, plus a fifty-cents-a-day bonus if you lasted the whole season. Don was a boy among men. But he earned his bonus—for three straight summers. The job not only put more money in his wallet but more muscle on his body; he was average height, 5'8", but tougher than many. And decidedly handsome.

In high school he fell in love with Bernice Franetovich, whose honor he defended valiantly. When, at Star of the Sea Catholic School, Leland Wesley made a sideways remark about Bernice, Malarkey slammed him against a locker. "Do that again and I'll kick the hell out of you," he said.

Don Malarkey wasn't a rebel without a cause. Sure, like a lot of guys, he had started smoking and "gone off the deep end," according to his mother, with his infatuation for Glenn Miller, Tommy Dorsey, and other musicians who played hip-swiveling music. But he had a more serious, contemplative side, too, though he would never admit it to his buddies.

Besides politics and current events, he was drawn to poetry, including Rudyard Kipling's "Gunga Din" and William Ernest Henley's "Invictus." Don liked the way the latter poem suggested that you shouldn't wait around for someone else to tell you who you were, what you needed to do, or where you needed to go. He liked being the captain of his soul; nobody was going to tell Don Malarkey how to live his life.

Raised Catholic, Malarkey attended church mainly to honor his mother Helen and grandmother Ida, both of whom he revered. Though he believed in God, he was too much the swashbuckler to be tied to anything that fenced him in.

In 1938, after Malarkey's father's insurance business folded, the family lost their house. Don, now attending Astoria High, went to live with his grandmother in Warrenton, across Youngs Bay from Astoria. His freewheeling days of adventure gave way to a rhythm of must-do responsibilities. His dreams of playing basketball for the legendary Astoria High Fishermen vanished; he couldn't get rides to and from practice six miles away.

While still going to school, he got a night job at the Liberty Grill. It was owned by his girlfriend's father, Louie Franetovich, who thought Malarkey was an OK guy. On breaks, Don would take time to read Astoria's daily paper, its pages often smudged with ketchup and mustard. In November 1938, the *Evening Astorian-Budget* reported about rioting in Germany. The article widened Don's eyes. Synagogues torched, windows shattered, women raped—by Nazi soldiers, on behalf of the German government? *What the hell was going on in the world?*

The news of Kristallnacht chilled many Americans. This was the German government attacking a segment of its very own people. "Mobs Wreck Jewish Stores in Berlin" read a headline in the *Chicago Daily Tribune*. "Nazi Mobs Riot in Wild Orgy" reported the *Los Angeles Times*.

President Roosevelt, who initially shrugged off the event as a "State Department matter," ultimately condemned the act, saying he "could scarcely believe that such things could occur in a twentieth-century civilization." But not everybody empathized with the Jews. Father Charles Coughlin, a Catholic priest in Boston whose anti-Semitic tirades could be heard on his popular radio show, took a "they-had-it-coming-to-them" attitude. He wasn't alone. And even if a broader swath of Americans condemned the attacks on Jews, few took action.

By now the Depression was all but over, and Americans were ready to feel good again. So were Germans. Two months before Kristallnacht, German leaders had bullied their way to annexing German-populated borderlands from Czechoslovakia with the Munich Agreement; the next month the German army occupied what they called "Sudetenland." Hitler's ambitions to exact revenge for the humiliation of World War I weren't exactly hidden.

As Don's teachers discussed rising concerns about Germany, he started to see where the situation was headed. The Third Reich, he realized, was a sleeping giant—and in the 1930s few Americans were eager to confront it. Even as the dark clouds of fascism roiled on the horizon, Americans were not eager for another war. The men who had survived World War I were now turning forty; though the United States' WWI war dead of 116,708 was a sliver of what other nations had lost—five countries lost more than a million men each—the memory was still fresh. And it was their sons who would fight a second world war.

Americans were engrained with a deep sense of individualism. With U.S. flying hero Charles Lindbergh hobnobbing with German leaders and going on about a German "sense of decency and value which in many ways is far ahead of ours," it was easy to be an isolationist, to believe the United States, as Lindbergh said, could be "a lone island in a world of force." Unlike European countries near Germany, America had two huge allies to protect it from enemy attacks: the Atlantic and the Pacific Oceans. Americans favored beefing up their Navy, Army, and Air Force and helping other countries militarily, but they didn't want to go to war. A 1938 Gallup poll showed 69 percent of Americans supported the statement that the United States should "do everything possible to help England and France win, except go to war ourselves."

Don was only seventeen years old, but just as he'd assimilated into an adult work world, so had he matured in political thought. As he read more about Hitler's saber-rattling, his interest deepened.

When Don was a senior at Astoria High, a teacher finished writing on the chalkboard and turned to the class.

"Did any of you see the editorial in last night's paper?"

Only one hand went up—Don's.

"Good for you, Mr. Malarkey. And what was it about?"

"The chances of Germany invading the 'Low Countries.'"

"And what countries are those?"

"Belgium, Luxembourg, and, uh, uh—"

"The Netherlands."

"Right."

"And just how good did the editorial writer deem those chances to be?"

"Unfortunately, ma'am, real good."

This was not the kind of conversation Don had at home with his grandmother, whose relationship with her grandson leaned more to the day-to-day logistics of getting him to and from school. He rarely saw his mother and almost never saw his father, who had slipped into his own personal depression. So the perspective he was developing on the war likely wasn't shaped by his parents; the biggest influences were school, peers, and, most notably, two dead uncles who'd served in World War I.

Gerald, barely nineteen, had been killed by German troops in Château-Thierry in France on August 11, 1918. Bob had been gassed by Germans in the Argonne Forest and, with his lungs singed, never recovered. He died in 1926 at thirty-one, when Don was five.

One evening, Noland, a Liberty Grill regular, saw Don at the restaurant. Nearby sat two men in suits, customers Don had never seen in the place. *Suits in a place where half the people walked in wearing rubber boots and smelled like fish?*

"So, whataya think, Donnie?" asked the bar pilot. "Germany gonna swallow France?"

Don stopped wiping the table he was cleaning.

"Mr. Noland, Germany's like the Notre Dame football team of Europe," he said with unabashed certainty. "Powerful. France is in trouble. So's all of Europe." He then backed up his opinion with detailed facts. Amazement lit up the bar pilot's face.

The next day, Don's boss Louie warned him to be careful. "After you left, those two men were asking questions about you," said Louie in his Croatian accent. "They said they were with the FBI. Wondered how the hell you knew so much about the goings-on in Europe."

Suspicion and fear were on the rise around the world. In America, people were still cool on the idea of involvement; a 1939 Gallup poll showed that 88 percent of Americans opposed going to war.

On September 1, 1939, Germany confirmed the world's fears. Hitler's army invaded Poland. German tanks headed east in a lightning war, or *Blitzkrieg*, annihilating whoever or whatever got in their way: soldiers, civilians, and livestock. Two days later, France, Britain, Australia, and New Zealand declared war on Germany. In the next week, Nepal, Canada, and South Africa did the same.

Although the United States did not join in declaring war at that time, the world was at war. Hearing the news, Don's grandmother, with whom he still lived, recoiled in grief. She had lost two sons to World War I. She didn't want to have to grieve her beloved Donnie, too.

CHAPTER 3

Off to War

Fritz

When Fritz showed up at Hitler Youth gatherings, it was always with a tinge of guilt—not because of his involvement, but because of doubts about whether he was committed enough to the cause. He still harbored the secret that his parents were helping Seligmann the Jew—and had been for nearly a year. His lack of courage grated on his conscience.

By now, he had heard the stories of others so much bolder than he—an eight-year-old girl who had marched home from Hitler Youth meetings and told her parents that she no longer belonged to them anymore, she belonged to Hitler. The student who had reported his teacher for refusing to have his students say their "Heil, Hitlers." The young man who had turned in his father for calling Hitler a "crazed Nazi maniac." In that last case, the father had been sent to the Dachau concentration camp. The son? He had been honored with a Hitler Youth promotion in rank.

Why couldn't Fritz do what he knew was right and report his parents to the Nazi authorities? Why couldn't he take action to back up the words he sang: "For the flag we are ready to die!" Die? He couldn't even muster the guts to file a report on his own parents.

His relationship with his father was an irresistible force meeting an immovable object. Fritz Sr. was like a boulder in Ferndorf Creek, Fritz Jr. like the current pressing against it—and, by necessity, going around it. In family photos, it was almost always just Fritz and his mother, seldom all three of them. At dinner, Fritz said little and, when he did, talked only of school, running, or life at the inn. The small stuff. Never about the important things that were talked about at Hitler Youth.

Fritz did not hate his father. Not at all. He simply did not understand the man and his allegiance to the Social Democratic Party, which opposed Hitler. Germany was finally positioning itself to emerge from its ugly past, to take its rightful place of dominance, to create a new Aryan nation that would make all things right. His father was stuck in the past, an old man too busy pumping gas, chopping firewood, and bagging groceries to see that the world was changing. An old man so skewed in his thinking that he found honor in secretly giving produce and milk and cigarettes to an old Jew. An old man who had forgotten how to dream.

What's more, father and son were rooted in the German region known as Siegerland, where the river Sieg flows into the Rhine. People of this region had not only their own dialect but, it was said, their own stubbornness.

When Germany invaded Poland in 1939 to begin World War II, the war invigorated Fritz and others in Hitler Youth with a renewed sense of purpose. Suddenly, the promise was in the process of being fulfilled. Some youth leaders—ages fifteen to twenty-one—were sent by train to Poland to help German families settle into homes from which Poles had been evicted. Fritz and other boys went door to door collecting all sorts of material to aid the war effort, from copper to scrap metal, razor blades to bottles. Blonde-haired girls with pigtails, wearing Bavarian dresses, collected money in coffee cans. At last the country was coming together in a crescendo of oneness, a collective effort to help the Führer make good on his promise to restore Germany to greatness. One people. One country. One leader.

Amid such excitement, Fritz would look at his father and wonder what the man was thinking.

At day's end, when the last guest was taken care of, the last load of firewood delivered, and the last gallon of petrol pumped, Fritz Engelbert Sr. would come into the house for dinner. He would bend over the wash basin, wash his face, and wonder how, in a peaceful, beautiful place such as Hilchenbach, he could feel such commotion in his soul.

It was not enough that he was a fifty-eight-year-old father trying to find common ground with a fifteen-year-old son fanatically devoted to Hitler. Granted, Anna's miscarriages couldn't be helped, but why, dear God, had he and his wife been so old when they had their son? At the dinner table, he and Fritz would talk about everything that didn't matter and nothing that did. To talk of Hitler and war, of right and wrong, of staying true to a more noble cause than totalitarianism, would only be to draw the line in the sand deeper. And now that Germany had invaded Poland, the father–son tension only wound tighter in the guts of both.

Fritz Jr. now had justification for the militaristic bent of the Hitler Youth: *We are at war. Shouldn't we support our own country?* After the invasion, Fritz was champing at the bit to serve Hitler and his country. At seventeen, the minimum age, he aspired to be part of the Waffen-SS, the armed wing of the Nazi Party's SS organization. But his father refused to give his consent to let him do so.

Fritz Jr. argued that, at 5'10" tall, he was already an inch over the minimum height requirement; he was from a long line of Aryan blood; he had no criminal record; and, of course, he was not married.

"Nein!" said his father. "Nein! Nein! Nein!"

Fritz's son had an independent streak that he and Anna had instilled in him when he was young. What his son didn't have, thought his father, was historical perspective. Eight years old when Hitler took power, Fritz Jr. had never had the chance to experience a life of freedom: to read the books you wanted to read, to think how you wanted to think—if you were a Jew, not to have your business ransacked and your skull crushed. The Nazi oppression of the Jews was Fritz Jr.'s "normal"; he knew nothing else. How could he miss what he had never had?

His son, he believed—oversold on gallantry, honor, and idealism by Hitler and the Nazi youth leaders—also had a glamorized view of war. To attend a paramilitary summer camp wearing shorts, brown caps, and neckerchiefs was one thing. Actual war was another.

Fritz Sr. knew. Like his father—yet another Fritz, who had fought against France in 1870 and 1871—he had gone to war. At age thirty-three, he had done battle in World War I, the so-called "war to end all wars." And he had not found the experience full of gallantry, honor, and idealism but of death, gore, and gangrene, surgeons sawing off the hands and feet of the wounded. (At times in World War I, the need for amputation was so high that surgeons resorted to using guillotines.) He had seen much of his action in the snow-chalked Vosges Mountains, where the Germans and French turned a pristine alpine mountain into what looked like a moonscape—for meager gains. Nearly ten thousand died.

"Henceforth all these names will evoke repeated engagements, bloody alterations of advance and retreat," wrote Joseph Belmon, a captain in the French Army, of one battle. "And it seems sad and curious that, on both sides, such sacrifices should be made for the possession of a few yards—or even less—of territory."

Fritz Sr. remembered not only the war, but its aftermath. Germany was inexorably changed—for the worse. Two million soldiers dead. One million civilians dead. For what? A vain attempt at European dominance, for political leaders and military higher-ups to be able to lord their sense of righteousness over neighboring countries?

He remembered seeing the disabled veterans show up at his inn, begging for cups of soup or a few paper marks—not that the money had much value after the war. Nearly three million disabled vets spread out into a country that wasn't equipped to take care of a sliver of that number, many roaming aimlessly, sleeping in barns, begging for bread. Men with missing arms, missing legs, missing whatever glamor war was supposed to have bestowed on them.

The millions of widows and orphans could physically blend in, but the maimed vets could not. Their obvious plight added to the grief of a country that had not only the blood of its own on its hands, but the blood of six million more who had died in the war, soldiers and civilians alike.

Germany, he believed, had become a volatile mix of guilt, grief, and poverty, its desperation making it vulnerable to anyone with a promise of something better. And into that vacuum—that insecurity—came a man to lead the easily led. In the 1938 election more than 99 percent of Germans had voted for Hitler, but the very thought of the man made Fritz Sr.'s blood boil. He had heard what was happening to the Jews—the gold stars, the death camps, the thousands being loaded onto trains in big cities while most of the non-Jews paid little attention.

Does nobody pay attention to history? Does nobody see the futility of the war we fought more than two decades ago? Does nobody understand that obedience can be the language of sheep on their way to the slaughter? Does nobody think it strange that our children are more Hitler's than ours?

What he wanted to say to his son at the dinner table was: *This is why I question your bowing to Hitler: Because you're following a madman. Because your uncle the schoolteacher gets beat up in front of his class for doing nothing wrong. Because you do not understand the blessed value of freedom. Because in five years, you may be that one-legged panhandling vet—if you're lucky. If you're not, you will be buried, like so many of our losses in the last war, in some field far away. And your mother and I will die of broken hearts.*

But what he said instead was, "Kannst du mir bitte die Schweinshaxe reichen?" ("Can you please pass the roasted pork hocks?")

On April 1, 1941, just short of his sixteenth birthday, Fritz entered an apprenticeship training program for a company just outside Hilchenbach called SIEMAG, which specialized in machines that rolled steel and other metals into sheets. He impressed the company. "He is willing and honest," his supervisor wrote on his review. He was told to come back when he was done with his military duties; clearly they thought the young man had potential.

Meanwhile, the war widened and deepened, dragging in other countries along the way. On December 7, 1941, Japan, a German ally, attacked the U.S. fleet at Pearl Harbor in Hawaii, and the United States quickly declared war on the Asian country. Four days later, citing provocations against Germany by a U.S. government that had declared its neutrality, Germany declared war on the United States.

As Germany invaded the Soviet Union, it used special mobile death squads called Einsatzgruppen to kill Jewish people. The civilians would be taken outside of town, where nobody besides the victims would be witness, and forced to dig their own graves. Then they were stripped, shot, and buried. Children watched their parents die this way. Parents watched their children die this way. From June 1941 to December 1941, the Einsatzgruppen killed nearly half a million Jews.

But Hitler and his staff came to believe that this approach lacked efficiency. The Einsatzgruppen system was overly stressful on those doing the killing. And, more significantly in their eyes, it wasn't "lowering the reservoir" of Jews fast enough. Jewish women were still having babies. Suicides of distraught Jews helped the German effort: some jumped from windows, some ate matchsticks, some hanged themselves. But such deaths were drops in a much larger bucket that needed draining. Thus did the Nazi leaders realize they needed what they would come to call the "final solution."

The flames of Fritz Engelbert's youth reached high into the night sky, like the fires that ravaged the houses, businesses, and synagogues of Jews. In Fritz's mind, those fires represented a righteous response on behalf of Nazi Germany to an obstacle that had prevented the old, tainted, inferior Germany from becoming a new, pure, superior Germany. That was what he had been taught in Hitler Youth. The Germans had no choice but to act to erase the country's World War I failure in the eyes of the world and help imbue their country with a greatness to which the rest of the world would someday bow.

Fritz Engelbert was going to war.

Don

One late afternoon in early September 1939, the Pacific Ocean fog crept up the Columbia River, shrouding Astoria in a veil of uncertainty. Don Malarkey was working the evening shift at the Liberty Grill when the paperboy—boxed paper hat on his head, canvas bag over his shoulder—dropped off the *Evening Astorian-Budget*. As usual, Don snuck the kid a piece of blackberry cobbler wrapped in a napkin and unfurled the paper. Then he all but gasped. "Fighting Underway!" said the headline.

Germany had done what he thought it might do: started what could become a world war. Don's idea of the cozy world of college—which he hoped to enter after working for two years so that he'd be able to afford it—was suddenly less realistic, with the growing uncertainty in the world. The U.S. military was soon looking for young men like Malarkey to go to battle for the country if necessary. And young men like Malarkey were soon contemplating doing just that.

In September 1940, the United States enacted the first peacetime draft in the 174-year history of the nation. Reserve Officers' Training Corps (ROTC) classes became mandatory for male students on college campuses, including the University of Oregon in Eugene, where Don entered in the fall of 1941.

Now twenty, Malarkey did not have to register for the draft; that wasn't required until age twenty-one. But three months into his freshman year, when Japan attacked Pearl Harbor on December 7, 1941, and the United States declared war on Japan, everything changed. Legislation lowering the draft age to eighteen was quickly passed.

Malarkey saw the handwriting on the wall. Ultimately, nearly two-thirds of U.S. soldiers in World War II would serve because they were drafted. After the attack, Malarkey's fraternity brothers at the Sigma Nu house could talk about little else besides who was going to enlist in what branch.

In America in the 1930s, patriotism was pronounced but not unconditional. For years, starting early in the decade, students had protested against going to war on the very University of Oregon campus where Malarkey attended school. And when his ROTC instructor flunked him for missing his final—he was sick and in the student infirmary—Malarkey didn't hesitate to argue the decision.

"I couldn't be there," he said from across the man's desk.

"That's not good enough."

"I had A's all fall. Can't I just take the test? I can prove that—"

"You'll need to repeat the course, Mr. Malarkey. Case closed."

Don turned abruptly, walked back to the Sigma Nu house, grabbed his olive drab army uniform, and returned to the office. The receptionist tried to stop him, but he blew by her like a sirens-on fire truck ignoring a red light, dropped the uniform on the instructor's desk, and left.

In other words, though Malarkey considered himself a patriot, enlisting wouldn't be about blind faith in authority. It would be about deeper things, among them his father and his uncles. Beyond adventure, he wanted to avenge the deaths of his two uncles killed by German soldiers. And he *didn't* want to be like his father—a quitter—which is why quitting ROTC had left him feeling less than satisfied.

Leo "Tick" Malarkey had deeply disappointed Don. He had been a star football player at the University of Oregon and, after suffering an eye injury his senior year, served as an assistant coach, helping Oregon earn a bid to the 1917 Rose Bowl, where the Webfoots beat Pennsylvania. (Leo's brother, Bob—Don's uncle—played halfback.)

After marrying, Leo and his wife Helen raised four children, and "Tick" made enough money to provide them private school education and the family with a membership at Astoria Country Club. He was a life-of-the-party guy who often drank too much. Once, after one too many at a downtown tavern, he stumbled over to the Liberty Grill, took one look at Don bussing tables, and said, "There's my no-good son."

When his insurance business folded in the Depression, so did Leo. Though he and Don's mother never divorced, he faded from the family picture. The house was repossessed. The family reconfigured.

Don never forgot his father's "no-good-son" comment. But what bothered him more was simply that the man had given up on his business, his family, his life.

"Malarkeys," Don liked to say, "don't quit."

His disappointment in his father only accentuated his reverence for his uncles, even though of the two he had known only Uncle Bob—and he had died when Don was five. If his father wasn't going to be there for him, dammit, his uncles would be his heroes—even if they were dead.

By now, he knew his uncles' stories by heart; the scrapbooks about them were fixtures in the Malarkeys' living room. Don had all but memorized his grandfather's letter to his Uncle Gerald in France, written July 10, 1918.

"I do not know when you will be at the Front. However, I wish to state that, were I your age, I would be there. . . . Son, you are as much a crusader as any knight of old who wore the cross and went to battle with the slogan 'God wills it.' Therefore, notwithstanding the tender heart of your dear Mother, don't forget that we both want you to do your full duty and know that you will."

Gerald Malarkey died a month after the letter was written, riddled by shrapnel from a German shell in eastern France. He had just turned nineteen, a year younger than Don was now. Back home, Astoria's mayor requested that businesses close for an hour before Gerald's funeral service at Ocean View Cemetery. Virtually all did.

Eight years later, Bob Malarkey, thirty-one, was laid to rest beside his brother Gerald at Ocean View. He had struggled for nearly a decade from the effects of having been poisoned by mustard gas fired by the Germans in the Argonne Forest. He had been gassed in France not far from where Gerald had died. Now, above the vast Pacific Ocean, they were back together for good. The *Evening Astorian-Budget* editorialized them under the headline "Two Graves":

> Today, the tired, battle-scarred, pain-racked body of Robert Malarkey is laid to rest amid the peaceful dunes of Ocean View. The new-made grave close beside an older one, beneath whose mound there lies in sleep his eternal younger brother, Gerald, who died on the field of Château Thierry.
>
> In those graves lie the broken bodies of two young heroes and there, too, the broken hopes of a father and mother. There is grief and sorrow there, but there is pride and joy, too, and there is victory and triumph and glory. But there must be something more than this if "the dead shall know that they have not fall'n in vain" and if the mourning parents shall know that the big price they have been called to pay is not wasted. Those graves and others like them must remind us that peace is the fruit of war and that the victory such graves have brought is a vast defeat unless it shall become an enduring victory for the cause of peace.

Now, back home for Christmas break 1941, Don once again read the stories he had read so many times growing up. The one about Gerald got him every time. An army honor guard, the *Evening Astorian-Budget* reported, had "fired a parting salute to the youngster who proved his mettle when his country called and who, in asking permission of his parents to enlist, said simply, 'Somebody must go.'"

A generation later, Don decided it was his turn to be that somebody.

The fires of Don Malarkey's youth had reached high into the night sky from Ben Gronnell's farm. The night he had helped save Ben's farm always reminded Don of the uncomfortable truth that the winds of the world sometimes carried sparks that torched the lives of the innocent. That was one reason he would fight. This is how communities—and countries—worked. In times of desperation, you grabbed your bucket just like your uncles had and joined the brigade to help protect what your neighbors and fellow Americans had worked so hard to create, and to preserve the freedom that was the envy of the world.

Don Malarkey was going to war.

PART II

WAR

War makes strange giant creatures out of us little routine men who inhabit the earth.

—World War II correspondent Ernie Pyle

CHAPTER 4

Into Battle

Fritz

In May 1943, as the winds of war blew across the world, the Nazi military sent Fritz Engelbert to Austria to serve as a leader of a *Kinderlandverschickung* (KLV) camp for German children who had been evacuated because of Allied bombings. He had already been drafted; after his stint in Austria, Fritz would return to Germany for basic training.

The higher-ups liked his eagerness. They liked his sense of commitment to the cause. Had his father not refused to allow him to enlist early, the young man might have become one of Hitler's elite. And, of course, they liked his Aryan blood. Now eighteen, Fritz was six feet tall, blond, and sturdily built.

The Hilchenbach train station near Ferndorf Creek buzzed with people coming and going: soldiers headed to military training, Hitler

Youth en route to assignments, children on their way to KLV sites, and Europe's Jews being herded like cattle to death camps. Germany's railroads had never been busier.

Fritz purposely strode ahead of his parents, as if he couldn't check his luggage and board his car soon enough. As if he didn't want to be embarrassed in front of the other Hitler Youth boys by not leaving for camp on his own. As if his parents were holding him back. It wasn't anger at his father that drove him, though Fritz still hadn't forgiven the man for standing between him and his desire to join the Waffen-SS. It was simply the passion of a young man anxious to test himself in adventures, to be on his own, to do his part for the Führer. Having spent almost half his life in Hitler Youth, he was tired of practicing and pretending. He was anxious for the war exercises to be real. And though in this assignment in Austria he would only be supervising children, he knew it was the last step before he would join the Wehrmacht.

Fritz Sr. trailed his son and wife. Now sixty-two, he was both physically and emotionally weary. He had won the battle to prevent Fritz Jr. from joining the Waffen-SS, but he had lost the war; one way or the other, it was obvious his son was going to wind up on some front line somewhere. Fritz Sr.'s anger was a quiet anger, a brooding that rarely exploded but seethed just beneath the surface. It was fed by Hitler's Sunday radio speeches—as when the Führer had said: "When an opponent declares, 'I will not come over to your side,' I say calmly, 'Your child belongs to us already. What are you? You will pass on. Your descendants, however, now stand in the new camp. In a short time, they will know nothing but this new community.'" *How dare he.*

Anna, as always, found herself caught between her son and her husband: on one hand trying in vain to keep up with her son's long strides, on the other trying not to allow herself to be swallowed by the defeatism that was suffocating her husband—and, as always, serving as a buffer between the two. She was now fifty-seven. In the eight-year war between her husband and their son, she had long ago given up any hope of surrender by either side. Meanwhile, even if the battles were quiet, they were battles, nevertheless. And she was tired of being caught in the crossfire.

Fritz, in May 1943, in his Hitler Youth uniform (Hitler Youth Camp in Anger, Styria, Austria). *Courtesy of the Engelbert Family Collection*

They parted politely on the platform, Fritz offering a quick hug to his mother and an even quicker handshake to his father. The whistle blew. Steam filled the sky. The train slowly pulled away, children waving small swastika flags out of their open windows. Anna waved. She simply wanted her son to find his adventure, get it over with, and come home to Hilchenbach. Even if she subscribed to the "distant" relationship between parent and child encouraged by Dr. Haarer, she was still a mother. A mother who just wanted her son to be safe.

Fritz Sr. watched the train grow smaller and smaller with a sense of resignation and, if he was honest, regret. This was it. The end of the war between father and son, or at least a ceasefire, whether temporary or permanent. He and Anna were losing their son—if, amid the powerful pull of the Third Reich, they'd ever really had him.

The year 1943 marked a transition not just for the Engelberts but for Germany and its efforts to regain all that it had lost in World War I. Hitler's staff was implementing its "final solution" extermination camps—the largest of them in Poland—in which prisoners, mostly Jews, were being murdered by poison gas.

The German military effort wasn't proving to be as successful as its "concentration camps," whose efficiency was earning raves from the brass. On the Eastern Front, Germany had lost the long and bloody Battle of Stalingrad to the Soviets in February, only months after Germany had given up its conquered territories in North Africa to the Allies. Meanwhile, Allied troops were advancing into Italy, and there was word that an all-out invasion of France might soon come by way of the English Channel.

All this was costing hundreds of thousands of soldiers. In order to replenish the ranks, Hitler Youth was called upon to take a role in the war itself. In 1942, Hitler established *Wehrertüchtigungslager*, mandatory military training camps, to train boys ages fifteen to eighteen. (Presumably including Fritz, though it isn't known when and where he trained.) And starting in January 1943, anti-aircraft batteries were manned solely by Hitler Youth boys for the first time. Most welcomed the responsibility, seeing it as a vote of confidence. It affirmed what the organization had taught them from the start: "He who serves Adolf Hitler, the Führer, serves Germany, and whoever serves Germany, serves God."

Members of Hitler Youth were also used as couriers. They were sent to raid synagogues and destroy sacred Hebrew scrolls and texts. Girls served in administrative positions in Nazi offices and as nurse's aides, farm laborers, and munitions-factory workers. A British prisoner of war told *Time* magazine in 1943: "Hitler has made the youth and the youth are ruling Germany."

Not all young people followed Hitler obediently; some opposed him so vehemently that they paid the ultimate price. The most famous resisters were Hans and Sophie Scholl, a brother and sister—twenty-four and twenty-one, respectively—who headed up the distribution of anti-Nazi leaflets by their underground resistance group at the University of Munich. They were executed by guillotine on February 22, 1943.

Fritz's train chugged toward the KLV camp in Anger, Austria. Some of the children would be housed with individual families, others at the camps hastily set up for these young refugees. Fritz's train had been packed with such children, little boys and girls with cardboard identification cards around their necks, names stitched on their clothing, and sad looks on their faces. It was not easy leaving their mothers and fathers—especially for those still in diapers. But, despite pushback from parents, Nazi leaders deemed it necessary, with Allied bombs dropping. Between 1940 and 1945, nearly three million young people were sent to camps in places such as Austria and East Prussia.

On the train, seventy-seven children buzzed around Fritz like mosquitoes. With only a few toilets, some of the younger children had wet themselves, soiled themselves, or both. The ones that wouldn't stop crying were given sugar cubes laced with egg liqueur to make them drowsy. Finally, as they neared their destination, calm settled in.

Fritz, who had never had a sibling, was far more at ease with a rifle in his arms than with a child. But he found himself sitting across from one little girl whose sad eyes and tear-stained cheeks touched something inside him that he hadn't known was there. Her blue eyes were framed by pigtails the color of winter wheat. She looked to be about eight or nine years old. Her lips were quivering.

"Schokolade?" he asked, offering her a piece of chocolate in a paper wrapping.

She dropped her chin as if she felt unworthy of the offer or afraid of the one offering it.

He widened his eyes to encourage her. Tentatively, she reached out, took the candy, bit into it, and smiled a slight smile.

"Danke," she said.

"Hast du Angst?"

She nodded.

He told her not to be afraid, that he would be her *Schutzengel*—"guardian angel."

She smiled big.

His gesture earned him a summer-long friend. Once they arrived at the camp, the girl followed him each day as if he were the train and she the caboose: wherever he went, she went.

"Wie ist dein Name?" he asked.

"Gerda."

"Ich bin Fritz."

In what was otherwise a frustrating experience for Fritz—too many children, not enough leaders—Gerda was a bright spot. She sat next to him at lunch. He taught her to play jacks. She would come up behind him, tap him on his elbow, and run, giggling. He would pretend he didn't see her when she knew he did.

In a May 19, 1943, letter home, Engelbert asked about his mother's garden, sought details of what he'd heard about British planes bombing a couple of dams, and suggested that things weren't ideal in Austria. But he was an optimist. "Grit your teeth and you'll get through," he wrote. "Where there is light, there is shadow and vice versa."

Fritz at age eighteen after becoming a soldier, August 1943 (*Panzergrenadier* armored infantryman in Kassel, Germany). *Courtesy of the Engelbert Family Collection*

In his off time, Fritz gathered with other Hitler Youth leaders, once posing for a photo with two pals. The trio is standing on a ragged road flanked by trees and an A-frame structure. He is in his Hitler Youth uniform: a dark three-button coat covers a shirt whose collar peeks out up top, a tie cinched with it, a hat, binoculars strapped sideways over a shoulder—and, of course, on his left arm a band with a swastika on it.

The face is part man, part boy. His expression betrays longing, as if he hopes the machismo he is modeling will "take," become permanent. And yet beneath the bravado there still seems to live a little boy who has never had the chance to "come out and play." It was as if Gerda connected him, if only on a subconscious level, to the child he had never been allowed to be.

At summer's end, he was surprised—and slightly embarrassed—by how hard it was to say goodbye to the little girl. His summer in Austria had allowed for a brief return to the childhood he'd never had, but now it was time to put that childhood permanently to rest.

After his stint in Austria, Engelbert was sent north to Kassel, Germany, for basic training. It was a highly choreographed process to separate the wheat from the chaff and, if a man proved he was the right stuff, to decide where he best fit.

Serving in the German armed forces (Wehrmacht) had been compulsory since 1935. But with few exceptions, Fritz and the others arrived wanting to be there. For the young men who had been funneled into Hitler Youth at age ten, life in the military had become not only an expectation but a highly anticipated honor. Soldiers were held in high esteem. Civilians tipped their hats to them and cut them slack. Women sidled up to them at pubs. People thanked them for their sacrifices, for helping Germany rise from World War I's ashes. Thus, for the majority of young men who arrived in Kassel, this was the fruition of a dream. Any individualism had long been scrubbed from them like lice.

"You are nothing, your *Volk* [your country, your people] are everything!" their superiors had been telling Fritz for the past eight years.

"We were born to die for Germany!" he and the others had cried at Hitler Youth rallies.

Americans trained hard. Germans trained as hard or harder, and certainly for longer, counting the Hitler Youth "minor leagues." Basic training was demanding, disciplined, and, at times, dehumanizing. But it worked.

"Few armies were more effectively trained than the Wehrmacht," wrote Stephen Fritz in *Frontsoldaten: The German Soldier in World War II.*

By August 1943, when Engelbert began his basic training, Germany had been at war for nearly four years; its military leaders knew what worked and what didn't, be it tactics, equipment, ammunition, or bonding. They were hardened by war itself, and they knew how to turn fresh recruits into effective soldiers. Early in the war, many U.S. soldiers, in contrast, were ill-prepared for combat and thus got on-the-job training. In 1941, when Japan bombed the Philippines shortly after attacking Pearl Harbor, soldiers in Manila—when not playing golf—were drilling with outdated World War I rifles and, in some cases, broomsticks. Not that they didn't think they could whip any country's finest soldiers.

At Kassel, everything was done to make drills seem as close to war as possible. Ammo was live, physical challenges exhausting, and weather ignored. "Germany accepted the one-percent fatality rate suffered in training as the necessary price to pay for saving more soldiers' lives later on the battlefield," according to *The German Soldier in World War II*.[1]

American officers were often funneled from colleges and ROTC; the German army was more open-minded about choosing its officers—what mattered wasn't the past but the present: who was sharp, who was fit, who was dedicated.

The sense of belonging was overwhelming. "I soon felt really at home," wrote a soldier named Martin Poppel. "[A]ccepted into that special circle of men. . . . From the officers down to the last driver, we have become a family."

Four weeks of basic training had prepared Fritz to fight, but what fueled him was his allegiance to the Führer, his love of *Volk*, and his respect for his comrades, some of whom weren't even as old as he was (eighteen). On the brink of war, nothing reflected the discrepancy between German men and boys in the military as much as the items each received as rations. The older soldiers got cigarettes and alcohol, while those Fritz's age and younger—young men who would soon be putting their lives on the front line—were given candy.

On September 5, 1943, Fritz Engelbert was sworn in as a Wehrmacht soldier. "It was very moving," he wrote to his parents. "After the announcement by our company leader, Lieutenant Andrä, the battalion commander, Major Hutelbeck—by the way, a great guy—walked off the front. Then the band played 'We Are Going to Pray.' Six comrades came forward, one from each platoon. They swore on a lieutenant's saber.

"The Battalion's Adjutant read the oath formula. We raised our right hand and took the oath. [It] reads: 'I swear this holy oath to God that I shall unconditionally obey the Leader of the German Reich and of the German People, Adolf Hitler, the Supreme Commander of the Wehrmacht, and be willing to commit my life to this oath any time.'"

Fritz liked the feeling of being part of something—something beyond the humdrum family back home. Unlike his father, these men lived in the future, not the past. And their spirit invigorated him.

Though shy, he won favor among the men for his commitment, strength, and smarts. Fritz made a handful of good friends, foremost among them Fritz Döring, just a year older than he was. The two had known each other back home because—although Döring was from Siegen, about ten miles from Hilchenbach—they had attended the same school, Höhere Handelsschule. They had been in the same Spanish class.

"Wir müssen immer zusammenhalten," Döring said on their final day at camp.

Engelbert slapped a hand on Döring's shoulder.

"Ja immer!"

Yes, no matter what, they must stick together. Friends for all time.

Over the next year the German military did no favors to Fritz Engelbert as a young man eager to fight. He trained; he was transferred. He trained; he was transferred. First to Orleans, in the south of France, country the Germans had occupied since Fritz's fifteenth birthday, May 10, 1940. When he had heard word of the occupation as a teenager, he'd been "filled with regret," as he would say later, at not having been one of "our victorious soldiers." And more than three years later, his experience in Orleans was as sour.

"It was a hard time for me as an eighteen-year-old recruit," he remembered decades later, "with hunger and some unworthy treatment by superiors." He was forced to lie down for hours, made to clean toilets, and "treated like a dog."

He was relieved to be transferred to Brittany, near picturesque Mont Saint Michel, a castle that rises from the northern coast of France like a sand structure made by a child at the seashore. But there he became jaundiced, apparently as a lingering result of the poor nutrition in Orleans, and he was sent to a military hospital near Rennes for a month. Meanwhile, his unit shipped out for Italy. Because of his illness, Fritz was left behind.

When he finally recovered, he was dispatched to St. Malo, another town on the English Channel, to help build the Atlantic Wall. As a young man who had expected to be going important places and doing great things, he felt like a leaf in an eddy, twirling in circles. Three places, three disappointments.

The Atlantic Wall was an extensive system of coastal defense and fortification. "The goal," said Field Marshal Gerd von Rundstedt, "must be to meet the enemy on the same day he lands and throw him again into the sea." Germany had been fighting on the Eastern Front since 1939, and in North Africa and the Mediterranean and Middle East Theater since 1940. When the war turned against Germany in the Mediterranean in 1943, the chances of an Allied invasion of Western Europe went from a likelihood to a certainty. With military personnel able to be spread only so thin, such fortifications were deemed necessary to deter—and defend—attacks from the sea. But there was a lot of coastline to fortify—nearly three thousand miles, most of it in France, whose proximity to England across the English Channel made that stretch the most likely point for an Allied landing.

And so German soldiers went to work. Fritz Engelbert was an anomaly; those working the wall tended to be soldiers at least thirty-six years old, Indian prisoners taken in the North African campaign, or men captured in the fighting in Eastern Europe: Armenians, Ukrainians, Cossacks, and the like. This wasn't what Fritz had signed up for; there was no heroism in pouring concrete—17.6 million cubic feet would be used on the wall—or helping drive "Rommel asparagus" logs into the sand to rip the bottoms off landing craft.

He was happy to be transferred to a small town near Paris, and happier still to learn that he had been given a four-week leave. The fact that Fritz chose to return to Hilchenbach suggests that if his relationship with his father was strained, the two had not cut ties.

When he got off the train, his uniform prompted smiles from young women, nods of approval from civilians, and an occasional "Heil Hitler!" or "Sieg Heil!" ("Hail victory!") But the honor he was shown boomeranged; he felt undeserving of praise. He wore the uniform, yes, but what had he actually done for the cause? Nothing. His time back home did more to frustrate than affirm him.

His leave was unsettling. And when he was ordered back to Kassel his spirits sagged all the more. This was where his military journey had begun; he saw his return as pathetic irony: after nearly a year, he was right back where he had started. He felt like a *Pimpf*, a neophyte in the jargon of Hitler Youth.

Fritz felt little of the "Live Faithfully, Fight Bravely, and Die Laughing!" gusto that had been instilled in him during his time in the Hitler Youth. He hadn't encountered a single enemy soldier. Instead he had cleaned toilets, mortared a wall, and fallen sick because he had been fed so poorly. He had seen more of the insides of train cars than of combat.

One night as Fritz was lying on his bunk, the sleep-hall door swung open and in rushed three soldiers.

"Die Amerikaner sind in der Normandie gelandet! Die Invasion hat begonnen!"

Fritz sprang up in disbelief. But it was true: the Americans had landed in Normandy. The details unfurled over the next few days, making it clear that Fritz's war—his real war—was about to begin. Allied forces—Americans, Canadians, British—had come by sea and by sky. Thousands of ships had disgorged tens of thousands of men who were trying to thwart the German resistance beyond the beaches. Thousands of paratroopers had jumped into the Normandy darkness to help secure those beachheads.

Among them was a young American private, Don Malarkey, not that Fritz knew or cared about the invaders' names—or, for that matter, had even considered that they might have names. Like the Jews, they were just a faceless enemy standing in the way of Germany's return to greatness.

It was simple. If they threatened his *Vaterland*, they needed to die.

Don

In the black of the night, some 1,500 feet above the English Channel, Don Malarkey and most of the other 101st Airborne paratroopers had been lulled to sleep by the thrum of the C-47 and by sleeping pills. When Don awoke, it was just after midnight on June 6, 1944. As the plane headed toward the coast of Normandy, France, Don, ready for the drop, was thinking of two things: the nearly two years of training in which he had prepared for this moment, and the prospect that if he wasn't careful, he could die.

He remembered having a beer back in England with a guy from the 82nd Airborne, Bob Niland, who had seen action in Sicily and had an eerie take on German soldiers. "If you want to be a hero," he had told Malarkey, "the Germans will make one out of you—*dead*."

The remark hit Don with the kickback of a mortar tube; adding to his fear was Bob's mention of the fact that his brother Edward Niland was missing in Burma. Malarkey mentally gulped: the Niland story. The jump into the dark. The not knowing what he'd find when he landed—or even if he'd be able to find the other guys in the 506th's E Company. It was easier, he decided, to think back than ahead.

Back to the little boy who had jumped off the roof with the umbrella, to the faded newspaper clippings about his war-hero uncles, to the young man who had stormed out of the ROTC director's office as if to say: I quit. But he hadn't quit. He couldn't quit. He had a score to settle with the Germans who had taken the lives of his uncles.

He had chosen Army Airborne after kicking the tires of a few other branches of service and reading an article on paratroopers in

Reader's Digest. The Russians and Italians had tried using military parachutists in World War I, and Germany had already used them in World War II. The Americans first tried it near Oran, Algeria, in North Africa, on November 8, 1942. But no such attempt was close to the magnitude of what was taking place on this night. More than 13,000 American paratroopers from the 101st and 82nd Airborne units were jumping behind the enemy lines on the Normandy coast. Among their objectives? To take out the Germany artillery that would be hammering the five beaches where 150,000 Allied soldiers would be storming ashore.

After the attack on Pearl Harbor, when Malarkey had told a friend from Astoria about his decision to become a paratrooper, the friend had said: "You're jumping out of a friggin' airplane going a couple hundred miles an hour—right into enemy territory. It's a death sentence, Malark."

His grandmother Ida, with whom Don had lived for two years, didn't like the idea at all. World War I had taken two of her three sons; because of his eye injury, Malarkey's father had served stateside, in an Oregon lumber mill, shaping wood for gliders. "If anything happens to you, Donnie Malarkey," she said, "it'll be the end of me."

Pearl Harbor had changed everything. On the University of Oregon campus where Don was going to school, men were enlisting right and left. Women began finding themselves outnumbering men in classes. And Japanese Americans were being rounded up and shipped to internment camps.

Tom Hayashi, a good friend of Don's from Astoria, was among them. He, too, had been attending the University of Oregon, but had received notice that he had to leave. Back home in Astoria, he told Don, people were throwing rocks through the window of a store his family owned. People on the West Coast were panicking, afraid of an aerial attack from Japan. Civilians volunteered to man lookouts over the Pacific Ocean. Oregon State's Rose Bowl game against Duke in January 1942 was shifted from Pasadena to Durham, North Carolina.

Malarkey looked down the line of his "stick," the guys in this particular load of paratroopers, among them Bill Guarnere, Buck Compton, Salvatore Bellino, Joseph Lesniewski, Dewitt Lowrey, Rod Bain, and Joe Toye. Guys from all over the country. Everyday guys.

He had been with these same young men now for nearly twenty months. He had thought he'd been tight with his Sigma Nu fraternity brothers at the University of Oregon in Eugene, but preparing for war, he had found, bonds men in a way that preparing for the fall all-fraternity chorus sing-off does not.

Part of it was attrition. Two out of three men wouldn't make the grade; those who did took pride in it, pride they had in common with the others. Easy Company, as the 140-man E Company was known, had bonded on 6-mile runs up and down 1,736-foot Mount Currahee at Camp Toccoa in Georgia, on a 118-mile hike from Toccoa to Atlanta, on their first jumps above Fort Benning, and over a shared "distaste" for a certain Captain Herbert Sobel.

Don, left, and his best friend
Skip Muck in Fort Benning in
1943. *Courtesy of the Malarkey Family Collection*

It wasn't that Sobel was too tough; every U.S. Army captain was tough. It was that the men thought he was unfair; he would revoke passes for the slightest of deficiencies—a rusty bayonet, lint on a chevron. He would reward the men with a big dinner and then, halfway through it, tell them to "get your asses up Currahee—now!" He got a thrill from ridiculing a soldier in front of the other men.

But more than that, the men were afraid that Sobel was just bullheaded and plain stupid enough that he was going to get some of them killed in the war. He didn't seem blessed with an ounce of savvy when it came to tactics; once, in a war game, he made an error that led his unit right into enemy hands. He looked at maps as if he had never seen one before. He made decisions out of an obvious enjoyment of lording power over his underlings, rather than from logic.

Malarkey cut Sobel more slack than most; Don thought, as tough as the man was, Sobel's standards for excellence might be the difference between life and death for some soldiers, himself included.

Skip Muck, a new friend of Malarkey's, disagreed. "The guy's the devil in jump boots," Muck told Malarkey one day, blowing smoke rings from a Lucky Strike cigarette.

Malarkey and Muck were as close as any two men in Easy Company. Though they couldn't have grown up farther apart—Oregon and New York—they were happy-go-lucky guys with a lot in common: their Catholic backgrounds; their shared love for Big Band music, especially Glenn Miller and Benny Goodman; girlfriends back home, though Skip's was the more solid bet for marriage; families that had been turned upside down by the Depression; fathers who had bailed on those families; and a love for adventure.

Every crazy story Don could tell—about rogue ocean waves and salmon the length of ironing boards—Skip could equal or exceed. Don's favorite was how Skip had swum across the Niagara River, just above the falls—at night. They decided each would experience the other's world when the war was over: Don would take Skip salmon fishing in the Pacific, and Skip would show Don where he had crossed the Niagara.

On the three-day march to Atlanta, Malarkey developed shin splints and blisters. When the unit camped at the eighty-mile mark, he needed to crawl to get his food. Muck saw him and cringed.

"No friend of mine crawls anywhere," he said, after fetching Don's dinner for him.

"That's just the kind of guy he was," said Malarkey decades later. "In some ways I was closer to Skip than to my own two brothers."

In England, before the paratroopers left for France, Sobel was replaced as Easy Company commander by First Lieutenant Tom Meehan. And Don and Skip made a vow.

"Friends no matter what, right?" said Muck.

"No matter what," said Malarkey.

Once the plane got beyond Guernsey Island, it started taking the first tattering of enemy fire, nothing serious. As the C-47 arced over mainland France, however, the sky opened up. German 88mm artillery guns blasted fire. Tracer bullets lit the darkness. Shells exploded, rocking the plane. Looking down from the now-bumpy aircraft, Don saw fires on the ground, presumably from downed aircraft—eighty-one had taken off from England—or gliders. That did nothing for his confidence. Neither did his sense that the plane was dropping too fast and too soon. The plan had been to fly at about 1,500 feet, then descend to 600 for the drop. But the plane was already down to 300 feet. *I gotta get out of this airplane.*

The paratroopers stood and readied themselves for the drop.

"We're gonna throw a scare into those Krauts tonight," said Lieutenant Buck Compton to Malarkey. Don gave him a thumbs-up and flashed a smile.

The men lined up and hooked their chutes to the static line. If everything to this point had had a veneer of the surreal to it, that click triggered something in Malarkey: *This . . . is . . . real.*

As the jumpmaster, Compton was first. *Whoosh*; gone. Don waited eagerly. Suddenly, out of nowhere, a stanza from "Invictus" came to him:

> Out of the night that covers me,
> Black as the pit from pole to pole,
> I thank whatever gods may be
> For my unconquerable soul.

Next came Guarnere. *Whoosh*; gone. Sal Bellino. *Whoosh*; gone. Malarkey was next. He crouched, exhaled, and jumped into the great unknown. *Open, open, open, please, God, open my chute*, he thought in half prayer, half desperate plea.

When his chute opened at last, he floated down in the darkness as if caught in the middle of some Fourth of July fireworks show gone horribly wrong. Below, German machine-gunners, artillery gunners, and soldiers who could make out the parachutes in the flashes of exploding shells sprayed small-arms fire at the invaders. When daylight broke in a few hours, one of the most sickening sights for newly arrived troops would be dead paratroopers with their chutes hung up in trees, one in Sainte-Mère-Église caught on the pinnacle of a church tower. In some cases the Nazis had used the helpless men as target practice, bloodying their bodies beyond recognition so that they offered an ominous welcome to their fellow soldiers.

Malarkey soon caught the faint image of the earth below. He slammed into the lower reaches of an elm tree, a jolt of pain piercing his upper body. He grimaced. He was momentarily stuck. He tugged here, tugged there, and slid down, his boots touching French soil.

Finally. It was time to stop these marauders he had read about each night in the *Evening Astorian-Budget* at the Liberty Grill. He shed his parachute and began seeking others from Easy Company. It was time to go after these faceless enemies daring to spit in the face of freedom and human dignity.

Dammit, thought Malarkey, *if these fascists threatened the democracy of the world, they needed to die.*

In Le Grand Chemin, a small patrol of D (Dog) Company soldiers led by First Lieutenant John Kelly discovered a German machine gun position protecting a battery of four 105mm German guns poised to hammer troops coming ashore at Utah Beach, and reported the find.

Lieutenant Dick Winters had arrived that morning with a mixed bag of about three dozen paratroopers, who were mostly from Dog Company but included Don and about a dozen other Easy Company men. Winters had been charged with knocking out the cannons. Against a German force that Winters estimated to be about forty-five men, the initial assault would be made by fourteen troopers who would later be reinforced by eleven more.

The cannons boomed, reloaded, boomed, reloaded. Winters huddled with Malarkey and a few other men to share the plan of attack.

"Hail Mary, Mother of God," said Don, just in case the adrenaline wasn't enough to get him through this, and set out to follow his orders.

He, Compton, and Popeye Wynn tossed grenades into a machine gun position, waited for the explosion, and then killed the surviving members of the crew. Winters, Guarnere, and Toye hit the first cannon position, then moved into the same position as Don and his companions.

That's when he saw it: a dead German soldier out in the open with what appeared to be a holster on his hip. Don figured it likely contained a souvenir Luger. The kind of gun you could bring home to remind yourself that you had avenged your uncles' deaths—and, history would prove, the kind of gun that, if it was found in your possession when you became a prisoner of war, would earn you a bullet in the head.

Years later Malarkey would suggest it was the stupidest thing he'd ever done, and Winters wouldn't disagree. Don raced for the dead soldier and reached for the holster, only to find it was a case containing some gun-sighting device. Later he would surmise that the only reason he hadn't been machine-gunned to death was that the Germans assumed he was a medic and thus off limits per the Geneva Convention—not that it wasn't sometimes ignored.

Cleveland Petty, who had been just down from Malarkey on the C-47 flight into Normandy, was manning a machine gun when he took a bullet in the neck. Winters motioned for Don to take over the gun. He fired it for almost an hour and lobbed half a dozen grenades to clear out a cluster of German troops. Like a baseball player trying to hit for the cycle, he took over a mortar next and started firing it.

Lieutenant Lewis Nixon managed to commandeer a couple of Sherman tanks coming off Utah Beach, which were used to snuff the remaining machine gun nests. But nobody could top Winters and his command of the entire attack, which would become known as the Brécourt Manor Assault.

Twenty-five American soldiers, including Malarkey, had whipped an estimated forty-five Germans, killing about fifteen and capturing a dozen. In the process, the 506th lost four men and had six injured. Winters was awarded the Distinguished Service Cross; Compton, Guarnere, and Gerald Lorraine, Silver Stars; and Malarkey and eleven others, Bronze Stars. It was a great start for Easy Company.

A few days later, at Carentan, Don Malarkey popped up from a foxhole only to see Fritz Niland, part of the 101st Airborne's 501st Parachute Infantry Regiment, running his way. Niland was a close friend of Malarkey's buddy Skip Muck. Both men were from Tonawanda, New York. Niland was the guy whose brother, Bob, had struck fear in Don with his story about how the Germans would be more than happy to "make you a hero—dead." His other brother, Ed, was apparently missing in action in Burma.

Earlier, Malarkey had seen Niland huddling with Father Francis Sampson. Now Niland dropped down beside him, looking, Don would remember, "solemn as all hell."

"What's up, Fritz?"

"It's Bob. He got it on D-Day. Barely made it past the beach."

"My God. I'm so sorry, Fritz."

"But that's not the worst of it. I went to tell my other brother, Preston—Fourth Infantry—about Bob and . . ."

Niland's head slumped forward into his hand. He was weeping.

"And Father Francis said he'd died, too. The next day. On the Atlantic Wall."

"Jesus, Mary, and Joseph," said Malarkey. "And Ed missing in Burma?"

"They're sending me home, Malark."

"As well they should. Be safe, Fritzy. God, I'm so sorry, pal."[2]

After two weeks on the main line of resistance, Malarkey wasn't the only one who felt the need to decompress. As Easy Company prepared to sail back to England, his buddy Alton More came across an American motorcycle and sidecar that appeared discarded. Malarkey was only too happy to help him get it aboard the transport ship. As if he were his thirteen-year-old self signaling his buddy in Astoria to let the tire roll, Malarkey flashed hand signals from the ship to his buddy on shore just before it cast off.

"Got one more coming, cap'n," said Malarkey to a sailor overseeing the loading.

From behind the beach grass on a foredune, More peeled out on the cycle, headed down the beach, and drove onto the ship's ramp. The sailor just shook his head. The ship's props engaged, and Easy Company's men—and hundreds of others—were on their way.

Once in England, More drove and Malarkey sat in the sidecar, whoopin', hollerin', and pumping fists in the air as if they had left the war behind forever.

But they hadn't. Malarkey realized that when he went to pick up his laundry from the two young women who did their wash in Aldbourne. Would he be willing to take some back for the others? Of course, he said.

"Meehan?" she said, holding a stack of fresh-washed clothes. At first Don was too busy swooning over her beautiful British accent—and cute figure—to tell her that the company commander's plane had crashed and burned on D-Day.

Malarkey shook his head sideways.

"Burgess?"

"Wounded. Sent home."

"Evans?"

"No."

"Bloser?"

He could see where this was going. Malarkey swallowed hard and nodded a polite goodbye. He couldn't keep doing this. It wasn't just Evans and Bloser who wouldn't ever be coming for their laundry; Sergio Moya, Everett Gray, Richard Owen, Herman Collins, and dozens of others were gone, too. One hundred and forty Easy Company officers and soldiers had jumped from those planes on D-Day. After two weeks in Normandy, only seventy-four of them were still alive.

CHAPTER 5

The Horrors of War

Fritz

"**S**ie sind verhaftet!"

In Kassel, Germany, in early June 1944, Fritz Engelbert awakened in the night to find a flashlight shining in his face and a member of the Feldgendarmerie—a military police officer—telling him he was under arrest.

"Hast du mich gehört? Du bist verhaftet!"

Engelbert was discombobulated. After nearly a year of bouncing around France and Germany like a pinball, he had learned the previous day that he was being sent to fight on the Eastern Front, in Romania, where war was being fought with unremitting harshness. It was essentially a death sentence; eight of ten German military casualties in World War II—5.5 million—came on the Eastern Front. The clash between Germany and soldiers of the Soviet bloc—Romanians among them—was the largest military conflict in world history. Fritz had already been issued a new uniform, including new boots, and they had already been swiped from where he had tucked them near his bunk before going to bed. He reported them stolen the next morning.

Now he was being arrested?

"For what?" he asked.

For not reporting the theft of his boots in a timely manner, he was told.

"But it happened only last night," he said. "I waited until this morning to make sure a comrade wasn't simply playing a joke on me."

How did they even know they'd been stolen? Was this some sort of setup?

"Mitkommen! Jetzt!"

"But I—"

"Aufstehen, sofort!"

He got on his feet as instructed. He threw on his uniform. He would spend three days in jail for this "offense," all the time muttering to himself about the injustice. When released, however, he learned that while he had been incarcerated, his unit had shipped out to Romania. Had he not been detained, his chances of surviving the war would have been far slimmer. Rather than face the bloodbath of the Eastern Front, he was being transferred to Erfurt, southwest of Berlin—away from both war fronts, to the country's interior. It was yet another strange twist in what was beginning to look like a conspiracy to keep him from what he wanted most: to fight. It was only later that he learned the reason for his new orders.

Since 1943, a group of conspirators—Wehrmacht generals and officers in key positions—had been developing a plan to assassinate Hitler
and establish a new German regime that would immediately seek accord
with Allied forces. If successful, Operation Valkyrie would put the conspirators in control of the Wehrmacht and in a position to give orders to
subdue and overwhelm the Waffen-SS, Gestapo, and Nazi party leaders
who were sympathetic to Hitler. Fritz and the rest of the 901st were being
positioned to implement such orders—in Fritz's case, to become an unwit-
ting turncoat and help defeat the Nazi Party to which he had been loyal
since age ten.

Not that he and his comrades knew it at the time. Had he known,
Fritz would have been livid: how dare Germans conspire to kill the very
man who had finally given hope to their hopeless country!

But it never came to that. On July 20, 1944, Claus von Stauffenberg
and an inner circle of co-conspirators arranged for a bomb to go off in a
meeting the Führer was attending. Hitler, however, was only grazed by
the blast, whose masterminds paid the ultimate price. SS and Gestapo
personnel arrested 7,000 people in relation to the assassination attempt.
Stauffenberg died at the hands of a firing squad the next day; ultimately
4,980 people were executed in connection with the assassination attempt.

The next night over the radio, Hitler assured the German people that
he was fine. "I take this as confirmation of the mandate of providence,"
he said, "to continue to pursue my goal in life, as I have done so far."

In an attempt to show the solidarity of Hitler and the Nazi Party
despite the assassination attempt, the Wehrmacht—Fritz among them—
marched through the streets of Erfurt. Knowing their leader had almost

died, the soldiers' goose steps were crisper; their arms snapped "Heil Hitler" with an enhanced sense of admiration and gratitude for the leader they had almost lost.

Meanwhile, Germany's war had gotten more complex. On top of their vain attempt to stem the Soviet advance toward Berlin from the east, German troops now had to meet the formidable threat from the Western Allied forces that had landed in Normandy six weeks earlier. Some of Germany's best military minds considered this the beginning of the end. Hitler believed otherwise; he would fight to the finish.

New orders arrived for Fritz Engelbert: he would be joining the *Panzergrenadier* (armored infantrymen) in the Panzer Lehr Division. The assignment excited the nineteen-year-old soldier; the Panzer Lehr was an elite unit, the only Wehrmacht Panzer division to be fully equipped with tanks and half-tracks—vehicles that were part tank, part truck—to transport its mechanized infantry. Many of its men—unlike Fritz—were experienced warriors, having won honors for bravery fighting on the Eastern Front or in North Africa, Sicily, or Italy. Engelbert felt honored—and a bit intimidated—to be included among such soldiers. But after a year in limbo he was eager to do his part and excited to experience what he had waited a lifetime for: war.

As instructed, he took a train as far west as possible at the time, Versailles—the rail system was in such chaos that it took him fourteen days. Along with nine comrades, he posed for a lighthearted photo in Place d'Armes, around which wrapped the largest castle in Europe. It would be the last time he would laugh for a long time.

The 901st's replacements were to be trucked from Versailles to the venerable town of Argentan, France, south of Caen and about a hundred miles inland from the English Channel. The Americans' surge inland needed to be stopped.

As Engelbert approached the truck, his eyes grew wide. Among the German soldiers there to meet him and the other replacements was Fritz Döring.

"Well, if it isn't my favorite pal from Spanish class!" said Döring, tossing Engelbert's duffel in the back of the truck. "Uh, bienvenido viejo amigo!"

"I can't believe it's you, Döring!"

"And just where in the hell have you been since Kassel? Heard you'd been sick."

"Where *haven't* I been?" Engelbert made a quick visual sweep of the train platform to make sure no officers were lurking. "I find my quarters, open my duffel bag, then it's, 'Come, Herr Engelbert, we're sending you to Orleans, Mont Saint Michel,' and on and on. I even got kicked back to Kassel! Felt like I was back in *Volksschule*."

"Well, glad you've finally rejoined the outfit. Remember, we're sticking together."

"Friends for all time," said Engelbert, slapping him on the back.

They got into the truck and sat across from each other on the metal benches.

"So, how's it been?" said Engelbert. "Heard we're getting hit hard."

Döring lit a cigarette, blew the smoke, and looked off to the distance.

"You don't want to know."

"That bad?"

"Worse."

Corpses. Engelbert hadn't been out of the truck for more than ten seconds when he saw them: hundreds of them. Bodies of German soldiers scattered across the fields, around the farmhouses, along the road. The graves registration soldiers—bandanas across their faces—were fighting a losing battle, a more macabre version of shoveling snow in a blizzard. Engelbert's gut was fighting a losing battle, too. Stomach roiling, he leaned over a mangled tractor and puked.

Here: the charred remains of a tank crew that had been trying to escape. There: the bodies of French civilians alongside a road who had been fleeing from Argentan after Allied planes shelled the village. Sprinkled among them: the bodies of horses and cattle, full of maggots in the August heat.

Fritz had never imagined such horror. He covered his mouth and nose; the smell was overwhelming. The waves of horror kept coming: the bodies of mothers, fathers, children, dogs, and cats among crumbled houses—lives silenced by war. The moans of the wounded in a makeshift hospital only deepened his despair.

"The spirit I encountered here was different from anything I had experienced before," Engelbert would write decades after the war.

Those in the 901st who'd survived the aerial and artillery shellings were bloody, tired, and beaten. Commander Fritz Bayerlein of the Panzer Lehr Division had used a single word to describe the status of his outfit after the attack: "Annihilated."

U.S. general Dwight D. Eisenhower, after observing the scene a week later, would put it more graphically: "The battlefield at Falaise was unquestionably one of the greatest 'killing fields' of any of the war areas. I encountered scenes that could be described only by Dante. It was literally possible to walk for hundreds of yards at a time, stepping on nothing but dead and decaying flesh."

Some of the dead had perished in Operation Cobra, an all-out American aerial attack during the breakout from Normandy in the last week of July, others in the Battle of Falaise Gap that followed. In places, Argentan had been reduced to rubble. The regiment Engelbert was joining, the 901st, had been decimated. A thousand men had died.

Operation Cobra, which would go down as one of the greatest air raids in history, had torn a hole in the German line. Bombs from American, British, and Canadian planes had pounded German troops for nearly a week. Following that, ground troops had encircled most of the eighty thousand German troops within a lasso about five by twenty miles in size. Those who hadn't surrendered—and despite Hitler's insistence that they not, tens of thousands had—were killed with fish-in-a-barrel expediency. Allied pilots who flew above Falaise reported that they could smell the rotting corpses from the sky.

By now, mid-August, the small remains of the German army— including the Panzer Lehr Division—were locked in a narrow pocket on the eastern edge. If there was any silver lining to the dark cloud shrouding the Panzer Lehr Division, it was its location. The division was in the pocket's lone gap—and on a main road on which it could retreat east. There was hope for escape before the Allied forces surrounded them.

On August 17, three days after he arrived, Engelbert and his unit began falling back amid constant barrages by American fighter bombers from the sky and an occasional skirmish on the ground. They were the fortunate ones. Within a week, all German forces west of the Allied lines were either dead or POWs. By then Fritz and the 901st were out of harm's way. The U.S. 80th Infantry Division liberated Argentan on August 20, 1944.

Operation Overlord, the Allied assault on France, was successful. After ten weeks of fighting—struggling mightily in the beginning—the Allied forces had prevailed. The liberation of Paris began on August 19. By then Engelbert and the 901st were safely back in Germany, in the Eifel area. Spent. Tired. Defeated.

Though he still hadn't seen much "action," the experience near Argentan had rattled Fritz. Until August 1944, his obsession had been about his participation, or lack thereof. Despite a September promotion from a *Panzergrenadier* to a *Gefreiter* (private, second class), he still felt worthless. Even if Argentan hadn't scratched that particular itch, he had seen a side of war that he hadn't known existed.

He had seen the dead. Smelled the dead. Realized that the innocent died right along with the soldiers. For the first time he began to wonder about this thing called war—whether it was as glorious as he had been led to believe.

The warm Normandy summer had given way to the torrential downpours of autumn. Roads turned to mud. Jeeps got stuck. French prostitutes complained that the weather was hurting business. Fritz's unit continued to hopscotch around: from Sinspelt north to Hanover. From

Hanover to Hunsrück. From Hunsrück to a position near Pirmasens, Germany, just across the border from France.

"It's your fault, Engelbert," joked Döring. "Ever since you hooked up with us, we hop around like frogs."

"Hey, we're alive."

"For now."

It was uncomfortable for soldiers to have their backs to the wall. On October 21, Allied troops had captured their first German city, Aachen. It had come at a high price—five thousand casualties, almost as many as the Germans had suffered—but it was a boost to American morale. When word got to Engelbert and the 901st in Hunsrück, they deplored the fact that German troops had not only been backed into their *Vaterland* but had lost their first struggle to defend a major city. By early November, the so-called liberators were occupying territory along the border that they hadn't planned on reaching until May 1945.

Engelbert was still writing the occasional letter home, beginning each with his trademark "My dear parents" and ending with: "Greetings to family and friends. For today I send you my love, Yours Fritz."

The letters suggested that he was unsettled by a lack of purpose. "The uncertainty of where we will go now is a bit depressing," he wrote.

Many Allied units, particularly to the south, were also in a holding pattern. After the breakout from Normandy, the Third Army had moved so quickly across France that fuel supplies couldn't keep pace—and an army couldn't effectively advance without gas.

But the struggle for territory had slowed, not ended. On December 1, 1944, the 901st prepared for an attack on American soldiers who had broken through the German line to capture Weislingen in the Alsace region of northeast France. Germany wanted it back.

Up to this point, Fritz said in a letter home, casualties in his unit had been light. That was about to change. Two platoons—twenty men in trucks and half-tracks—eased to the outskirts of the village; they had been told that reinforcements would soon arrive. Each half-track was capable of transporting about ten soldiers. But the half-tracks were vulnerable to shells coming in from above: the rear part of the interior was exposed.

At 3:00 a.m., a quarter moon shining through the clouds washed the farmland in just enough light that 5th Company could see the scattered houses, barns, and church spire in the village. Recon suggested that the Americans suspected nothing. Ten men, including Fritz, dismounted from one half-track. They set up a command post in an abandoned house far from the main village. Fritz would work as a messenger from there but be ready to join the attack if needed. His stomach lurched; as he would write to his parents, "We looked forward to the dawn of the day with some concern."

Döring noted Engelbert's nervousness. He leaned against the half-track and crushed his cigarette.

"Geht es dir gut?"

Engelbert nodded, though tentatively.

"Ja, mir geht's gut."

Or at least he was pretending to be all right.

Up ahead the platoon leader nodded toward the first house they would attack. He crossed a cobbled path, his head swiveling left and right.

Once at the house, he shattered a window with a well-placed kick and tossed in a stick grenade.

Kaboom! The battle was on. It turned out that the Americans had been cloistered in cellars and attics. There was shouting. Panic. Finally, gunfire. Soon the village was alive with a maddening medley of machine guns, small arms, grenades, bazookas, and an occasional scream and moan. Engelbert was quickly ordered to join the fight.

"Some houses were smoked out with hand grenades, machine guns, and bazookas," he would write to his parents. "It was a mad shoot-out."

The German patrol leaders knew they didn't have enough strength to take the entire village, so they concentrated on one section, still expecting the reinforcements to arrive soon. The *crack-crack-crack* of a carbine sent one of Fritz's comrades twisting to the earth, his gun flying; he screamed in agony. *Blam. Blam.* Another German, Staff Sergeant Rudolf Schrader, was dead before he hit the ground. It was the first time Engelbert had seen a man die.

Whit, whit.

A platoon leader whistled to Engelbert, signaling to him to move forward and take cover behind a half-track. The leader's hand signals indicated where to fire and how many Americans might be inside. Fritz wheeled around the edge of the half-track and fired, then jerked back, the rush taking the edge off his nerves. But it seemed that the Americans were too well-hidden for him to get a good shot. The battle raged on. One hour. Two. A hint of morning light began to slowly steal the Germans' cover.

The radio squawked; the company commander was to report to the battalion immediately. He fell back. Engelbert didn't like the look of things. One soldier dead. One wounded. The company commander gone. Their cover of darkness disappearing. And the promised reinforcements nowhere to be seen. He glanced at the other helmeted men in gray coats to his left and right, behind the cover of rock walls, outbuildings, and haystacks. The return fire from the Americans was relentless. Fritz exhaled.

Another squawk from the radio. A whisper: *Engine noise. Middle of village.*

"Our foreboding had been confirmed," Fritz would say in a letter home.

Soon an American tank rolled through the early-morning mist like a pirate ship, its snout swinging left and right as if it had eyes. Engelbert bristled with fear. A shell shattered the earth nearby, showering him in dirt, gravel, and a gray-coated arm. His stomach lurched.

"When it got light, hell was going on," he would write to his parents. The Germans had underestimated the size of the American unit.

The half-track that had been an asset was now a liability; the Americans had clearly zeroed in on the cluster of soldiers in and behind it. Engelbert fired a few shots, then scurried to cover behind a cluster of wagons.

"At first everything was quiet, then suddenly the tanks unleashed three shots in a row. At each one, one of our half-tracks exploded. Shortly thereafter, wild infantry fire lit up the whole village."

Had Engelbert stayed, he would have been torn to pieces. The enemy fire only increased, bullets whizzing left and right. Grenades exploded. Men yelled. It was sheer madness. Fritz's chest heaved with anxiety. His neckerchief was soaked in sweat.

The platoon leader barked a panicked order. "Jeder für sich!" ("Every man for himself!") Men left their positions and ran. The gunfire spiked to an even more intense level. Engelbert looked across at Döring, who pointed to a grove across a field. Fritz nodded. Together they fled.

Amid the panic, a memory flashed back from basic training—*if you must run from the enemy, be the ship with a submarine on its ass. Never go in a straight line.*

"I jumped in a zigzag like a rabbit," he wrote to his parents. "The bullets were whistling around my ears."

Döring tilted his head back, his teeth clenched, no less desperate than his friend. For just a moment Engelbert was back in Hilchenbach and Döring was his rival, the boy to beat to win the town cup. He dug deeper. His pace quickened even as he jutted left, then right. He was leaving Döring behind. His lungs heaved; his legs ached.

It was just another hundred feet to the grove. Fritz had never felt such panic, such fear, such vulnerability; his legs and arms pumped madly, fueled by sheer desperation. To his left and right, he made out the jiggling blurs of others fleeing—and falling.

Crack. One man dropped.

Crack. Crack. Two more.

Fifty feet.

Ch-ch-ch-ch-ch-ch-ch-ch.

An American machine-gunner had joined the shooting gallery. Engelbert waited for the bullets to hit his back. None came. Instead, he heard a voice behind him.

"Oye, hombre!"

It was Döring! He hadn't given up. The two were soon even. Stride for stride, like two schoolboys—the two Fritzes—in a village race. For just a millisecond they flashed each other nervous smiles.

A flurry of bullets tattered the ground, left, right, behind, and beyond. The two ran harder.

Twenty-five feet.

Out of nowhere, a lifetime of buried emotions rose deep within Engelbert. He could see them in the woods, reaching out for him, and despite everything, he reached, too.

Mutter! Vater!

Fritzy!

Crack!

It wasn't the sound of the rifle shot that shocked Engelbert; he had been hearing gunfire for hours. It was the realization, with a frantic glance to his right, that Döring had been shot. His friend's face contorted in a collage of shock, pain, and helplessness, as if he desperately wanted to stay with Fritz but could not. He dropped like a drowning man sinking into the sea.

Fritz crashed through tall brush and into the woods, safe—for now. He bent over, wheezing, hands on his knees, face drenched with sweat. He glanced back to see if Döring was still alive, if he could go back, rescue him, drag him—

"Quick, in the half-track!" yelled Staff Sergeant Hubert Solke.

"But Döring, the oth—"

"Now!"

Fritz piled in along with three other soldiers. The vehicle rumbled away. Where was everybody else? He peeked above the armored sides of the half-track. Scattered across the field were his comrade's bodies.

"Down, Engelbert!" yelled Solke. "You'll get your head shot off."

The 901st rolled back to Pirmasens. On the way they were met by their company commander, Lieutenant Karl Neupert. Engelbert had great respect for Neupert, a man committed not only to The Cause but also to his men. He was thirty-one, twelve years older than Fritz, who saw him as not just his commanding officer but his mentor, too.

Neupert grieved at what he saw—a single half-track with only four men in it.

"Sir, four armored vehicles lost," said the only platoon leader still alive. "Sixteen men dead, captured, or missing."

Neupert looked down and rubbed his brow with his hand. Writing home to his parents, Engelbert remembered: "Tears came to his eyes. The only thing he said was, 'My beautiful company...'" The lieutenant buried his face in his hands.

Back in Hunsrück, Fritz could think of little beyond the war in general and the death of Döring in particular. Always a quiet young man, he now turned silent. Even if he had wanted to talk, there was hardly anyone left in his platoon. "Our division is heavily shattered," he wrote. The Weislingen debacle had been a "heavy blow."

With every new experience since basic training, Fritz's illusions about war and honor had unraveled. First the inhumane treatment by his superiors in Orleans, then mass death in Argentan, now the decimation of his platoon and the death of a close friend. One moment he and Döring were together stride for stride; the next, his friend was gone. By this point in the war one of every three German soldiers had been wounded or killed.

For a young man who had pined for war, Fritz Engelbert was ready to be done with it. "Christmas is in two weeks!" he wrote to his parents. "Let's hope and pray that it's the last Christmas in the war!!!!"

Winter was deepening in Germany's Eifel region. The first snow fell. One afternoon, Neupert placed an Iron Cross Second Class pin in Engelbert's hand. "For bravery in battle," he said. "At Weislingen." Fritz didn't think himself worthy of such honor. Why should he be lauded because an American soldier targeted Döring's back instead of his? Because Fritz had, in his desperation, survived? That said, he was gratified that a man he respected so deeply had felt him worthy of the honor.

"Have you heard?" a comrade asked him the next day.

Rumors were quickening the pulses of men who had grown up being told by Hitler that they—Germany's young people—were the reason that the Führer would be able to "make a new world." Hitler had no intention of surrendering. On the contrary, Germany was planning a surprise counteroffensive, a gallant do-or-die effort to reverse the results of the war.

That's all Engelbert needed to hear. The news rejuvenated him. He would gladly join that attack, for the honor of the Führer. His hopes rose.

Germany was going to win this damn war.

Don

"Let's go, Easy! Get your asses outta bed, ladies!"

Outside Mourmelon, France, on December 18, 1944, Malarkey was awakened in the night to find a flashlight shining in his face and an officer eyeing him with impatience.

"Get up, Malark!" he said.

Malarkey was discombobulated. *What the hell?* Was it the five grand he'd won in craps that night? Was someone claiming he'd cheated?

"Hey, I won that dough fair and—"

"Shut your pie hole, Malark. A major German offensive has begun in Belgium. Caught us with our pants down. Already put a helluva dent in our line. Pile your personal crap in the middle of the room and report to company supply to get whatever you can in terms of equipment."

Malarkey's reaction was the same response the nocturnal visitor was getting from everyone else: great reluctance to move. After fighting in Holland for six weeks, Easy Company had been at Camp Mourmelon in France for the last three. It was heaven. The men were sleeping in warm beds, vacated not too long before by German soldiers. For the first time in seemingly forever, the men in the 506th had been paid. The food was far better than the "mutton crap" of Holland. And there was talk of New Year's Eve in Paris. Who would want to leave a place like—

"Now!" shouted the officer.

Within hours the men of Easy Company were jostling knee to knee in the back of a high-sided cattle truck. The journey was a little over one hundred miles, the temperature not much above freezing. Men blew on their hands, flipped their coat collars high, anything to ward off the mid-December chill. Nobody was prepared for winter fighting. Nobody was prepared for fighting, period. They had been issued no wool overcoats, no long underwear, no wool socks. And MPs breaking up bar fights in Paris had more ammunition than they did.

For Malarkey, war was getting old. Normandy had been novel and triumphant; the victory at Brécourt Manor had infused him and his buddies with confidence. Going back to England had been heaven. But Holland had been hell.

It had started off well enough—a daylight jump on September 17, 1944. Don was a newly minted staff sergeant. The Dutch people showered the liberating forces with food, beer, and kisses. But if the game was off to a great start, war batted last.

Near Nuenen, Compton had taken bullets in the butt and pleaded for his men to "get the hell out of here! Leave me!" They didn't. At 220 pounds—he had played for UCLA in the 1943 Rose Bowl—Compton was tough to carry, so the men ripped a door off a farm outbuilding, lashed him to it, and dragged him to safety.

Near the Veghel-Uden Highway, the British were running five U.S.-made Sherman tanks, one of whose commanders made a terrible tactical error. A German Tiger picked off all five like beer cans on a stump. The tanks were ablaze. With help from others, Malarkey climbed the turret of one and yanked out a couple of survivors. The commander's hands had been blown off.

Atop a dike one night, Lieutenant Frederick "Moose" Heyliger was seriously wounded by one of his own men who panicked, mistook him for a German, and shot him.

Malarkey was soon sick of Holland. The casualties were one reason; Easy had jumped with 154 men, including replacements, and a third were either dead or wounded—some, like Joe Toye, had been sent back for medical treatment for the second time. The food was terrible. And military life had gotten boring. A nighttime river rescue helped ease the boredom—Don helped get 125 British soldiers, 10 Dutch resistance fighters, and 5 American pilots back from across enemy lines and the Lower Rhine—but Malarkey had a hard time seeing any pattern or purpose to the fighting in Holland.

All of which had made Camp Mourmelon in newly liberated France such a godsend. For a while, the war simply went away. Men practiced for a football game they had planned for Christmas Day. Slept. Gambled. Drank. And warmed to the idea of not being at war.

Now, as the truck bounced toward Bastogne—and back to war—it hadn't escaped Malarkey that Mourmelon was centered roughly between two places of significance to him: Château-Thierry, about sixty miles west, where Malarkey's Uncle Gerald had died in World War I, and the Argonne Forest, about the same distance to the east, where his Uncle Bob had been gassed.

Had Don avenged their deaths? It wasn't a question that haunted him, but now and then it nagged him for an answer. Malarkey's answer was no. Only one thing would avenge their deaths: victory.

Soon, Mourmelon was far behind. After nearly three hours, the men's shivers had turned to numbness, their stomachs uneasy from the bouncy ride and exhaust fumes. Some lost their breakfasts.

A cold rain fell as they entered Belgium's Ardennes Forest. Easy Company's boys bailed out of the trucks a couple of miles north of Bastogne. As they walked toward the front line, haggard American soldiers—elements of the 28th "Bloody Bucket" Infantry Division and the 10th

Armored Division—were walking away from it in retreat. Their heads were down, shoulders slumped, some with arms in slings or bandages around their heads.

Bit by bit, the Easy Company men heard the rumors, news that quickened the pulses of these men who had grown weary of war but bristled at a challenge. The Germans had run over an entire American army, and they couldn't be stopped.

"The Germans will kill you all," said one retreating American soldier, with a dismissive lift of his head.

That was all Malarkey needed to hear. He would gladly take that challenge—for the honor of Uncle Gerald and Uncle Bob. And, yes, for his country. His hopes rose.

The 101st was going to win this damn war.

CHAPTER 6

Casualties and Chaos

It was the not knowing that quickened the heartbeats of Private Fritz Engelbert and his comrades in the fog-shrouded grove of pines. That made their mouths go dry as they waited to make the attack. That whispered possibilities of disaster amid hopes of victory. At times a man in the 5th Company of the Panzer Lehr Division, Regiment 901, would hear something from the Americans in the village—a jeep or tank rumbling to life—and wonder if the forest-protected Germans had been seen. For now, amid the stillness of bone-chilling cold and dark, was the waiting. Anticipation. Worry.

It was the morning of Wednesday, December 20, 1944, the fourth day of the German counteroffensive. History would remember it as the Battle of the Bulge, but at the time the Germans called it Operation Wacht am Rhein (Watch on the Rhine). Hitler's prime goal was to create a breach between British forces in the north and American forces in the south by capturing Antwerp, Belgium, a major Allied port for supplies. Taking Bastogne, a key transportation hub with seven major roads running through it, was a means to that end.

Nearly a million troops were fighting on the seventy-mile-long line, with Germany holding an initial advantage in troop strength. The Germans had all but surrounded four Allied armies. General Heinrich von Lüttwitz was considering sending an ultimatum to the Americans in Bastogne demanding surrender of the town; otherwise, he would threaten, Germany would massacre the trapped soldiers.

The previous week, hearing of the Germans' surprise attack, U.S. general Dwight D. Eisenhower had decided to defend Bastogne at all costs, and the U.S. 101st Airborne Division was ordered there.

The German encirclement of the 101st—and Don Malarkey—would be complete before day's end. Wounded soldiers needing medical attention wouldn't be able to be transported out, and food, ammunition, and medical supplies wouldn't be able to be transported in. Meanwhile, a heavy cloud cover was making it unsafe, if not impossible, for air drops of supplies.

Although the Germans had "lassoed" the Americans, they still needed to split the front and take Bastogne, whose last defense to the southeast was Marvie. The village was being defended by the United States' Team O'Hara, from Combat Command B, 10th Armored Division, and it would be reinforced—unbeknownst to 5th Company of the German 901st—by the U.S. 2nd Battalion, 327th Glider Infantry Regiment, 101st Airborne.

Taking Marvie would put the Germans on Bastogne's front porch. And 5th Company was confident it could be done. "At the beginning of our offensive in the Ardennes," Engelbert would say decades later, "we could not even begin to doubt that the victory would be ours."

Fifth Company would roll forward with four Mark IV tanks, six half-tracks, and one self-propelled gun—basically a tank without a turret for protection from enemy fire. And just short of a hundred men.

"Gott mit uns!" a soldier yelled. Yes, thought Fritz, God is with us! First Marvie, then Bastogne, then Antwerp, then victory in Europe! As the German soldiers talked, their confidence grew. Lieutenant Karl Neupert, their company commander, nodded his head in approval; this was just what he had been hoping for.

Fritz looked at his comrades. Döring was no longer among them. God, he missed his friend. But others remained, and by now the routine of war had bonded them in a desperate quest for victory. There was Neupert. There was Solke, who had rescued Fritz in the half-track after his sprint across the field at Weislingen. Engelbert had now been part of 5th Company for nearly six months, and he was proud to go to battle with such men.

Neupert turned to his *Landsers*; it was time. Engelbert grabbed his Gewehr 43, a semi-automatic rifle similar to the American Garand.

"Kompanie, aufgesessen!"

Men grabbed rifles and rushed to their half-tracks. The tanks rumbled to life. Smoke belched into the sky. And without delay the unit forged forward toward Marvie, the front tires of the half-tracks bouncing and the treads clanking on the muddy road. In front of the triangle formation:

four tanks and a self-propelled gun; in the second wave, three half-tracks, each with ten to twelve face-to-face soldiers in the open-roof back; in the third wave, two half-tracks; and at the rear, one half-track, Engelbert riding in the back, Neupert and the driver up front, able to see forward through the vehicle's loophole squint "eyes." It was the commander's job to observe and conduct the assault from the rear.

They crossed a ditch and moved across an open pasture, going slightly uphill in the vicinity of a little creek. The tanks opened fire on the village. Solke's half-track growled forward, its 7.5cm cannon firing fast and furiously. Walls of houses collapsed. Roofs caught fire. American soldiers scurried for cover.

"Der Ami rennt! Der Ami rennt!" Adrenaline-pumped soldiers screamed in glee that the Americans were running. Fritz remembers thinking: *This is it. The tide is turning.* "We raged forward like an excited bull!" he would say.

Then it happened: Hidden U.S. tanks emerged from cover and began returning fire. From the north, on the road to Bastogne, four Sherman tanks from the 10th Armored Division (Team O'Hara) rumbled through the fog and began blasting. One of the Mark IVs took a direct hit.

Ka-boom, ka-boom, ka-boom!

Soon the German's front wave was getting hammered. The half-track with Solke in it exploded in a tangle of steel, fire, and flesh. Engelbert reeled. *Oh, nein, Hubert!* On the Germans' flanks, reinforcements from the Americans' 327th Glider Infantry Regiment—Neupert hadn't planned on them—had dug in and were peppering the pursuit with small-arms fire and bazookas.

But guns blazing, 5th Company continued its attack on the Americans defending Marvie. Engelbert saw some of his comrades emerge from the open back doors of the half-tracks a few hundred yards to the east of the town and overrun some of the Glider infantry and take them prisoner. The Americans were forced to follow the half-tracks, hands in the air.

But as the fight continued, the Americans' Sherman tanks were firing broadside at the first line of Mark IVs and half-tracks. The German tanks and half-tracks were pulverized, bursting into flames, the few surviving soldiers scrambling for cover.

Ka-boom, ka-boom, ka-boom!

Again, a glimmer of hope: the self-propelled "Hetzer" on the right flank reached the village's edge and turned its snout toward the line of Sherman tanks. Like two cowboys in a Western duel, each drew for his gun. The Sherman drew faster. The Hetzer exploded in a fireball. Beyond, barns, houses, and outbuildings roiled in flames, smoke adding to the surreal atmosphere of the battle. A close-range bazooka ignited a Mark IV. Engelbert, from his place in the German rear, realized the situation had become life-or-death. The field was littered with his comrades.

Ping! Ping! Ping! Bullets hammered the sides of the half-track he was in. He rose and fired an occasional shot, even though he sensed it was too little, too late. A shell whistled overhead—*boom!*—barely missing the half-track, a geyser of dirt and shrapnel pounding down. Gusts of artillery shells burst even closer. The Shermans were relentless. *Ka-boom! Ka-boom! Ka-boom!* From somewhere, an American machine-gunner joined the cacophony of madness: *ch-ch-ch-ch-ch-ch-ch-ch-ch-ch-ch-ch-ch-ch-ch-ch-ch-ch.*

Tanks rumbled. Soldiers screamed. Bullets zinged. Engelbert's ears rang from the noise. Amid the firestorm, he realized that machine-gun bullets had so thoroughly peppered the armored walls of the half-track he was riding in that the heat was peeling the paint and rust off the *inside* walls. Across from his bench, some of his comrades were frozen in fear. One was praying out loud.

Gott beschütze uns! Gott beschütze uns!

Engelbert silently asked his mother for strength.

Mutter, hilf mir, bitte!

A German machine-gunner spotted a cluster of Americans in foxholes and blurted fire from close range. In the smoke that now hung over the body-littered pasture like a death fog, Commander Neupert's half-track with ten soldiers inside rumbled ever forward, a wisp of hope. Two half-tracks had somehow reached the first farmhouses. A family of Belgian civilians watched in horror from their hideaway in a stable as German soldiers bailed out of the back of the other half-track and started engaging the Glider infantry in hand-to-hand combat. Neupert was buoyed by the aggressiveness of his men; this battle wasn't over yet. The Germans could still prevail.

Suddenly, a surprise: to his right, one of the German Mark IVs—commanded by a *Hauptmann*, a captain who outranked Neupert—suddenly stopped. It pivoted right. Pivoted right again. And headed to the rear, obviously in pursuit of the safety of the woods.

What the hell? Neupert couldn't believe what he was seeing. His half-track—Engelbert in back—pushed relentlessly forward, even though he and the few others still alive suddenly had less firepower—and the

Americans could concentrate better on their targets. Amid the concussion of bombs and spraying of machine-gun fire, he saw the carnage: German vehicles were on fire, on their sides, stalled, or—taking the lead of the captain—retreating. The smell of charred flesh assaulted Engelbert's nostrils.

Lieutenant Neupert, in a front-row seat, had seen even more than Fritz had seen—and it had sickened him. He swiveled his head to the pale faces of the ten young men in the back, the 901st's last, best hope. Some were barely half his age. The plan was to have them deploy from the half-track, take cover in the barns, and fight. But in the last fifteen minutes, the Mark IV's retreat had sounded a death knell. For the Germans, the challenge was now like trying to kill a bear with a pocket knife.

"Kehrt marsch, marsch!" he barked to the driver.

Amid the flashes and booms, it wasn't a call he wanted to make, but retreating at least gave his men a chance to regroup and live to fight another day. This battle was lost. The half-track turned crazily in an arcing about-face and headed for the woods, shells dogging it.

Two hours after they had attacked, the last of 5th Company limped back to the woods; only a handful of soldiers were still alive.

Safely in the grove, Fritz leaned against a tree in bewilderment. "I'd never been in a battle with such fury," he would say. Nor had he seen a retreat like that. It was another crack in his Third Reich armor: *Maybe the men around me aren't as deeply committed to the cause as I thought.*

Lieutenant Neupert flew to the captain of the retreating tank in a rage.

"Sie Feigling! Sie haben uns im Stich gelassen!" he shouted in his face. ("I promise I'll never attack side by side with your tanks!")

Engelbert was stunned at his commander's nerve. The captain was two notches above Neupert on the military pecking order; this was like a student rebuking his teacher. In the German army, men were sometimes shot on the spot for insubordinate behavior. But Neupert wasn't through.

"Sie sind ein Feigling!" ("You are a coward!")

The captain's face went from anger to, oddly, acceptance. Or was it shame?

"I can only excuse your imputation to your excitement and anger," he told the lieutenant. "And I will not pursue any action against you."

Engelbert concluded that deep down, the captain knew he had cowered in battle. And he respected the lieutenant who had dared to call him out.

Engelbert looked around at the tattered remains of 5th Company. Ninety-six men had gone into the battle and seventy-nine had become casualties. Seventeen men were left. Later, when the accounting was done, it was determined that twenty-nine had been killed while still in their vehicles, thirty had died in hand-to-hand combat, and twenty had been taken prisoner. Of their eleven vehicles, only Neupert's half-track and the Mark IV had made it through.

Darkness descended on 5th Company, accompanied by light flurries of snow. It would be the longest night of Fritz Engelbert's life. He was rattled by what had just happened, shivering from the cold, and fearful about what the next day might bring.

Could it get any worse?

Don

In the Ardennes Forest, it was the quiet that spoke loudest. That spooked. That whispered doubt as the men of Easy Company waited. A man would hear something, lunge for his rifle, and realize it was only the clink of a canteen or the fluttering wings of a nuthatch that was starving in the cold, just like these newcomers to the woods. For now, amid the bone-chilling cold was stillness, waiting, anticipation, worry. Some men preferred all-out fighting to waiting, which carried with it a fear that the chaos of combat did not.

Waiting is a huge part of war. But this waiting came with an extra chill—and not just from the freezing temperatures. By now word had sprinkled through the 101st that, three days before, Waffen-SS soldiers had gunned down eighty-four U.S. POWs clustered together near Malmedy, Belgium. The Easy Company men had seen the thousand-yard stares of the men walking from the line, the men from the 28th Infantry and 10th Armored Division whom they were replacing. And they had arrived to see the remnants of war in the forest of the Bois Jacques.

"You could see that they had a hell of a fight there," Bill Guarnere would write in his memoir, *Brothers in Battle, Best of Friends*. "The ground had craters from the 88s, shell cases, and tree branches all over, dead GIs, and limbs—an arm here, a leg there, blood, and guts."

Now it was two days later: Wednesday, December 20, 1944. Hunger was already gnawing at the men's stomachs like starved rats. Arriving at Bastogne from Mourmelon, some men in E Company had bummed K-rations from soldiers in retreat. Others were making nocturnal missions to local farms, pawing through gardens and chicken coops to dig out potatoes or grab eggs. And smoking their cigarettes to the final nub.

The men of Easy Company didn't have enough of anything: food, warm clothes, ammunition, or, for the moment, ambition. Even hydration was a problem; men would wake to find the water in their canteens frozen solid. And to think, mused Malarkey, that just a few days ago he had slept in a warm bed with scotch on his breath and $5,000 worth of craps winnings in his back pocket.

He tried to dig his foxhole deeper with an army shovel, but between frozen soil and pine roots it was like digging through Haystack Rock back home on the Oregon coast.

"Malark, whataya got in terms of ammo?" Lieutenant Buck Compton asked, his breath not only heard but seen in the cold.

Don searched his pockets.

"One clip and a couple of grenades. No Tommy gun ammo at all. In other words, squat."

Compton tossed him a clip, then went on to the next guy, blowing on his hands to keep them warm.

The men in E Company of the 101st Airborne's 506th Parachute Infantry Regiment were perched in the forest just east of the Bastogne-Foy road, three miles north-northeast of the town the Americans occupied and the Germans wanted: Bastogne. Easy Company's 140 men were spread thin along a 500-yard stretch of the front.

Five miles south, the church spire in Marvie rose above the trees near where the 5th Company of Panzer Lehr Division, Regiment 901, had awakened that morning. If Bastogne was the center of a round clock,

Malarkey was at one or two o'clock and Engelbert at four or five o'clock, each fighting a different battle.

Compton was distributing ammo to his men; he had heard that the Germans had nearly encircled the Americans, which would make the 101st the proverbial "hole in the doughnut." To the northeast, beyond the Bois Jacques and beyond the fields, lay the village of Foy, temporary home for an ever-increasing number of German troops.

With their field glasses, scouts from the 101st in the outpost position (OP) could see the armored vehicles in the villages, their numbers growing each day, the German soldiers scurrying about in white camouflage to blend in with the snow. (Presumably their heavy artillery was tucked behind outbuildings or trees.) Each day, the GIs would watch with envy as trucks and tanks rolled in with more supplies. Not that all German units had it so good, but in Foy smoke curled from the chimneys of Belgian homes that the toasty warm *Landsers* now occupied.

To the 101st, it looked like a spoil of riches. Malarkey was wrapping his boots in burlap bags to keep his feet from freezing. Some U.S. soldiers were wrapping themselves in Belgian bed sheets for camouflage when making forays across snow-covered fields. And at night the Americans were curling up in foxholes, not in houses with fireplaces. With their supply lines cut, E Company had no way of getting the food, water, and ammo it needed. And it effectively had but a single piece of artillery to cover the entire Foy area.

What the Germans couldn't have known was that every day that the 101st repelled an attack—every day the Germans weren't able to punch a hole in the line—was giving General George S. Patton and his huge

Third Army time to advance from the south. And America's flyboys an opportunity for the skies to clear so they could get their birds in the air, allowing the now-grounded aerial attack to resume.

The question was: How long could the 101st hold on?

What the Americans lacked in resources, they made up for in resolve. When Staff Sergeant Malarkey took a jeep into Bastogne to pick up what limited supplies he could, he learned that the Germans had completed the circle. The 101st Airborne was officially surrounded. There was no way out—except by fighting their way through the enemy, which, against huge odds, they were just cocky enough to believe they could do.

"They've got us surrounded," said a 101st medic while giving a wounded man crème de menthe for pain because they were out of morphine. "The poor bastards."

On Thursday, December 21, snow began falling—beautiful, swirling, mesmerizing snow, flakes the size of poker chips. A few skirmishes broke out, though nothing serious. It was a chess game, the Germans probing here, the Americans probing there. The unknowns kept everyone on alert. Easy Company might have guys up front on patrol, but that was no guarantee that a German patrol couldn't slither through—or, for that matter, that the Germans wouldn't start lobbing 88mm shells from the villages below.

The next day, December 22, snow fell even harder, almost a foot deep in some places. Shivering in his foxhole, Malarkey recited "Invictus" to himself to keep his mind off the cold. The stubble on men's faces grew. The impatience deepened. The stalemate continued. The Germans must have suspected that the 101st was in no position to mount an all-out assault on the villages below; they didn't have enough ammo. Or perhaps they were banking on the Americans' surrendering; the German lines were rife with the rumor that any day an ultimatum would be made to the Americans: *surrender Bastogne and live, or keep fighting—and die.*

Meanwhile, Malarkey and the others went on patrols, dug their foxholes deeper, and shivered. GI field shoes weren't waterproof; across the entire line, trench foot was felling soldiers by the thousands. It got so bad that some developed gangrene and had to have one or both feet amputated. Between November 1944 and April 1945, forty-five thousand American soldiers were hospitalized for trench foot.

The other type of injury that medical personnel were getting in droves was shock. Psychological wounds. For every three men killed or wounded, one was hospitalized for combat exhaustion. A few took their own lives, or tried to. Others intentionally shot themselves in the foot so they'd be unable to keep fighting—and might get a "ticket home." It was the coward's way out. Then again, it was a way out.

Besides Skip Muck, Malarkey's closest E Company friend was Joe Toye. Malarkey thought Toye was the toughest man in Easy Company— despite his "softer side," which came out when he sang guys to sleep with off-key Irish ballads or his favorite, "I'll Be Seeing You." Joe hailed from a coal-mining family in Reading, Pennsylvania, his rough-hewn personality hiding insecurities known to few beyond Malarkey. Toye hadn't finished high school. His vocabulary was straight from the coal mines. He had wanted to play college football but his father forbade it; "You belong," he said, "in the mines."

Back in England, Joe had had one too many one night, and Malarkey had to talk him off the roof of a hotel atrium. When Malarkey calmed him down, Joe broke down about feeling like a failure.

"I'm not just blowing smoke when I say this, but you're the most admired man in Easy," Malarkey told him. "Ask any of 'em. They'll tell you."

Not long after that, when a drunk Easy Company soldier pulled a knife on Malarkey, it was Toye who pinned the guy to a wall and threatened to kill him if he laid a finger on Don again. Twice Toye had been wounded seriously enough to get a ticket home; twice he'd returned to the front lines. And he had just been wounded a third time, in the Bois Jacques, taking shrapnel in the wrist when a German plane swooped low and dropped an antipersonnel bomb.

"You lucky SOB," Malarkey said to him, thinking that Toye's war was over.

"I'll be back, Malark."

Less than a week later, Malarkey was shivering in his foxhole early one evening—half asleep, half awake—when he heard the baritone voice with an Irish lilt, almost on key: *"I'll be seeing you in all the old familiar places. . . ."* He smiled to himself.

Toye was back.

On December 23 came a sound from the sky. *Planes!* Sure enough, the clouds had broken up and C-47 transport planes—the same type of plane from which E Company had bailed over Normandy—were making supply drops with parachutes. Ammunition. Food. Clothing. More than eight hundred tons' worth. The cheers were loud. The resupply did wonders for the men's morale. So did a one-page newsletter written by General A. C. McAuliffe and delivered by jeep on Christmas Eve. It was about how, two days earlier, the German commander had had the gall to demand the surrender of Bastogne.

Four Germans—two officers and two enlisted men—had headed for Bastogne, white flags waving, but were stopped by Americans at a farmhouse on the outskirts of Marvie. Their message was forwarded to McAuliffe. It was printed in English on a single sheet of onion-skin paper and dated December 22, 1944:

To the U.S.A. Commander of the encircled town of Bastogne.

The fortune of war is changing. This time the U.S.A. forces in and near Bastogne have been encircled by strong German armored units. More German armored units have crossed the river Ourthe near Ortheuville, have taken Marche and reached St. Hubert by passing through Hompre-Sibret-Tillet. Libramont is in German hands.

There is only one possibility to save the encircled U.S.A. troops from total annihilation: that is the honorable surrender of the encircled town. In order to think it over, a term of two hours will be granted beginning with the presentation of this note.

If this proposal should be rejected one German Artillery Corps and six heavy A.A. Battalions are ready to annihilate the U.S.A. troops in and near Bastogne. The order for firing will be given immediately after this two hours' term.

All the serious civilian losses caused by this artillery fire would not correspond with the well-known American humanity.

McAuliffe had told them "Nuts." *Shove it. Go to hell. No!*

The formality of the German request and the informality of the American response underscored a notable difference between the two armies. Because of the years of systematic training provided by Hitler Youth and a continued emphasis on discipline, camaraderie, and high expectations, the German army had an almost robotic confidence embedded in each soldier from the get-go, now bolstered by a final burst of do-or-die pride. What the Americans had was ingenuity, faith in themselves, and a brashness that they tended to back up with action. On paper, they were already beaten, but how do you measure bravado—the against-all-odds confidence that you will prevail no matter what?

On Christmas Eve, Winters was trying to keep his men's spirits up.

"Hang tough," he'd say, going from man to man.

Temperatures dropped. The wind picked up. Malarkey and the others huddled in their foxholes, knowing that the Germans were out there, in the dark, waiting. They sang "Silent Night"—the Luftwaffe bombs over Bastogne adding uneasy percussion.

Christmas Day brought gloriously blue skies for flying, and the American Thunderbolts rocked German troops—and, unfortunately, civilians—in dozens of villages surrounding Bastogne. The next day, when Patton's Third Army punched a hole in the southern edge of the "loop" that was threatening to strangle American troops, the 101st had a way of getting supplies in and the wounded out. And the Allied force in general had a ton more firepower. The breakthrough bolstered everyone's moods, though the 101st wasn't buying this crap about "being saved" by Patton's boys. Said Malarkey: "Nobody in the 101st will ever say we needed rescuing."

By New Year's, Easy Company under Captain Winters had been on the front lines in Belgium for fourteen days. The nights seemed endless. Darkness fell shortly after four o'clock in the afternoon.

Meanwhile, the back-and-forth with the Germans became a deadly game of Russian roulette. Late in the afternoon on January 3, light was beginning to fade and Easy Company was returning to its positions in the woods after yet another "probe" north to test the Germans and see where a weakness might be exploited. Suddenly, German 88mm shells started exploding around the troops.

"Incoming!" yelled Winters. "Take cover!"

Ka-boom! Ka-boom! Ka-boom!

The forest shook. The noise was deafening. Men fell on their faces in the snow and scurried toward foxholes that didn't always exist. The attack was like a storm; the rockets howled like the wind. It was harrowing enough being shelled by the 88s, but worse in a forest. The shells were designed to explode on contact, and they would often hit high up in the trees, detonate, and create "tree bursts" that flung shrapnel and knife-like splinters of wood in all directions. The trees themselves had become weapons, snapping and falling to compound the chaos.

Ka-boom! Ka-boom! Ka-boom!

Nothing in Malarkey's hundred-plus days of battle had been as intense, as loud, as incessant as this. He would say the barrage made his "head reel, ears pop, and . . . his heart stop beating." He found a foxhole. Through the smoke, he saw someone curled in a fetal position. Noise pounded—*ka-boom, ka-boom, ka-boom.* The concussion threatened to shatter Malarkey's eardrums. He could hear only faint voices. Instructions. Warnings. Fear.

Ka-boom! Ka-boom!

The shells thundered down in relentless pursuit, as if each man had one with his name on it. Each shell packed thirty-two pounds of metal and high explosives. The bombs ripped through the snow, sending dirt, hot metal, and wood fragments into the sky and then raining down in chaos.

"I'm hit, I'm hit!"

The voice sounded familiar to Malarkey.

Oh, God, no. Please, no!

"Joe, that you?"

It was Toye, every instinct in his coal miner's blood raging against defeat—even if his left leg had been blown off and lay by itself in the snow.

"Gotta get up, gotta get up."

"Medic!" Malarkey yelled. "Medic!"

"Gotta get going. Gotta keep going."

Seeing a wounded man out in the open, alone and in pain, was an invitation for disaster: every man in the unit wanted to rush to his aid. The Germans exploited such empathy—with glee. Guy rushes out to help. *Blam!* Two for one.

But as Toye kept trying desperately to move, Bill Guarnere couldn't help himself. He crawled out of his foxhole and started for his best friend.

"No! Ge' back, Bill!" someone yelled. "Stay down!"

But Guarnere couldn't take seeing Joe in such pain. So vulnerable. So helpless. He rushed to him, grabbed him, and had started to slide him when—

Ka-boom!

The earth once again quivered, the concussion jolting every man in the area. A burst of shrapnel, tree shards, dirt, and snow darkened the scene. When the geyser was over, there, in the smoke and mist, was a horrific scene: two men in the snow, Toye's leg gone, and one of Guarnere's all but detached from his body.

Malarkey whirled in horror and—*life be damned*—rushed to help. So did others. Mercifully, the shelling stopped.

"Kraut bastards!" someone yelled.

Guarnere wriggled in the snow like a wounded snake, moaning, mumbling amid the smoke and mist.

"My leg, my leg, my leg."

Medic Eugene Roe and buddies from the platoon gathered around Bill, others around Joe.

"Malark, gimme a cigarette," said Toye, his words strained.

"You're gonna be okay, Joe," said Malarkey.

"God, what's a guy gotta do to die, Malark?"

Medics shot Toye and Guarnere with morphine and got them onto stretchers, then to a jeep. The rest of the Easy men ultimately dispersed, less to grieve—this was war—than to move on and try to forget.

Malarkey just stood there, alone, looking at the blood-stained snow. It had been like looking at horrific View-Master slides—*click*, Toye lying alone in the snow minus a leg; *click*, Guarnere mangled; *click*, everyone gone and the beautiful white woods torn all to hell.

Later, as afternoon turned to evening, Malarkey stood as numb as a statue, his right hand cupped around the cold stock of a P38 pistol in his pocket. He could tell people it was an accident; that he had had the gun in his pocket and it had just accidentally gone off. A man with a bullet in his foot was a liability to his unit; he would be sent to England. And he'd be out of this cold, bloody, hopeless hell.

Malarkey looked around at the tattered remains of the 506th's E Company. Then he looked at the remains of himself. His feet were numb. His stomach empty. His spirits as shattered as a hundred tree bursts.

Could it get any worse?

CHAPTER 7

Hidden Wounds

Fritz

Snow fell across the Ardennes, blanketing the woods and rolling farm-land in a beauty that belied what lay beneath it: bodies. Corpses turned to grotesque ice sculptures in the night. To a man, the soldiers of 5th Company weren't muttering about Neupert's decision to turn back. They were quietly praising him for it, nobody more ardently than Engelbert.

It was Thursday, December 21, 1944. The German soldiers turned their uniforms inside out so their white interior linings would camouflage them in the snow.

"Er hat unser Leben gerettet," said Fritz. Others agreed. Neupert had saved their lives. It had been a decision not of cowardice but of courage. The commanding officer knew he would be bad-mouthed for falling back, but his men's lives were more important than his future with the Wehrmacht, than his reputation, than *him*, period.

The day after their horrible defeat, Neupert informed his tattered bunch that this would be a day to rest and recharge. Wait for reinforcements. Get wounds patched in the battalion medical station. Keep a close eye on the village. And figure out a plan.

Men slept inside the few remaining half-tracks, ate some of the putrid food that was still left, and puffed on cigarettes. In an exercise that brought them back to their Hitler Youth days, they built log-wrapped lean-tos to stay dry from the snow.

All was quiet, the fears of yesterday muted by weariness and wounds. After what the Yanks had thrown at them the day before, what could possibly scare them?

They heard it before they saw it—what sounded like a freight train hitting its brakes at full speed, the sound jolting them with a fear they thought they'd exorcised but clearly had not.

"Achtung, volle Deckung! Granatwerfer von 10 Uhr!"

Neupert yelled that the fire was coming from ten o'clock. The mortar cracked high above them like a bolt of lightning. Other shells followed.

"Alle Mann, hinlegen!"

The men dove into the snow. High up, a mortar shattered a pine tree as thick as a telephone pole, sending shards slicing down on 5th Company like hot, jagged raindrops. Some of those shards sliced into the backs of Lieutenant Karl Neupert and two of his soldiers. Men screamed. Moaned. Groaned. Engelbert turned toward his commander, lying beside him within arm's reach, his gray overcoat already blotched in crimson, his eyes languid. He was alive, but barely. As the hot shrapnel met the cold snow, steam made the scene a misty montage.

"Sani, Sani! Wir brauchen Sanis!" yelled Engelbert, though he wasn't even sure whether the 901st still had living, breathing medics.

Then, to Neupert: "Halt durch, Leutnant! Halt durch!"

In the end, Engelbert's encouraging Neupert to hang on didn't matter. The lieutenant hung on long enough to be carted off to a medical tent. But by morning he was dead.

On that day, Friday, December 22, Engelbert was tangled in emotions. Three weeks after losing his closest friend, Fritz Döring, he had now lost the superior officer he esteemed most—a man who had taught him more than a little about courage and conviction. And the 5th had lost 80 percent of its men in a single battle. In all his imaginings about what it would be like to go to war, Engelbert had never conjured anything like this.

"The rest of our company got into a mortar attack," he wrote to his parents. "Again, some of us were wounded. Our commander Lt. Neupert was hit, too. We all are very, very sorry for that. Now there's just a handful of us left."

Lieutenant Johannes Jähningen was appointed the new company leader. The wounded got only cursory care; most of the medics were dead. Unlike the Americans, the Germans had no penicillin, and many of their wounded suffered serious infections.

And yet when Engelbert was ordered to the command post in Marvie to confirm whether the English translation was correct in a letter demanding the Americans surrender Bastogne, his spirits soared. *This could be the beginning of the end! The war could soon be over! We could be going home!*

By nightfall, word trickled back: the Americans had refused to surrender. Fritz felt as if he'd been kicked in the gut but clung to whatever optimism he could muster.

"Bastogne is encircled," he wrote home. "Today a parliamentary from our side was over there. They refused to surrender. Tonight, our artillery will soften up Bastogne. Tomorrow it shall be taken. So much for today. Good night! In my thoughts I am always with you."

The fight for Marvie wasn't over. With reinforcements arriving, Lieutenant Jähningen sounded the cry from on high to take Bastogne—and taking Marvie was a means to that end. On Saturday, December 23, the weather cold and crisp, the 901st attacked from the south, instead of from the east as in its previous attempt; by midday the Germans had taken nearly half the village. The open-field battle turned into house-to-house fighting. Engelbert was in a command post in a farmhouse to the south of the village.

At one point the Germans sent their self-propelled gun charging toward the Americans. A medium tank fired on it. Direct hit. The vehicle became a virtual blowtorch. When a nearby loft filled with hay caught fire, the heat was so intense that the Americans were forced to retreat. The battlefield was once again tinged with thick, black smoke.

With help from the village priest, Father Vanderweyden, the Americans had evacuated civilians from the village the previous day. After hastily packing their food and belongings, the three hundred occupants had formed two large groups—one making its way northwest to Bastogne, the other crossing the German lines to find shelter in Lutrebois to the south.

A fierce battle raged in the snow-tinted village, hour upon hour, both sides suffering heavy losses. The main road through the village was blocked by an American half-track that had been accidentally destroyed by friendly fire—the silver lining being that it would slow any German advance into Bastogne.

Day became night. Night became day. The fighting continued. Hunkered down in a farmhouse, Engelbert had little idea that the outcome stood on a knife's edge. On his Kettenkrad, its tracks giving him grip in the snow, Engelbert delivered messages from one commander to the next. Meanwhile, soldiers—many fresh-faced replacements younger than Engelbert—holed up in the farmhouse, tired, freezing, frightened.

The only things that lifted spirits were the small treasures left behind by the Americans: chocolate, cookies, flashlights, and even a postal bag of Christmas presents. With roads choked by ice and snow, it was getting harder for the Germans to get food, ammunition, and fuel to the front lines. "We felt as if Christmas had already arrived," Engelbert would report in a letter to his parents.

Just when the tired, freezing, and fearful soldiers were finding warmth and rest in the cellars, officers burst through the door brandishing pistols.

"Raus, Ihr faulen Bastarde! Kämpft!" ("Out, you lazy bastards! Fight!")

On Hill 500, German troops encircled an outpost from the Glider Infantry's Company F and killed them all. But the Americans held the line. By Christmas Eve, both sides had taken shelter in the cellars of whatever was left of this house or that.

Still holed up in the cellar of the command post, Fritz was more than happy to receive orders to take a message to Lutrebois. As he walked alone in the snow, he gradually shed the noise and madness of war.

"It was magnificent outside," he would later write home. "The fir trees were so beautifully covered with snow. Just like home!"

The scene drew him back to Hilchenbach. "In my mind, I was at home with you," he wrote. "I had to think of former times. And of the future! I felt that you were with me in your thoughts."

Seeing the dead American had touched him, but he had to remind himself: *You mustn't be touched. You are a soldier.*

On Christmas Eve, the Belgian parents in Lutrebois had their children sleep in their clothes in case the bombs should come in the night. When Christmas Day arrived with blue skies, it wasn't a present but an omen of doom. The Americans would have their Thunderbolts in the sky—and the Germans' Luftwaffe, or whatever was left of it, would have no answer for them.

Having seen no signs of the aerial invaders by noon, however, soldiers and civilians lined up in the street, anticipating a special Christmas dinner to be fixed by the German field kitchen. Soldiers would be fed first; civilians would get leftovers—if there were any. But what happened next made that a moot point: it was hell from on high, in the form of American Thunderbolts.

Ka-boom! Ka-boom! Ka-boom!

Debris shot into the air, then rained down terror in the form of brick, rock, dirt, and splintered wood. People screamed. Walls collapsed. Dust billowed.

"In Deckung gehen!" yelled German officers, imploring their men to take cover.

"Enzo! Alexia! C'est papa!" yelled a Belgian father in search of his missing children.

It was chaos in two languages—German and French.

Everywhere: panic. Civilians and soldiers ran, dove for cover, prayed. *Ka-boom! Ka-boom! Ka-boom!* The deafening thud of bombs pounded. Fires broke out. Smoke smudged the sky and tainted the snow with soot. Everywhere people hunted frantically for shelter. Engelbert found it in the cellar of a house. Fifty meters away, more than a dozen found it in the village's chapel, Germans and Belgian civilians crammed into the small church, brought together by a desperate will to live.

German soldiers could be cruel to Belgian civilians. But perhaps Christmas softened their hearts—Engelbert remembered an odd sense of civility in Lutrebois. Soldiers and civilians were all in the same boat, trying to avoid being victims of Americans in the sky.

Ka-boom! Ka-boom! Ka-boom! The shelling was relentless, as if the American pilots were venting their frustration at having gone more than a week without being able to fly. Fritz felt the cellar walls shudder. Muffled thuds. Then quiet. Muffled thuds. During a window of quiet, the men were ordered into the woods, where they waited out the rest of the attack. Finally, the bombing ended. Engelbert and his comrades wandered back to the rubble. Despite a haze of smoke, it was obvious: little was left of Lutrebois. His heart pounding, Fritz ran with other soldiers for the chapel, where many of their comrades and civilians had taken shelter. When they saw where it had been, they stopped in their tracks.

It was gone. Crushed. Reduced to fragments of stone and brick and jagged shreds of wood, flames licking it here and there.

"Direkter Treffer," said a comrade.

Direct hit, indeed. In the tangle, Engelbert could see the occasional gray wool of a uniform, a splash of blood, what once had been a man and was now a tangle of flesh and entrails. But what tugged at him most was a face he had seen, then quickly told himself he hadn't.

"Wir können nichts tun," said an officer.

He was right. There was nothing they could do. As Engelbert went from house to house looking for scraps of food per the officer's orders, the man's words seemed to mock him.

This was war. When bad things happened, there was never anything anyone could do. Not even stop to grieve for a split second. You just followed the next set of orders. And, in Engelbert's case, pretended you hadn't seen that face in the rubble.

After night fell, Fritz Engelbert was finally able to finish his letter to his parents: "Now it is 7 p.m. and thank God it is dark. I had to interrupt because shortly before twelve o'clock we had a Jabo [Jagdbomber: fighter bomber] attack. Half of the village is on fire. The church received a direct hit, no stone was left standing. We sat in the basement. During a break we escaped into the forest and stayed there freezing until dark.

Just now a truck with provisions has arrived. We got thirty cigarettes and some schnapps."

The handwriting was on whatever walls in Lutrebois hadn't been blown to pieces: there would be no taking of Marvie, Bastogne, or Antwerp. Only cloudy skies had allowed Germany to make the inroads into the American lines that it had. With air power, the Americans were fighting with two arms, the Germans with one tied behind their back.

A week later, after the 901st had retreated east to near the Luxembourg border, Engelbert wrote home again. "Today on the last evening of the old year I am especially with you in my thoughts," he told his parents on December 31. "From the bottom of my heart I send you my good wishes for the New Year, all the best and God's blessing.

"Yes, the year 1945 will begin in two hours. What will it bring for us?!? Hopefully the peace!!! I will stay up till midnight to hear the Führer's speech."

Hitler gave two New Year's speeches, one to the public at large and one to soldiers in particular. Both brimmed with optimism and bitterly blamed the "Jewish-international enemy of the world" for Germany's "misery" and the Allied bombings for the "defilement of culture," which he called "shameful."

Germany, he vowed, would not lose the war. "Like a phoenix from the ashes, so the strong German will all the more rise up anew from the ruins of our cities," he said. "Once this time of suffering is over, every German will be incredibly proud of being allowed to be a member of such a *Volk*."

He told the soldiers, "I cannot close this appeal without thanking the Lord for the help that He always allowed the leadership and the *Volk* to find, as well as for the power He gave us to be stronger than misery and danger."

He thanked "Providence" for protecting him during the July 20 assassination attempt and concluded with, "The Almighty, who has led our *Volk* in its previous fight for life and weighed, rewarded, and judged it in accordance with its merits, will this time encounter a generation worthy of His blessings. You are the unfading witnesses for this in the past years, my German soldiers, and you will be that all the more in the coming year!"

After listening to Hitler, Fritz finished his letter, without adding any conjecture, analysis, or opinion. In contrast with his once-fervent zeal for Hitler, the muted tone of this letter spoke volumes. In fact, for the first time, Hitler's words had raised doubt in Fritz. The Führer, safe in his bunker in Berlin, seemed completely out of touch with the reality of the war, which clearly was not going well for Germany. It was as if Hitler believed that he could will Germany to victory with grand rhetoric. The carnage that Fritz had just endured in Lutrebois and Marvie suggested otherwise. Germany was losing the war. Not that he would share these doubts in his letter.

"The speech is over," he wrote. "You will have heard it, too. In this hour I have just one wish: may the good Lord give his blessing and support this year again to us, our sorely tested German homeland—to you there at home and to us here at the front line."

His letter was in stark contrast to the one he had written from near Weislingen on December 5, less than a month before. At that time, despite having just watched Döring die, he had been able to see a light at the end of the proverbial tunnel. "Let's hope and pray that it's the last Christmas in the war!!!!" he had written, optimistic about a German victory.

Now, as the year ended, he no longer had that hope. He had lost most of the men in his platoon. He'd heard Hitler's out-of-touch assessment of the war. And he had seen something in the rubble of the church in Lutrebois that had sealed his hatred of war: framed by shattered stone, the dusty, swollen, sweet face of a little Belgian girl.

Don

Don Malarkey didn't shoot himself in the foot. He couldn't. Apart from anything else, it would have been a dishonor to his World War I uncles—a self-inflicted wound to send a selfish soldier home. Beyond that, Malarkey looked at the men around him, the ones still left. He had lost eight buddies since they'd gone to war, not counting the wounded ones such as Toye and Guarnere. Buck Compton had just been given a breather; the shelling had pushed him over the edge. He couldn't take it anymore. But as much as Malarkey wanted to leave it all behind, he realized something: those who were left needed him. If he quit, it would be easier on him but all the harder for the others. He couldn't do that. He was a Malarkey. He couldn't quit. He owed something to his uncles. To Easy Company. Hell, he thought, to himself.

Soldiers just soldiered on—even after January 10, when Roe, Easy Company's medic, came to him.

"Malark, I'm sorry," he said, "but it's Skip. He's dead. Penkala, too."

Don's disposition didn't change. It was as if he was frozen in grief. Or numb. Maybe both.

"How?" he asked softly.

"Direct hit . . . shell found them like it had eyes."

Again, no collapse. No angry fists to the sky. No tears. He was already past the breaking point. For Malarkey, the moment wasn't just about Skip. It was about a hundred-plus days on the front line, seeing bodies torn apart and broken and smashed, bloated in summer's sun and frozen by winter's cold. It was watching Fritz Niland, right there in your foxhole at Carentan, break down and weep after believing all three of his brothers had been killed in the war. It was the legs of Toye and Guarnere in the blood-splattered snow. All of it had flooded Malarkey with so much unexamined pain that Skip's death was just one more set of unclaimed laundry in England that he couldn't deal with. After a while, you learned to use the pain almost like an anesthetic, to protect yourself from more. By the time he heard about Skip, he had the emotional dry heaves. Nothing left to come up.

"Here," said Roe, pressing the cross of the rosary beads into Malarkey's hand. "He'd want you to have these."

Malarkey held onto the cold cross. All around, men's eyes were wet with tears; Muck was clearly a favorite, and there was nobody closer to him than Don. Winters noticed that Malarkey had the "thousand-yard stare." He offered him a break at the rear.

Thanks, but no thanks, Malarkey said. Every man still left in Easy Company was at a breaking point, and there were no time-outs in war. You couldn't stop and talk about the death of your best friend, the guy who had wanted to introduce you to his fiancée and show you where he had swum across the Niagara. The guy you were going to take salmon fishing over the Columbia River Bar and treat to dinner at the Liberty Grill afterward.

For all practical purposes, the Battle of the Bulge was over. Between Foy and the town of Noville, airborne soldiers on graves-registration duty worked overtime. "The bodies were stacked twelve to a pile," one paratrooper would recount, "with the Germans in separate groups from the Americans."

Though the Americans had been taken by surprise and were slow to respond, their resiliency—particularly the 101st Airborne's—had made the difference. They had held off the Germans just long enough that Patton's Third Army could help turn the tables.

The cost was great. U.S. casualties in the Battle of the Bulge exceeded eighty-seven thousand; German casualties, sixty-eight thousand. More than three thousand civilians died. And fifty thousand soldiers were simply never accounted for: buried in rubble, ground into the earth by tank tracks, obliterated by shells, lost in plane crashes, spirited away in ways that only war can imagine. Fifty thousand men. *Vanished.*

And there was never a statistical category for the other casualties: those with hidden wounds. Wounds buried deep. Like the ones already infecting the souls of Don Malarkey and Fritz Engelbert. Not flesh wounds. Soul wounds.

CHAPTER 8

The End of Battle

Fritz

On January 31, 1945, Fritz Engelbert became one of the last German soldiers to withdraw across the Luxembourg-Germany border to the *Vaterland*. For the 901st's 5th Company, it had been a month of fighting and falling back, fighting and falling back. If the pattern was militarily honorable, the end game was destined to be the same for the 5th as for every other company of German soldiers: defeat. The Third Reich was now in its death throes. It was not a matter of whether Germany would be defeated by the Allied Forces, but when.

But officers, if perhaps secretly pessimistic, kept flying the swastika with boldness. In the German Army, after all, it was not uncommon for openly defeatist soldiers to be executed. And back in Berlin Hitler was not about to surrender—particularly since U.S. president Franklin

Roosevelt and Soviet leader Joseph Stalin were adamant that they would only accept an unconditional surrender. The war was going badly for Germany, but Hitler had assured the public and the military that Germany would prevail.

Against this backdrop, Engelbert told his folks he just wanted to be done with war. In an early January letter he said that he had a "great longing for home, for another life. Enough!" He told them that the life of a soldier goes in waves.

> Currently I'm on the crest of that wave again. We are located near the German border in a small cleared village and are waiting for the realignment. Despite the fact that we live for the moment here, I am satisfied; grateful for every quiet hour I have been granted. . . . The only thing that weighs on you like a soft shadow is the question of how it will look in the next wave hollow.
>
> Right now, the weather is favorable for us. The clouds are hanging low, it is snowing outside. I am now sitting in our little room, the stove crackles. It's pretty cozy. How nice it was at home at this time! If I could find skis, I would have the opportunity to ski here. The landscape is like at home.
>
> It is almost noon. Hopefully the truck will come with food soon. It is not particularly rosy with food at this moment. Our kitchen truck had an engine failure and couldn't keep up with us. So we were fed by another company. For a while we didn't get any warm meals.

Fritz and his comrades were pushed deeper into Germany. A shell exploded near Engelbert in a skirmish with Canadian troops on the lower Rhine, but the shrapnel sliced into his G43 rifle, not into him. With his rifle unusable, he was issued an Italian Beretta submachine gun. But he never fired a shot with it. Not one. The 901st was constantly on the run—frantically on the run—from the Allied forces advancing from the west. On February 19, Fritz's commander, Lieutenant Jähningen, was killed in action; Engelbert was now serving under his third commander in six months.

Beyond his roiling stomach—he had learned that combat messed with his digestive system—Engelbert worried about lots of things, as his letters home suggested. Among them: that enemy planes were bombing in the region of Westphalia, of which Hilchenbach was part, perhaps putting his parents in danger. And that his own unit could be bombed—they were staying in a house whose basement provided insufficient cover. When the 901st did travel, they would go by night; otherwise they were prime targets for aerial attacks.

This "on-the-run" pattern continued for weeks, though the 901st scored occasional small victories. Fritz's unit attacked the American-held village Schiefbahn—at night, with tanks. Twenty-three Americans were taken prisoner, and Engelbert was ordered by Lieutenant Jähningen's replacement to escort them to the back of the line.

Taking nearly two dozen prisoners to the rear lines wasn't a responsibility Engelbert had had before, and he made the most of it. He was, after all, within earshot of his commander; perhaps the man would be impressed with Fritz's English. He couldn't resist.

"For you boys," he said, looking at the American GIs, "the war is over."

A few of the soldiers looked puzzled: a kraut speaking English? Decades later, Fritz said the Americans were surprisingly friendly.

"Cigarette?" one asked, offering him a smoke.

The tables turned the next day. Engelbert and two of his 5th Company comrades found themselves holed up in a barn. Through the window, a comrade of Engelbert's reported more than half a dozen GIs approaching—intently, as if they'd seen the Germans scurry to their hiding place. Fritz and the other two would be fish in a barrel.

"Wir müssen müssen die weiße Fahne hissen! Kapitulation!" said Engelbert to his comrades. ("We must wave the white flag! Surrender!")

Had he just said this? Was he turning his back on his beloved Hitler and bowing to the *Schwein* Americans? Taking the way out of a coward?

"Bist du sicher?" said another.

Yes, he was certain, said Fritz—as if saying it might convince himself.

According to Gerald F. Linderman in *World within War*, the soldier's worst fears were "that he would be wounded, would remain alone and unaided, and would die a forlorn and solitary death; and that, if taken by the enemy, he would be killed rather than held captive, or that, if made a prisoner, he would be treated with cruelty."

Though he was only nineteen, Engelbert had seven months of combat under his belt and was the most experienced soldier of the bunch. The three quickly hashed out their options in nervous staccato statements. The Americans, Engelbert said, were not the Soviets, who often killed POWs on the Eastern Front. Surrendering to the Americans was, they quickly agreed, the best hope of survival.

The men frantically leaned their three carbines together to form a tripod, barrels pointed skyward. A piece of bedclothes atop the summit signaled their intention to surrender. Standing outside, they figured, would likely mean getting shot on sight. Huddling in the barn with the surrender sign out front offered them a chance.

A GI soon kicked in the barn door, and more than half a dozen rifles were suddenly pointed in their faces like the backside of a porcupine.

"Kapitulation," said Fritz, nodding his head in his eagerness. "Kapitulation."

His two comrades nodded their heads too.

Wait, what was Engelbert doing? He knew a little English.

"We . . . wish . . . we . . . want . . . surrender."

The American soldiers laughed.

"Hey, the guy must have played shortstop for the Yankees," said one GI.

"And his cousin's Mickey Mouse!" said another.

"Shut up," said the GI in charge. "Let's get them outta here."

The three Germans were loaded onto a tank, at which point Fritz started to light up a cigarette.

"Don't smoke, kraut," said one of the GIs.

Engelbert and his comrades represented one tributary flowing into the surging river of POWs that was swelling like the Rhine after spring snowmelt. In March 1945, an average of 10,000 Germans per day were taken prisoner. By April the total would soar to 1.8 million.

Engelbert was transferred to a prison camp in Attichy in northern France, about 270 miles southwest of where he had been captured. Later he would be sent to Amigny-Rouy and finally to Laon, all three just northwest of Reims, France. He was POW number 646130.

In Berlin, Hitler celebrated his fifty-sixth birthday on April 20 by making a rare appearance outside his Berlin bunker—to pin medals of honor on Hitler Youth boys. Ten days later, with the Soviets nearly having reached his bunker from the east, he committed suicide. Many Germans reacted much like Americans would when President Kennedy was shot. Lothar Loewe, who was a sixteen-year-old German soldier at the time, would explain: "It was like the whole world collapsing. Adolf Hitler's death left me with a feeling of emptiness."

Fritz's reaction was different—and surprising even to himself. He had loyally served Hitler for the last decade, half his life. But he had begun doubting the greatness of the man. He had begun wondering if he and his comrades had been pawns in a game in which the Führer made promises that he could not keep. Whether the man—who had committed suicide rather than face the Russians—had been as courageous as so many seemed to think. Whether he was a fraud. It was not a comfortable thought, because to accept it would be to accept the idea that he and his comrades had been duped. But Engelbert's once-clear thoughts of Hitler and war had been muddied by the madness.

Engelbert's personal defeat paralleled that of Germany. With no hope left, the Germans surrendered. An armistice was signed with Allied forces on May 7 in Reims, at a tiny schoolhouse across from the train station— less than an hour's drive southeast from the three POW camps where

Engelbert would spend time. War in Europe ended the next day, two days before Fritz turned twenty.

As a POW, Engelbert didn't have access to news; how much he knew about the "outside world" is debatable. At some point word filtered through the camp that Hitler had died and the war was over. But it's less clear how much the POWs knew of the darker truths about Hitler, particularly regarding the death camps where more than eleven million people died.

"At the prison, we talked of where our homes were, what we would be going back to, who we missed," said Armin Meisel, a fellow POW and close friend of Engelbert's, "but we knew nothing—*nothing*—of the Holocaust." The only hint that Engelbert got was an October 1946 letter from his mother, in which she wrote at the end: "Jews have not yet come back."

In hindsight, that may seem incredible. The almost year-long Nuremberg Trials, in which twenty-four German Nazi leaders were tried and convicted for their part in the Holocaust and other war crimes, took place while Engelbert and Meisel were POWs. But decades later, both men claimed not to have known about the atrocities.

Neither would complain of mistreatment—this despite post-war controversy about how the Allied forces treated German prisoners in Europe. Some believe Eisenhower broke Geneva Convention agreements by giving the prisoners too little food and incarcerating them for too long; few were allowed to leave within one month of the end of war, as convention rules required. The theory is that Eisenhower had prisoners redesignated as "disarmed enemy forces" to skirt such regulations, in part to appease the French, who wanted payback for the Germans' brutal treatment of French citizens during the occupation.

Whether or not Eisenhower was behind the "extended stays," Engelbert spent two years as a POW, all but two months of it *after* the war ended.

Decades after his experience as a POW, Fritz would say that food had been scarce, but he had never felt as if prisoners were mistreated; food had been scarce when he'd been fighting the war, too. Europe was in ruins, farmers among the victims, too.

Engelbert was among the younger prisoners. But when his section of the prison had to choose someone to entrust with their food, they unanimously chose him. Meisel, who would remain a close friend of Fritz's—and of the Engelbert family—for life, would explain: "He would have starved first before taking any food that belonged to anyone else. Honor. Integrity. That was Fritz Engelbert."

Fritz Koppenhagen, a fellow prisoner, became almost a father figure to Engelbert and Meisel. Forty years old, Koppenhagen was roughly twice the age of the young men. The three of them wrote and printed a weekly newsletter. And they worked together in the woods each day.

Forced labor was allowed by the Geneva Convention, and prisoners were sent on work detail into the forests of France's Champagne region to fell and split timber. "Be thankful," a guard told Engelbert. "In other camps, your comrades are clearing minefields."

Fritz at age twenty-one in
March 1947, a POW in France.
Courtesy of the Engelbert Family Collection

Work as a lumberjack was demanding. All day. Every day. Engelbert's
hands were blistered, his back sore, his stomach incessantly empty.

"But then, on your return to the camp, the French women—the
mothers—would see us and when the guards weren't looking, sneak us
loaves of fresh-baked bread," he said. Telling the story decades later, his
eyes would inevitably begin to mist. "They must have felt pity for these
famished young men," he told an interviewer, "and put aside that they were
the German enemies. I was always touched by this act of humanity."

The combination of physical labor and little food turned prisoners
into sacks of bones; many barely weighed 50 kilograms, or 110 pounds.
Engelbert got down to 130, 20 pounds below his normal weight. More

troublesome was a bout of typhoid fever, which wracked him with fever, stomach pain, and headaches. But even that cloud had a silver lining. At the hospital in Laon, he was treated by a Dr. Bertheau, a Frenchman who not only helped Fritz return to health but, once he was well, got him a job in the commander's house.

"Fritz is healthy," wrote Koppenhagen to Engelbert's parents. "He works in the hospital in Laon. Accommodation is very good, also the food. The doctor who Fritz now works for is a kindhearted man. He never lets your son feel that he's a prisoner. The jobs are all easy jobs in the commander's house."

As his time as a prisoner lengthened, so did Fritz's skepticism about the war—and of Hitler. "Here our fathers bled and we, their sons, soaked this floor with our sweat," he wrote home on April 3, 1946. "Oh, those damned wars! Hopefully mankind has finally learned from it."

As one year as a POW became two, Engelbert's longing for home increased. "How much longer will I have to stay behind barbed wire?" he asked his parents on March 5, 1946. "Don't you know anything about it? Every morning when the sun rises, my eyes fly east to home."

Two weeks later: "Today is the first beautiful spring day when home-sickness burns." That said, either his attitude was remarkably optimistic or he wanted to cheer his parents. "So far," he wrote, "everything is fine with me."

In November 1946, eighteen months after the war had ended, Anna Engelbert wrote to Red Cross authorities in Geneva, Switzerland, who were in charge of POWs and all but demanded the return of her son. She also wrote to Fritz that he was needed at home to help run the inn.

"We are both ill," she wrote. "Your father has a bad heart."

By the time Engelbert was finally released in early May 1947, he had not been home for nearly three years, since his leave in the summer of 1944. Eighteen when he entered the service, he was now twenty-two. He had traveled thousands of miles, and though he didn't believe a single bullet of his had killed an enemy soldier, he had seen death in nearly every conceivable form. He was tired. And if he didn't notice it at the time, broken. He was not the Hitler Youth boy who had left in August 1943 to "help restore Germany to greatness," who had smiled and waved as the train left the Hilchenbach train depot.

On May 9, 1947, Fritz Sr. and Anna Engelbert looked up from their work at the inn and there he was, standing in front of them: their son who had left as a boy and was now a man. Dressed not in military garb but in civilian clothes. Thin beyond belief, his face chiseled with unspoken horror, his eyes having seen too much.

The hugs and handshakes soon gave way to the rhythms of the past: quiet mistrust between father and son, Anna caught in the middle. Life at Gasthaus Engelbert was just as it had been when Fritz left, but at the same time it was nothing like it had been.

War, he had written back in January, was like a wave. "The only thing that weighs on you like a soft shadow is the question of how it will look in the next wave hollow."

He was about to find out.

Don

On February 5, 1945, Don Malarkey and what was left of Easy Company arrived in the city of Haguenau on the river Moder, which flows into the Rhine. By now, it was evident to any soldier carrying a gun that the Allied forces would win the war in Europe. What lay ahead was "mop-up" work: Fight through an occasional skirmish with the Germans. Take yet more POWs. And get the hell back home without getting killed.

But if a German surrender was expected soon—and Don had a future to look forward to again—why couldn't he quit thinking about the past? When a truck with Easy Company's 1st Platoon showed up, only eleven of the original forty men were in the back. But the only one Don noticed missing was Skip.

It didn't help matters when a group of fresh-faced replacements arrived, bouncing around as if they were at Boy Scout camp. None of them had seen the legs of Toye and Guarnere in the snow. It wasn't their fault, but they knew nothing about loss. Among Malarkey's closest friends: Muck and Hoobler, dead. Toye, Guarnere, Scotty Gordon, Frank Perconte, and Burr Smith, wounded. Compton, shell-shocked.

War got a grip on you and wouldn't let go. In Haguenau, Malarkey could have left the line; Winters had told him he'd paid his dues. But he had chosen to stay. So, unfortunately, had his memories. Standing in the shower—his first since Mourmelon, six weeks before—he closed his eyes, and just when he'd thought the warm water could take him away from this mess, he heard the words of the medic Eugene Roe: *Malark, I'm sorry, but it's Skip.*

He wrote a letter home to Bernice, who was now a singer in New York. Earlier, she had asked what war was really like. He decided to tell her.

When we were surrounded, I sometimes felt we would never pull out of it. Generally, I was confident—in spite of the suffering. Can you imagine, honey, living in a foxhole with ice on the side and hanging from an improvised roof? Outside the snow up to your knees. We had to wrap our feet in burlap bags to keep them from freezing—even then, many of [the men] had toes that wouldn't function. I can remember how my hands would freeze to my Tommy gun.

The fact that you're still alive is the only important thing. I know you don't know what it is to face death. It's the most punishing experience you can imagine. And when you're fighting, you're going through it 24 hours a day. It's hard, darling, to walk into those kraut tanks, machine guns, artillery, etc. when you know you've got so much to live for. It takes a lot of that stuff called "guts" that too damn few men have. Having been as lucky as I am, I begin to feel that I'm a fugitive from the law of averages, which isn't good. The war is hell all right.

How would you feel if you were walking down the street with a friend and, suddenly, she was blown into a thousand pieces? My best friend was killed at my side, the greatest little guy I've ever known. I was more broken up than I've ever been in my life but there's no turning back—keep drivin'—and for five days after we kept attackin'.

Each day more of my friends would leave for a better world. That's a sample of what I've been doing. I could never describe the terror that strikes you when you're under those terrific artillery barrages when the exploding steel seemingly pounds you into the ground and makes your head reel, your ears pop, and your heart stop beating. I would tell you a lot more about legs and arms, faces, eyes, etc. that are no longer usable. That's the kind of life I know—not an existence of a human being [but] the life of a madman.

Malarkey got a letter from Joe Toye, who reported that after the amputation of his leg he had gotten gangrene and had to have it cut again. "Tonight," he wrote, "they're cuttin' it for the fourth time, and if it's not successful, I've already been told that's it. I die."

After a cross-river skirmish that took the life of Eugene Jackson, Easy Company headed deeper into Germany, its war essentially over. Behind them: emotional rapids and waterfalls. In front: the smooth stretch of a lazy river. Malarkey started thinking of Faye Tanner, Skip Muck's fiancée back in New York. He traded letters with her. Skip's mother hadn't gotten an official telegram yet, and she was holding out hope that Skip was still alive. Sorry, Malarkey confirmed to Faye, he's gone.

"Perhaps we can console ourselves in that he is in a happier place where there is always peace and not the misery and horror of a crazy world at war," Malarkey wrote. "It's hard to believe that the Rhine is so far behind the lines these days. This damn war has been going so long that when it finally does end, I won't be able to believe it."

He promised Faye he would come visit her once he returned stateside.

Malarkey contracted what doctors called "Rhine River malaria" and was hospitalized in Liège, Belgium. He was released in early May 1945. He was having a beer at a sidewalk pub in Verviers, trying to figure out how he could get back to Easy Company, now far to the east in Germany. When he went to pay for his drink the bartender shook his head no; "Déjà payé."

"What the hell?"

The bartender nodded to a table of men, one of whom tapped Don's shoulder.

"Aigles hurlants!"

"Screaming Eagles," said an English-speaker on the next stool. "The patch on your shoulder. Bastogne heroes. They buy your beer to honor you!"

Malarkey might never have felt prouder. The people whose country the Americans had liberated from the Germans were saying thank you. It was May 7, 1945, nearly five years since German soldiers had goose-stepped into city after city. The Allied victory in the Battle of the Bulge had ended that Nazi occupation; as of February 4, 1945, Belgium was free again.

As Malarkey sipped his beer, bells started ringing outside.

"La guerre est terminée! Les Allemands se sont rendus!" people were shouting in French.

Instantly: Smiles! Hollers! Hugs!

"The war is over!" an English-speaker, face aglow, said to Malarkey. "The Germans have surrendered!"

The grateful Belgians bought so many drinks for Malarkey that when he saw someone who looked like Frank Perconte walk by outside, he wondered if it was only the buzz from the beer. But then Perconte saw Don, burst through the pub's door, and gave Malarkey a huge hug. The reunion only got better when Burr Smith, another Screaming Eagle, rolled by on a trolley—in fact, doing handstands *atop* the trolley—and joined the celebration.

What could be greater, thought Malarkey, than celebrating the war's end with guys you'd been with ever since Toccoa? The three locked arms.

"This is it," said Smith. "We're going home!"

Beyond Ocean View Cemetery, the waves of the Pacific Ocean rolled ashore. Malarkey got out of the car and popped his umbrella. It was late December 1945, and Astoria welcomed him home with a medium drizzle and temperatures in the low forties. Typical Oregon winter.

He had come to pay his respects to his uncles. He hadn't written a poem for the occasion or invited anyone else to come. He just thought it necessary, important, to stand before the graves of his two long-gone uncles and say: *We, the Malarkey boys, made it. We didn't give up. Didn't quit. And we won the war.*

It had been a wild month since his arrival in New York on November 29. He had seen Bernice, but both had said goodbye with uncertainties about their future together. He had decided not to go see Skip's girlfriend in upstate New York—for fear he that he might fall in love with her and forever feel as if he were taking someone only Skip had deserved. He'd found himself in an elevator with Lauritz Melchior, the premier tenor of the New York Metropolitan Opera, who had seen Malarkey's Screaming Eagle patch and said, "Sergeant, I salute you."

His arrival home in Oregon had been nice. It was Christmastime. His mother, aunt, uncle, and cousins had bear-hugged him at the train station in Portland. His father had shaken his hand; as Don would say, "It was as if he hardly knew me." Ida Malarkey, the grandmother who had said that if "Donnie" died, it would "be the end of me," had passed away. On June 6, 1944, after hearing about the D-Day landings, she had gone to bed and died in her sleep.

Malarkey looked out at the Pacific—or as much as he could see of it through the clouds. In its vastness, he didn't see endless possibilities, only uncertainty. In its winter wildness, not beauty but rage. In its frothy swells, not answers but questions.

What was it the bar pilot Noland had told him once when he'd asked him why he went to sea? "It's the adventure. It's wondering what's behind this wave and the next one and the next one."

Malarkey had no idea. But he was about to find out.

PART III

HOME

We are not youth any longer. We don't want to take the world by storm. We are fleeing. We fly from ourselves. From our life. We were eighteen and had begun to love life and the world; and we had to shoot it to pieces.

—Erich Maria Remarque, *All Quiet on the Western Front*[1]

CHAPTER 9

Reckoning Up the Damage

Fritz

In a German folktale that mirrors Engelbert's return from war, Karl Katz sips from a flagon and falls asleep for twenty years, only to wake up to a world unlike the one he remembered. The story, found in *German Popular Stories and Fairy Tales,* translated by Edgar Taylor, is the German equivalent of Washington Irving's "Rip Van Winkle."

Says one part of the story: *He went in at the open doorway; but he found all so dreary and empty, that he staggered out again like a drunken man. . . .*

Like Karl Katz seeing his home, Fritz found Hilchenbach "dreary and empty." In March 1945, a radio station in nearby Ferndorf had been a target for Allied troops trying to cripple Germany by attacking its infrastructure: communication centers, railroads, bridges, and the like. The war had been here, too. Engelbert's father had only recently finished repairing the gable on Gasthaus Engelbert, which had been riddled by artillery; the inn itself had been littered with glass from house-to-house fighting.

Even if Hilchenbach hadn't been hit hard like bigger cities and two years had now passed since the end of the war, people were still walking around in dazes. Families had been torn apart. Young people displaced. Children orphaned. Many fathers were never seen again; 4.3 million German soldiers died or went missing. Vets roamed the streets, many missing limbs. Homelessness was rampant. Half a million German civilians had died, mainly in the Allied bombings.

And, then, of course there were the Jews—or lack thereof. Seligmann had died of a heart attack in 1941, but the other Jewish families in Hilchenbach—in fact, essentially every Jewish family in Germany—had vanished. Two-thirds of Europe's Jews died at the hands of the Nazis. Engelbert wouldn't have known such numbers soon after the war's end, but as he began to stitch together the story of the death camps, it repulsed him. He was not the same man he had been, and Germany was not the country he had imagined it to be.

When he'd been thirteen, when his Hitler Youth leaders and his Hitler Youth comrades were making their snide remarks about the Jews, it had seemed natural to make the local butcher the enemy, the bad guy, the scourge that needed purging. Never mind a fact that he wouldn't learn until later: some 150,000 men of Jewish descent had fought for Germany in World War II just like Fritz.

Empty: Over the next few months, as Engelbert heard, read, and watched the newsreel horror of the Holocaust, as he realized that Hitler had been behind it all, as he put the pieces of the puzzle together, he looked at himself in the mirror and hated what he saw. It wasn't the gaunt, hollow-cheeked, typhoid-fever-wracked image that he despised. It was what he could not see: the insides. The mind of a fool. The will of a coward. The heart of a stone-cold statue.

He had heard how the Americans, after seeing the train cars full of bodies at Dachau, had rounded up Hitler Youth from nearby Munich and taken them to see the carnage, to witness what their Nazi leaders had done, the *Aktion*—mass murders. And Fritz held himself just as guilty as those leaders.

He saw the Hitler Youth loyalist who had considered reporting his parents to the authorities for helping Seligmann. And the Wehrmacht soldier whose war was responsible for the little girl dying in the rubble of Lutrebois.

Staggered: Alcohol wasn't—and never would be—Engelbert's Achilles' heel; shame would be. If, in his reintroduction to civilian life in Germany, he reeled, wobbled, floundered like Karl Katz, it wasn't because of inebriation but because his world had been upended by his realization that all he had thought was good, pure, and honest was evil, sullied, and dishonest. That the man he had modeled his life after was a monster. And if he was staggered—flabbergasted, shocked, unsteady—it was because all that he had once thought to be true turned out to be a lie.

At the time, that's how it seemed: a sudden, surprising turnaround. Looking back years later, however, he realized that it had been gradual: first, seeing more death than nobility in war; second, being pushed back by the Allied soldiers in a defeat that shattered the myth of German superiority that he had been fed since he was ten—and which Hitler was still crowing about on New Year's Day 1945; third, the news that Hitler had taken the coward's way out and killed himself; and, finally, with his return to Hilchenbach, the realization that the Jews were gone—not just four families in his hometown but millions of Jews murdered by Hitler's henchmen, of which he'd might as well have been one.

"It was," he would say years later, "a gradual process, over time, based on what I'd experienced and what I'd learned. But it happened. For the first time, I understood the man for who he really was."

Another line from the tale of Karl Katz: *A crowd of women and children soon flocked around the strange-looking man with the long gray beard; and all broke upon him at once with the question, "Who are you?"*[1]

Who was he, indeed?

A fool.

A lackey.

An accomplice.

An evildoer.

An imbecile.

A hired hand of the devil himself, the perfect example of Hitler's insistence that "people will more easily fall victims to a big lie than to a small one."

A *Mitläufer*—"a person lacking courage and moral stance."

Or so he considered himself. Day after day, week after week, month after month, the more he learned about Hitler, the more he quietly seethed—the operative word "quietly." In all things, Fritz Engelbert was composed, quiet, controlled. Never the go-to-the-head-of-the-class student. But, as his classmate Waltraud Menn would say, always the student with the right answer. Until now. Until he realized that he had the wrong answer regarding Adolf Hitler. He had been duped by the greatest con artist on earth. And what did that make Engelbert but an extension of the Führer's evil? Never mind that he had never killed a man in the war; whatever blood Hitler had on his hands, Engelbert had on his own.

A final Katz reference: *As to where he had been for the twenty years, that was a part of the story at which Karl shrugged up his shoulders; for he never could very well explain it. And seemed to think the less that was said about it the better.*

Yes, thought Engelbert, the less said about his participation in Hitler Youth and the Wehrmacht the better. Do not flaunt that for which you should be ashamed. When he had come to Hilchenbach on leave in the summer of 1943, heads would turn: the hat, the boots, the uniform. Instant respect, from pub owners who would slide him a free frosty Krombacher to young women who would slip him a smile. Now he felt like a ghost—invisible.

He was an anomaly; most soldiers had been home for nearly two years. When civilians looked at him, it was with neither deep respect nor derision. In some ways, German soldiers were regarded by civilians the same way they regarded themselves: as victims. Germans, including those who had been fervent Nazis, were now saying, "I was never one of them. I never trusted the man." Author and Holocaust survivor Primo Levi called it "willed ignorance."

"For the majority, the realization that they had worked and slayed for a criminal cause came with devastating slowness," wrote Gerhard Rempel in *Hitler's Children*.

Engelbert—a man whose integrity, people would come to say, defined him—was quick to take responsibility for his stupidity. Not, of course, that he was going to say that to his father, who never just came out and said it—"Ich lag richtig. Du lagst falsch"—but he might as well have: *I was right. You were wrong.*

If the war had shattered countries, lives, cities, and more—9.2 percent of Germany's population died in it, compared to 0.3 percent of the U.S. population—if it had changed so much for so many, Fritz Jr. and Fritz Sr. had picked up right where they left off. The quiet war between father and son continued. Never mind that, even if they didn't know it, the two had never been so closely aligned in how they viewed the world.

Fritz Engelbert Jr. had fallen asleep for a long, long time. Now he was awake, and the world was different. He was different. In one sense he was freer than he had been his entire life: no Hitler to follow, no commander's orders to follow, no jingoistic bent to follow.

So why did he still feel like a prisoner of war?

Don

On the "sleeping porch" at the Sigma Nu house at the University of Oregon, Don Malarkey was wide awake. The reason wasn't the sweet serenade of trumpet snoring and tuba farting coming from his fraternity brothers; it was the war. Easy Company. He got up, grabbed a photo,

found a pen, and, in T-shirt, pajamas, and slippers, padded down the
basement steps.

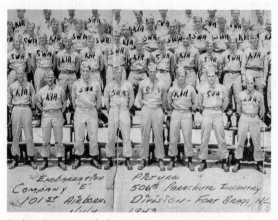

Back in Oregon, Malarkey wrote KIA or SWA on this photograph of Easy Company, noting which of his buddies had been
killed in action or seriously wounded in action. *Courtesy of
the Malarkey Family Collection*

There on the couch he looked at the group shot from Toccoa: 117
men of E Company, 506th Regiment, 101st Airborne Division, a couple
dozen having missed the photo session. Taking out a pen, he went to
work. If a man had been killed in action, he wrote "KIA" on his chest. If
he had been seriously wounded in action, he wrote "SWA." When he was
finished he went to add up the two numbers, but couldn't. The tears had
blurred his vision too badly.

When he had sufficiently wiped his eyes, the total came to ninety-one.
All but twenty-six. Only one in five of the original Easy Company men

had made it home unscathed. Four in five were either dead or seriously
wounded, guys like Toye and Guarnere, hobbling around on one leg.

Some people might have looked at the numbers and counted themselves lucky. Not Malarkey. Once, in a letter home to Bernice, he had
called himself "a fugitive from the law of averages." Now he asked: *Why
them? Why not me? Hell, I even asked for it—and lived. At Brécourt
Manor, I'd hot-dogged out in the middle of a firefight to grab what I
thought was a Luger, put my own men in danger to satisfy my own selfish
desires. Not a scratch. Then, at Foy, a corporal gets hit when it should
have been me taking that shot. How fair is that?*

Across the post-war United States, a wave of optimism blew from
coast to coast, a mood as light and sunny as Germany's was dark and
sullen. America was in better economic condition than any other country
in the world. The United States had emerged from the war as the domi-
nant force in the world. The middle class was swelling, unemployment
plummeting to historic lows, and "the American Dream" becoming a
reality for millions. The GI Bill of Rights, passed in 1944, allowed vets
to go to college and get low-interest house loans—something Malarkey
was taking advantage of. Pockets of suburbs popped up, first on the East
Coast and in California, then across the country. Life was good.

But a cold war like the one between the United States and the Soviet
Union was emerging deep in the soul of Don Malarkey. The memories
would not go away. They were with him when he was walking to the
McDonald Theater in downtown Eugene and a car backfired; instinctively, he dove into a bush as his friends' incredulous looks turned to

laughter. The memories were with him when he awoke on the sleeping porch at the Sigma Nu fraternity house sweating like a man in a sauna, having been sucked back to Bastogne in a nightmare: Muck exploding. Legs in the snow. The sixteen-year-old German soldier, an angel in all-white camouflage.

Malarkey began to wonder where the dividing line was between good and evil. He tried—God knows he tried—to default to what the army had taught him: dehumanization. *It was just another faceless soldier, the enemy that had to be thwarted.* And yet he had seen that boy's eyes, and his skin as smooth as Ardennes snow. Had Malarkey committed murder? Was he going to hell? Where was the purification for whatever curse he carried? Where was the absolution for the sin of having survived when others had not?

Those weren't the only things that frayed his nerves. There was also the loneliness. On the University of Oregon campus, he could be lonely while at a basketball game with 2,500 fans at McArthur Court. Lonely in a class of fifty students. Lonely anywhere.

Three years before, he had found life on campus as comfortable as a pair of well-worn saddle shoes. Now everything was different. It was as if he had "missing time." And everyone else had "missing experiences"— no idea what he'd just been through, acting as if life were nothing more complicated than jitterbug dancing, pep rallies, and panty raids.

Malarkey wasn't expecting a ticker-tape parade for him and others who'd fought; a beer and a listening ear would have been enough. But he found little interest in, or affirmation of, his experience in Europe. Everyone wanted just to "get on with our lives."

Few talked about the war or showed any interest in trying to understand it. Nobody got it. Nobody got him. Oh, outwardly, he was Joe College. A crooner with good looks, he directed the fraternity choir, starred on the Sigma Nu basketball team, and dragged his grades up from the depths of the Cs. But on a deeper level, he felt lost.

Things hadn't worked out for Don and Bernice, who wanted him to move to New York so she could continue her singing career. "I'm too damaged, too mixed up to even think about getting married, much less going to New York," he wrote her. Malarkey always respected how diligently she had written him during the war, and how willingly she at least tried to understand what he was going through in battle. Nobody on campus seemed to care. How do you explain the shellings in the Bois Jacques to a fraternity brother who thinks pressure is not being able to find a date for the homecoming dance?

In November 1947, Don met Irene Moor, a blonde Gamma Phi Beta. They had Cokes at the College Side Inn. "She had brown eyes you wanted to look at forever," he would say.

Her family was out of Don's league; she was from Portland, where her father was a member of Waverley Country Club. Don, meanwhile, had worked the seining nets, flipped burgers at the Liberty Grill, and worked the cash register at Spudnut's Doughnuts in Eugene. During the Depression, his father had blown away like a kite on a busted string. And Don was still dragging a war behind him like a ball and chain. But Irene was as smitten with him as he was with her, especially after he serenaded her one night with some Sinatra songs in the Pioneer Cemetery across from McArthur Court.

What he loved about her was that she was different from the others when it came to Don's war baggage. When he was suddenly in tears because someone reminded him of Skip Muck, she understood. She listened. She cared.

A grenade of bad memories could explode on Don, and he and Irene could pick up right where they left off. As if nothing at all had changed. As if she could love him, protect him, keep him safe from the war—for now and forever.

Never mind that Irene, like Don, was only human, and the ghosts of Bastogne were insidious. Years later he was asked what it was like for him after returning from the war.

"Tough," he said.

"Tough meaning what?" probed the journalist doing the interview.

"It was hell."

"What was the worst it ever got?"

"The worst?"

His eyes were misting before he opened his mouth to speak. He sniffed.

"Every evening after work," he said, "I'd go out for a drink. And at the bottom of my glass of scotch . . . I'd see the faces . . . of every man I left in Bastogne."

CHAPTER 10

In the Long Haul

Fritz

The plan—at least in his father's mind—had always been for Fritz to take over Gasthaus Engelbert. Not that his son had the slightest interest in doing so. Since he was young, Fritz had wanted to be an attorney, the profession of his uncle Fritz Pinkerneil, whom he admired deeply. When he arrived home from the war, however, he saw for himself what his mother had shared in letters to him at the POW camp. Both his parents were ailing.

The war, their age, and the years of nonstop work had caught up with them. Fritz Sr., nearly sixty-six, had heart problems and tired easily doing the simplest of physical chores. Anna, sixty-one, was in better condition but weary. If the inn was to stay in the family—where it had been since 1870—it seemed that Fritz would need to operate it. If he didn't, it would have to be sold. And then he would have not only the shame of Hitler on his conscience, but the shame of ending generations of family ownership. That was a one-two punch he wasn't willing to absorb—at least not now.

So, reluctantly, he took over.

It was not difficult work; it was just not work that Fritz had the slightest affinity for. With each room cleaned, beer drawn, and stack of firewood split, he was reminded of how much better the life of an attorney—or anything else—would be.

Beyond meeting guests' often lofty expectations, there was the pressure of his father watching him like a hawk—as if Fritz were an eight-year-old boy and not a twenty-two-year-old man. The pressure tightened Fritz's nerves like violin strings. And each day, it seemed, the tuning pegs were twisted ever so much more, making the strings tauter.

String one: a job he did not want or like. *String two*: what the job was preventing him from doing—building any sort of life to speak of, meeting women, challenging himself with school or a career, finding adventure. *String three*: the quiet disapproval of his father, nothing done by Fritz at the inn being done as well as the old man would have done it. And, finally, *string four*: the war shame, the bow drawn discordantly across the strings in a screeching rage at Hitler's betrayal.

"Forty years later, as I sit and look at these notes I wrote then, I can only shake my head in wonder at the way our young people were so inspired," another German soldier, Martin Pöppel, said after the war. Pöppel, too, had been caught up in the Hitler Youth fervor and gone to war. His words could have been Fritz's.

Hitler "ripped us out of our childhood and placed us in a struggle for our life," said an anonymous German soldier in the summer of 1944, as recorded in Stephen G. Fritz's *Frontsoldaten*. But at the time the young man had accepted the necessity. Because "the struggle was for our future."

In the post-war years, as Engelbert's perspective on the war grew, he realized the casualty count was beyond comprehension: between combat, genocide, massacres, bombings, disease, starvation, and civilians caught in the middle of it all, historians say Germany's decision to invade Poland in 1939 ultimately led to 75 million deaths, 55 million of those civilians. Six million Jews had been systematically murdered, and another 5 to 6 million ethnic Poles and Slavs, including Ukranians and Belarusians, were killed too. More than 1.1 million German civilians had died in World War II.

One of Engelbert's first questions after returning to Hilchenbach had been, "Where are the Jewish families?" The people knew, but nobody wanted to say. To tell of the death camps was to face an uncomfortable truth better left ignored: that the people's silence—their refusal to speak out against unspeakable evil—made them complicit in the mass murder. Many were silently ashamed that they had done nothing to stand up for the Hony, Stern, Schäfer, and Holländer families.

This only compounded Engelbert's sense of shame for betraying these people, first as part of Hitler Youth and later as a soldier in the German army. How could he not have seen the evil that was gathering like storm clouds in the skies above Germany in the late 1930s? Because, as his father told him, "Your Hitler Youth leaders would not allow you to look up, to look beyond them and the Führer."

But there was still serious strain between father and son. "Their relationship," Fritz's younger son, Matthias, would say, "was never dominated by love."

The connection had been stretched to its limits by each man's pride. Fritz Sr.'s had been bolstered by Fritz Jr.'s disillusionment with Hitler. Fritz Jr.'s had been wounded by that same disillusionment: he realized that his boyhood hero had betrayed his country for his own selfish gain. Not that father and son ever talked about it; theirs was a cold war, the salvos lobbed in silence.

Seeing his country in shambles made Fritz's shame all the more unbearable. Hilchenbach itself had been spared, but more than 160 German cities had been leveled by Allied bombing; 80 percent of Berlin's historic buildings were in ruins. At war's end, the Allied victors—the United States, the Soviet Union, France, and Great Britain—had divided Berlin into four occupation zones to try to help facilitate rebuilding, but there were huge obstacles. The European economy had collapsed. No central government existed. Refugees—Jews who had survived the death camps and POWs among them—wandered through the streets on foot with nowhere to go. Surviving German soldiers did what they could to stay alive: cleared rubble, patched holes in the roads, stitched the trousers of Allied soldiers against whom they'd just fought.

With so many German men having died in the war—soldiers and civilians alike—millions of women were widowed, many with children to care for. Food and water were scarce. Women sold sex for loaves of bread. Some were raped, at times by Allied soldiers from the occupying forces who, with no law enforcement to speak of, feared no repercussions.

Disease ran rampant, with survivors of the war succumbing to dysentery, typhus, and diphtheria brought on by the city's destroyed water and sewage systems. Hospital space and medicine were in short supply

Fritz's first winter back from war—1947 to 1948—was so harsh that it became known as "Hunger Winter." Record low temperatures froze the waterways, trapping ships with perishable foods imported from abroad in the harbors. A poor harvest meant less fresh food sent from the agricultural parts of Germany to the cities. Food was rationed. A coal shortage meant people had trouble heating their homes. Cold, starvation, and disease killed hundreds of thousands.

The Engelberts were among the fortunate ones. Fritz tried to remind himself of that when running the inn became particularly frustrating. Slowly, as the months passed, the rest of Germany started to rebuild, from infrastructure to attitudes and everything in between.

Under the Nazi regime, any book that didn't wholeheartedly support Hitler was banned; now, as bookstores rebuilt from the rubble and banned books became available again, Fritz cautiously began reading books he would never have considered before the war—as if lightning might strike as he turned the pages of Dietrich Bonhoeffer's *The Cost of Discipleship*, written by a theologian who had been executed for his defiance of Hitler. He also read the poetry of Wolfgang Borchert, an author and playwright who had opposed Hitler, served in the war, left his regiment, and ultimately died of liver failure eight months after Fritz returned home.

The post-war Soviet Union was emerging as a threat to the world. The Americans had long been wary of Soviet communism and of Russian leader Joseph Stalin's tyrannical rule of his own country and countries the Soviets had taken over; in Czechoslovakia, people had no sooner celebrated the defeat of Germany when Soviet soldiers started raping and pillaging. The Soviet Union, meanwhile, resented America's decades-long refusal to legitimize the USSR. After the war such grievances ripened into distrust as a cold-war chess match between the two countries began, with Germany as the pawn.

At dinner one night in early June 1948, Anna refilled the beer steins of her "two Fritzes" and mentioned radio reports of the Luftbrücke (Berlin Airlift) beginning soon. The Soviet Union had cut off all land and water transit routes between Berlin and West Berlin, turning the latter into an isolated island surrounded by East Germany. The Allies were preparing to drop food and coal from airplanes to keep the two million West Berliners from starving and, come winter, from freezing.

"How quickly friends can become enemies," said Fritz Sr. "It was not that long ago that the Soviets were helping the Allies defeat Hitler."

"And I, for one, am glad they did," said Fritz Jr. "Someone needed to stop him."

His father leaned forward in disbelief. His mother's eyes widened. His father dabbed the corners of his mouth with a napkin.

"And you are serious, son?"

Fritz nodded, surprised that he had spoken his mind as he had.

"Fritz, I do not wish to pour salt into a wound," he said. "I've been to war, and I know how it can change a man."

Fritz Jr. waited for the "I-told-you-so" lecture. His father paused, deep in thought. Anna's face froze in anticipation—of what, she did not know.

"It takes a lot of courage to change one's convictions, as you apparently have," he said, "especially when it means swimming against the unfortunate tide of our country—still."

Anna's stone face creased into the slightest smile, even that with a sense of uncertainty; these were uncharted waters for all three.

"Thank you, Father," Fritz Jr. said.

There was an awkward pause, as if something extraordinary had just happened and nobody knew quite what to do next.

Fritz Sr. lifted his beer stein.

"If, as I said, friends can quickly become enemies," he said, "so, apparently, can enemies quickly become friends. A toast to my son, a man with the courage to follow his heart."

And their two beer mugs clinked.

On December 13, 1948, Fritz Engelbert Sr. had a heart attack and died. He was sixty-seven. Like so many father-son separations, it triggered as much regret as grief in Fritz Jr.—in particular, regret that it had taken so long for them to find whatever tenuous peace they had found.

Not that his fragile reconciliation with his father had inspired Fritz to take any interest in running Gasthaus Engelbert. His sense of obligation to run the inn continued, and his sense of futility along with it. With his father gone, he might conceivably have convinced his mother to sell. But he didn't. Instead he split the wood, tidied the rooms, hired and fired the help, and pumped the petrol, day after day. He and his father might have reached an odd accord regarding Hitler and Germany, but as Fritz worked it was as if he could see the man off to the side, head tilted, eyes squinting slightly. *Are this month's books updated? Are you aware the Schumachers in No. 3 have been waiting for fresh towels for more than an hour? Have you restocked the bar?*

Fritz hated it all. And he hated that he hated it all. It only added another layer of shame: millions were without work, and yet here he was with a job that he wasn't in the least grateful for. Why should he have a job when German soldiers were polishing the boots of American soldiers in what was left of Berlin?

What had driven so many to Hitler in post–World War I Germany was the fear and hatred of their European neighbors that he had instilled in them. But, Fritz wondered, what if the real enemy was within? What kind of monsters had Hitler made of his own people by teaching them that fear and hatred? And if the enemy wasn't outside the borders but within, wasn't it the responsibility of Fritz and his fellow Germans to overcome such ignorance? To start anew?

Fritz would awaken at night in a sweat, thinking of war, Hitler, shame. He obsessed about not feeling better about his blessings at the inn. He was short with his mother. She would see him sitting alone behind the house, looking off into who knew what. He quietly seethed over apparently innocent remarks. And he would not smile, much less laugh. He tried going to gatherings of veterans' clubs, hoping perhaps to find some solace in the commonality of their shared experiences, but he always parted ways when the others were quick to defend Hitler. He soon tired of arguing with people so blind to what he now saw as obvious truth.

Three years after the war's end, the anger still boiled in his belly even as the loneliness deepened in his soul. The Allied command was carrying out its "De-Nazification program" to rid Germany and Austria of National Socialist ideology, but Engelbert had already carried out his own personal purge. The question was: What would he replace Nazism with? He had spent nearly half his life defined by Adolf Hitler.

Now that he was free to redefine himself, the prospect perplexed him—dare he admit, frightened him. When the door imprisoning a caged animal is opened, the animal doesn't necessarily bolt for freedom; it often clings to the safety of its familiar confines. Fritz, too, was hesitant to leave the cage.

In 1950, two relationships enhanced Fritz Engelbert's life—one a job, one a marriage. That they gave him direction, security, and satisfaction was obvious. That they failed to quell the demons inside was equally obvious.

When SIEMAG, the company Fritz had had an apprenticeship with before the war, offered him a job as a salesman, he approached his mother about a hybrid work life. Fritz proposed that he work at SIEMAG on weekdays, and work nights and weekends running Gasthaus Engelbert, bringing in some part-time help to operate the inn while he was away. Though she was skeptical about whether it would work, Anna agreed.

If that setup enriched and complicated his life, so did falling in love with Margret Messerschmidt, whom he met at SIEMAG. In some ways she was everything Fritz Engelbert was not: athletic, energetic, and social. What they had in common were wounds from the war, though she seemed far better at dealing with hers than Fritz was with his.

As a young woman, Margret had marched for the Wehrmacht as part of the Band of German Maidens (BDM), the girls' wing of the Hitler

Youth. Like Fritz, she had come of age just as such commitment was mandatory; she had never known a life without Hitler, and she had aspired to the Nazi ideal of being a good wife and producing the next generation of children for the Reich.

She had also been regularly forced to flee with her mother and sister into the woods to survive Allied bombings. And at eighteen she had heard her father, Robert Messerschmidt, a train engineer for the German National Railway, allude to atrocities he had seen in the Ukraine in early 1942. After Germany invaded the Soviet Union in 1941, two out of three of Ukraine's Jewish men, women, and children were killed in the next eighteen months. The German Einsatzgruppen rounded them up, transported them to remote areas, and shot them so they would fall into mass graves. Parents watched children killed, children watched parents killed.

"If we ever have to atone for what we are doing there we will all fare very badly," Robert told Margret, his other daughter Gertrud, and his wife Auguste.

His unspoken warning? *This was never to be mentioned again.*

After Fritz and Margret married on April 28, 1950, they tried to juggle a life that included both of them working at SIEMAG and Fritz trying desperately to keep the inn functioning.

During the day he did nothing but work. At night, amid his struggles to sleep, he inadvertently introduced Margret to all the baggage from his past; Fritz often woke in a sweat from war-related nightmares.

The pressure built. The violin strings tightened until one snapped. In December 1950, a particularly ornery guest had left the inn in a huff.

Fritz came into the third-floor apartment, not even bothering to knock the snow off his boots, and slammed the door behind him. Margret was making tea in the kitchen. Fritz unloaded an armful of firewood with a good-riddance toss, strewing kindling here and there.

"Are you all right?" she asked.

"No, I'm not all right," he said.

"What's wrong?"

"To think of doing this job for the rest of my life . . ." he sputtered, running his hand through his hair. "I would rather—I would rather hang myself!"

Don

On June 19, 1948, Don Malarkey skipped his graduation ceremony from the University of Oregon so he could marry Irene Moor. He had told her that however many children they had, one needed to be a boy so he could be named "Michael Malarkey." Always a fan of poetry, Don loved the alliteration.

They had that son in 1949. And three daughters—Martha the next year, Sharon in 1953, and Marianne eleven years later. "Our dangling participle," Don called her.

Age twenty-seven when he married Irene, Don felt he was too old to go to law school. They began married life in Don's old hometown, Astoria, where he sold cars. But after doing that and serving as an elected county commissioner, he decided neither was for him. He moved the family to Portland, where he got into real estate.

Don could be utterly charming, the life of any party. He was handsome, bronzed up well when Oregon's sun allowed, and stayed lean and taut swimming early morning laps. In some ways, he was straight out of Hollywood. Once, when Sharon was fishing with him on the Deschutes River, he saw something to her side, told her, "Don't move," pulled out a pistol, and shot a rattlesnake. He sang some great Sinatra, flirted shamelessly with younger women, and preferred what he called "forties girls"— thin waists, shapely legs, high heels.

He was never short on confidence—at least outwardly. It wasn't uncommon for him to tell people, "I was the best-looking guy in Easy Company."

And he had no patience for liberal politicians. Malarkey was a slim Archie Bunker. Each evening Irene delivered his dinner on a tray as if she were his own personal waitress, and sometimes a second dinner for their neighbor Ralph, who often joined him. He favored shows that made him laugh, *The Three Stooges, Carol Burnett, The Honeymooners*, and, yes, *All in the Family* after it debuted in 1971. He also watched the news.

As a staunch conservative, he felt that Richard Nixon won the September 1960 Nixon-Kennedy debate. Most disagreed. But Nixon had been vice president for Dwight "Ike" Eisenhower, and he was a Republican. That was good enough for Don.

When John F. Kennedy became president of the United States in 1961, Don was disappointed. The only thing he liked about the man was that, like Don, he was Catholic. Of course, he was saddened when Kennedy was assassinated, but he never warmed to JFK and his family.

In 1964, when Irene was pregnant with her fourth child, a grocery store checker who knew Don asked if they had any names picked out for the baby.

"'Jacqueline' is one we like," he said.

"Oh, wonderful, after Jacqueline Kennedy!"

Don hadn't thought of that; Jacqueline was a dear family friend. He came home and promptly told Irene their daughter was not going to be named Jacqueline. When she was born on August 3, 1964, they named her Marianne.

Don prided himself in his conservativism, but the Vietnam War brought out another side of him. Though he seldom voiced his opinion, he thought it was a mistake for the United States to be fighting what he saw as an unwinnable war. His son, Michael, would turn eighteen in 1967—and thus be draft-eligible.

The two had never had a strong relationship, the chasm between them dug not by their differences but by their similarities. Both brimmed with pride and stubbornness. However, when it appeared likely that Michael would get drafted and be sent to Vietnam, Don started working the phone. It wasn't as if he had a lot of political clout, but he knew people who knew people. The Malarkeys had lost two young men to World War I, he explained. And nobody in Easy Company had served on the front lines more days than Don. Word climbed the command chain that the Malarkey family had, in essence, given

enough. When Michael was drafted, he was stationed in Germany and
never saw combat.

As the war still festered within him, Don found peace in blackberry
picking. He and Irene favored wild Pacific blackberries (*Rubus ursinus*),
as opposed to the introduced and common Himalayan (called Armenian
blackberry, *Rubus armeniacus*) or the introduced, but less common,
Evergreen (*Rubus laciniatus*).

"He was fussy about that," his friend Dale Shank would remember.
"He believed the flavor of the native blackberry was the best."

Don took the family to the Nehalem River of his youth, showed the
kids how to dig clams on the Oregon coast, and cheered the athletic teams
of his alma mater, the University of Oregon. Every now and then he would
take the family to eastern Oregon—the high desert—where they would
help his friend Jack Collins on his ranch.

Meanwhile, he bumped from job to job, finding it hard to settle
into anything that satisfied him. But he could always find a bar, especially in December and January, the dark months. The Battle of the
Bulge months. The "I-made-it-back-and-the-others-didn't" months.
He liked whisky from Scotland, Johnnie Walker in particular. He
drank to forget two things: family finances and war, though, on a
deeper level, both might have been indexed under the category "Don's
inability to cope with . . ."

The war wasn't going away for him. He slept with a gun. He had
nightmares. Irene would hear rustling, awaken, and find that he'd had a
bad dream and was curled up underneath a desk.

As the years passed, money became an issue. Don's drinking got worse and the family's financial situation more desperate. Near the end of the month, it wasn't uncommon for Irene's well-heeled folks to slip her some money to help the family get by—which, of course, did nothing for Don's pride when he discovered it. Neither did Irene's going to work at a men's clothing store. *I parachuted into France and helped take out four artillery placements—all in the same day—but can't keep my family financially afloat?*

One night Irene heard a knock on the front door after midnight. It was the police bringing Don home because he was too inebriated to drive himself from the bar. Again. The officers knew Malarkey's address by heart. Neighbors would call; Don had showed up on their porch again and needed some help getting home.

"I remember walking down the stairs for breakfast one morning and there was a piece of trim from our car on the dining room table," his youngest daughter, Marianne McNally, would recall.

"What's this?" she asked her mother.

"Your dad pissed off someone at the bar again," said Irene. "They rammed our car in the parking lot over and over."

The car couldn't be driven. While it was being repaired—it was the family's lone vehicle—they had to get around by bus. Irene was at her wits' end. Her husband barely made enough money to keep the family afloat, and now this.

At the snap of a finger, Don could go from happy father to yelling at his kids. He grumbled at Irene. Growled at the sportscasters calling the game. Rolled his eyes if people were on time; he preferred them to be five to ten minutes early. Asked people to get up and get him a Coke instead of getting it himself. And hated seeing people cry because—not that he fully understood this—it triggered his war-connected emotions, brought to mind all the times that he had wanted to cry but couldn't.

"He hated the TV show *Lassie*," Sharon, the middle Malarkey daughter, would remember. "On Sunday nights when Martha and I would watch it, we would start crying when Lassie's life was imperiled and we thought she would die. The crying would infuriate Dad and he would forbid us to watch the show, but somehow, we always would."

When extended family gathered for Christmas, Don busied himself in the kitchen so that he wouldn't have to interact with the others. If one of the children slipped in to grab a few olives, he would utter the kind of admonishment that brought the conversations in the house to a hush. While the family gathered for the meal, he often took his food to the basement and ate alone. After dinner, he read to his family—not "The Christmas Story," but the story about how, when the Germans demanded surrender during the Battle of the Bulge, General Anthony McAuliffe, the 101st's commander, had replied "Nuts!"

"The worst day was always January 10," said Marianne. "That was the anniversary of Skip Muck's death. Once we got past that we thought we could breathe again."

Years passed. On a December night, after a long stint with Johnnie Walker at the American Legion Hall, Malarkey placed a long-distance call to Joe Toye. As Don would remember it, both he and Joe were "half-juiced." It was funny at the time, two old soldiers, shooting the breeze while badly buzzed.

But as time passed the drinking was no longer funny, particularly to Irene. Don could get away with it with Marianne, the lone child left in the house; when he had been drinking he would put her on his knee and recite "Gunga Din" or "Invictus" and everyone thought he was just happy and funny and swell.

"He was," Marianne would say, "a fun drunk."

Irene wasn't laughing. She was tired of having to send a neighbor friend to the Brass Monkey to retrieve her husband. Fed up, she wrote a note for Don, took Marianne, and left. With a friend and her friend's daughters, they drove a thousand miles south to Los Angeles, where they went to Disneyland.

"I remember the first night, sitting outside a phone booth while Mom talked to Dad and he was screaming so loud I could hear," said Marianne. "She told him we were leaving until he could get his act together. She was tired of him drinking their money away."

For better or worse, the war had defined Don Malarkey. He had seen its brutality up close. He wrestled not only with painful memories, but with a conscience that seemed to feed off his pain. Was he a good man? Was he a worthy man? Or was he simply a lucky man who hadn't been at the spot where, say, Skip Muck had been when that shell pounced on him like a lion on a mouse? And did that really make him lucky, or tormented? After a man died in Bastogne, he remembered, some would say: *They're the lucky ones. We gotta endure this hell. They're home free.*

Malarkey endured—and was determined to live, at least for now. He was fanatical about taking medicines and vitamins, in part because he didn't want to die. "He was convinced that he was going to hell because of all the German soldiers he'd killed," Marianne would say. And though nobody suspected it at the time, he was in the clutches of depression.

Though his marriage to Irene stayed together, things got worse for Don. One December night after work, he stopped at the Captain's Corner for a drink—or three. This time, however, when it was closing time, he didn't go straight home. Instead, his mind swimming crazily, he headed the car east from Portland on Highway 26 toward Mount Hood. At 11,250 feet, it is Oregon's highest mountain, the highway carved into the base of its snowy southern flank, Douglas firs towering beyond the twisting road. He had no business driving after the amount he had had to drink, but his mind wasn't attuned to precautions. He was back in the fog of war, trying to find some relief for the pain that wouldn't go away.

He had survived being surrounded by German troops—in temperatures so cold that his hand had frozen to his Tommy gun. But try as he might, he couldn't figure a way out of this one. Some twenty-five years after the Battle of the Bulge, he was surrounded once again, only this time not by German soldiers but by memories that wouldn't go away, faces that couldn't be forgotten, regrets that shouldn't have lingered but did. And so he had decided to choose the only option he felt he had left.

He already had the curve picked out. Above a drop-off. No guardrails.

CHAPTER 11

Walking Wounded

Fritz

Fritz Engelbert did not abandon Gasthaus Engelbert out of despair or for his own selfish ambition. Instead—taking a snowy walk after storming out of the apartment on that night in December 1950 and brooding on the problem—he came up with a solution that satisfied him, Margret, and Anna: the family would continue to own the inn, preserving the multi-generation tradition, and they would continue to live there, but they would lease it to someone else to operate. And he would be able to focus on just one job—at SIEMAG.

Meanwhile, Margret would quit work to stay home. She would soon be giving her attention to another new twist in their lives: a son, Volker, born in 1952.

In a letter written that same year, Engelbert told a former POW mate, Fritz Koppenhagen, about his compromise. As he explained, his sense of honor required him to consider his nearly sixty-six-year-old mother, and his wariness of materialism and blindly pursuing money made the choice to stay at the inn easier. Koppenhagen, a teacher, applauded his friend's decision. In an April 6 letter he wrote: "Through your letter, which let me take a very insightful look into the inner and outer design of your life, there is a good clear line to which I can only congratulate you. If God shaped our life for us so that we would have to deal with the management of material possessions in the course of our life, then he might have intended to give us the opportunity to learn how I, as a human being, stand on the matter. The question of whether you should give up your family life, your wife's health or even your mother's well-deserved retirement is quickly answered. In any case, the person who can be made a slave to a property will never be happy with his life."

Fritz loved his job at SIEMAG, perhaps too much. There Fritz did not have to serve guests who treated him like a butler, did not have to reckon with his father's criticism of his every decision (from beyond the grave), did not have to be pulled this direction and that. He simply had to convince people to buy enormous amounts of metal. He liked what he did. And SIEMAG liked him. They made him the company's purchasing manager at age twenty-nine, though some in upper management questioned whether someone so young could handle such responsibility.

As Koppenhagen's letter suggested, Fritz's love for his work wasn't about the money. It was because he liked the people, the process, the sense of accomplishment. At war, his "team" had been on its heels from the get-go; they had gotten the best of the Americans a few times during the tug-o'-war for Marvie, but there had been little to celebrate. And little to suggest he mattered. At his SIEMAG job, on the other hand, he was valued highly, he felt a sense of camaraderie, he earned good money, and he saw leaps of growth that represented success. What's more, his work left him little time to think about the past.

The only problem with his love of his work was that it consumed him—or he willingly let it, at the expense of his family. In 1956, a second son, Matthias, arrived. Fritz was neither an affectionate father nor an abusive father. He was mostly an absent father. Margret's mantra for the boys when they were young was "Papa arbeitet immer bei SIEMAG." ("Daddy is always working at SIEMAG.") The family's pet parakeet, Bubi, carried the same words into the 1960s: "Papa immer SIEMAG."

At work he could ignore the ghosts of the past. At home, not so much. In one nightmare he saw a little girl and asked her if she would like a piece of *Schokolade.*

"I can't have chocolate," she said. "Because I'm dead. Remember me? In the church rubble at Lutrebois? Your war killed me."

Engelbert bolted upright in bed, sweating, heaving, frightened.

"Liebling geht es dir gut?" asked Margret.

"Ja."

Engelbert was always "all right." He had to be. He was a soldier. Six days a week he dutifully got up and marched off to work, where he could forget. Then he came home, where he remembered—and where he would put in a half-day's work on Sunday.

He was reserved, modest, and respectful, his demeanor a thin layer of ice below which lurked the depths of Marvie and the Falaise Gap and Weislingen. His one recreation was Big Band music; he particularly enjoyed the German composer and band leader James Last and English-born Les Humphries. But he was never one to watch a soccer match on TV. "Nobody's watching me while I work," he once said. "So why should I watch them?"

The ever-active Margret loved to cross-country ski, something Fritz did only grudgingly. He would occasionally laugh at comedians Loriot and Hape Kerkeling, but for the most part he eschewed anything that smacked of silliness or triviality. He focused on work, not fun.

Sundays sometimes involved a gathering of relatives, a mingling of Engelbert's aunts and uncles and cousins and nephews and nieces. Conversations at such events would often return to the war, even though more than a decade had passed since its end. As if the gathering were scripted by a theater director, Fritz's brother-in-law, Heinz, would dig in to defend the honor of the Wehrmacht, and Fritz would rebut his arguments with an anger he only unleashed on such occasions.

"Ich bereue jeden Tag, dass ich ein Zahnrad in seiner hasserfüllten Kriegsmaschine war!" he would say. ("Not a day passes that I don't feel shame for having been part of Hitler's war machine!") If he was dour most of the time, he got particularly dark and quiet on three days of the year: September 1 (the anniversary of Germany's invasion of Poland, which had started World War II), November 9 (Kristallnacht), and December 16 (the start of the Battle of the Bulge).

In 1955, when there was talk of North Atlantic Treaty Organization (NATO) nations allowing West Germany to join and remilitarize, Engelbert seethed. "We should never have an army again," he said. "Never!"

"He was so very bitter," his son Matthias would say.

Fritz would fly into a rage at anyone who denied Hitler's responsibility for the death camps. He scoffed at those who tried to glorify the virtues and skills of German soldiers. He would shake his head in disgust when the German government dragged its feet in punishing the *Verbrecher* (criminals) who had supported the Nazi regime.

"At times," Matthias would say, "my father would wind up in tears. The regret simply would not go away. It ate away at him. Every. Single. Day."

Fritz hated the glamorization of war. At one gathering, his brother-in-law, Heinz, was regaling the family with stories of the gallantry of war when Fritz's face began to redden. "In Normandy, the Americans kept coming but our *Landsers* would not give in!" said Heinz. "Hedgerow to hedgerow, they fought courageously for the *Vaterland*!"

"And a few weeks later died like dogs," said Engelbert, remembering how he had first arrived to join his unit for combat. "At the Falaise Gap, there were bodies as far as I could see." His eyes began to mist. "It was like they were not even human beings. The Americans shot . . . them . . . like . . . dogs!" He trembled; his face was wet with sweat. The conversation around him quieted.

Heinz cleared his throat. "We must go now."

The party ended. More than one gathering ended the same way, with Fritz either too angry to enjoy his own family or too sullen to speak.

"Our mother suffered a lot when she saw our dad becoming so emotional," Volker would say. "She tried to avoid talking about, or listening to, the misery of war."

She didn't realize it at the time—Fritz didn't either—but he was experiencing what would be labeled post-traumatic stress disorder (PTSD) in the 1970s, following the Vietnam War. It occurs in many—though not all—of those who have been exposed to a traumatic event or, in Fritz's case, numerous tragic events. Such memories can translate into an array of PTSD symptoms, including isolation, emotional numbing, anger, depression, anxiety, and even suicidal thoughts.

But in Fritz's case, a second layer of psychological poison was eating through him like battery acid: what is known today as "moral injury." Fritz Engelbert may have been loyal to Hitler, but he experienced an about-face following the war, and his conscience had to deal with learning about Hitler's atrocities. That conscience felt deeply wounded.

Moral injury is about more than seeing corpses and smelling death; it's about one's most deeply held values being trampled. It can plague those who are forced to do something against their values—say, kill an enemy soldier even though society and religion say, "Thou shall not kill." By the time Fritz arrived in Marvie, his letters suggest, he had seen war for what it really was and just wanted it over. Instead, he was thrown into the horrific Battle of the Bulge, then into prison for two years.

Afterward, when he first understood the Third Reich from a broader perspective, he had no way of reconciling the wrong he had witnessed and participated in, no way to heal from this moral injury. With his post-war vision, he wasn't nostalgic for a Germany before the invasion of Poland, but a Germany before the rise of Hitler in 1933.

German doctors in the seventeenth century called this condition—a soldier's longing for a home that no longer is—*Heimweh*. The Spanish called it *estar roto*, "to be broken." After the Civil War, Americans used the term "soldier's heart," an indication that a soldier's deepest parts had been changed by war. Fritz knew no name for it, only that his heart had been broken, his soul withered—as much by Hitler as by the war itself.

"Modern warfare damages and destroys the youth and his character and threatens him with annihilation at the very time rites of passage are supposed to mature him in psychologically nurturing, socially useful, and spiritually enlightened ways," wrote Edward Tick in *War and the Soul*. It "leaves us with a huge population of partially transformed survivors," Tick argued.

Fritz Engelbert was among those survivors. "His conscience tormented him because he could not forgive himself for having fought for such an evil and criminal cause," his son Matthias would say. But there was nowhere to go where he would be understood, or where such feelings might be alleviated—and so, like many former soldiers, he suffered alone. Just Fritz and his conscience.

"The most profound experience of the self is the experience of the conscience. . . ." wrote Tick. "Modern war inevitably traumatizes this center of the self."

Fritz was a loner. He connected deeply with little beyond work and world news on the radio. (The Engelberts would not get a television until

1964, when Volker and Matthias pleaded for one to watch the Summer Olympics in Tokyo.)

In 1959, the German movie *Die Brücke* came out. It was based on an actual event in the final days of World War II, in which seven German boys in their mid-teens found themselves drawn into the effort to defend a bridge from oncoming Allied soldiers. They were not soldiers, but— caught up in the gallantry of war—they entered the fray almost as if it were a game. All but one died. Fritz seethed when it was over; to him, the movie represented the absolute futility of war, "the waste of lives for the glory of those too cowardly to fight themselves," he would later tell his sons.

Engelbert believed in sticking to one's convictions, even giving one's life for them, but his blind following of Hitler had proven that it matters what those convictions are. When his son Volker turned fourteen and was confirmed in the church, Fritz didn't give him a record album by his favorite band, the Beatles; he gave him a book by Bonhoeffer, the German pastor who had defied Hitler and been hanged on April 9, 1945.

In 1960, when Fritz was thirty-five, he moved his family, including his seventy-four-year-old mother, Anna, into a newly built house in Ferndorf, five miles from Hilchenbach. At the "roofing ceremony" to dedicate the new house, Fritz ended his short talk by saying: "May everything continue to work well on our site, so that one day we will be able to live happily in the still, cold walls and our two boys will grow up to be neat guys. Above all, however, my wish is that this building and all the houses of our beautiful Ferndorf Valley and our entire homeland may be granted deep peace for the future."

Fritz was a man of purpose, but he was built with "still, cold walls." He was good to his mother. Good to the boys. Good to Margret. But he could never get too close to any of them.

He was not a hugger. Not the father who kicked the soccer ball around with Matthias and Volker or went to their handball games. Not one to smile. For Engelbert, the glass was always half empty. He would not compliment Margret for her athletic success, would not encourage the boys—Volker with his bent for music, Matthias for sports—and would not engage in levity of any kind. He tucked his emotions deep inside—in fact, as Volker would say, he ran from them.

"We could never go back to the family house in Hilchenbach," according to Volker. "I came to realize that my father was afraid he would lose control of his emotions." As with Malarkey and *Lassie*, emotions were to be suppressed at all cost, lest he have to deal with his own. "He was a wooden person, not a heart person at all."

At SIEMAG, Fritz continued climbing the proverbial ladder, eventually becoming head of human resources. Forty-five-hour weeks became fifty, fifty became fifty-five.

He liked routines. Every day, Margret would have his clothes laid out for him for work. His coffee would be sitting on the table for him when he had dressed. When he finished at work, he would call fifteen minutes before leaving for home. When he arrived, Margret would be nicely dressed, with her makeup on. She would have a cookie waiting for him. At home, he read newspapers and listened to the radio, almost always the news. There was little he paid attention to beyond work, politics, and the economy. Those who knew him said he was brilliant. Stubbornly independent. Enigmatic.

In 1960, when John F. Kennedy was elected president of the United States, Fritz reveled in his victory. He loved JFK; if anyone could stand up to the communists and prevent World War III, Kennedy was the man. Many Germans felt the same way. JFK's June 26, 1963, speech in Berlin—"Ich bin ein Berliner" ("I am a Berliner")—ingratiated the country to him. By now, nearly two decades after the end of the war, some still clung to the old ways, lamenting the fall of the Third Reich, but most Germans did not. Eisenhower, whom Kennedy had succeeded, had been a World War II general and, at seventy, was the oldest U.S. president ever up to that point; he represented a past that a growing number of Germans wanted to forget. Kennedy, at forty-three, was the second-youngest U.S. president ever; handsome, energetic, and committed to peace, he represented a future for which many Germans longed.

"I still get goosebumps seeing the footage of Kennedy giving that [Berliner] speech after nearly sixty years!" Volker, who had had a magazine photo pullout of JFK stuck to his bedroom wall as a boy, would say. "The Germans would have torn down that wall with their bare hands if he had ordered it!"

Fritz felt a kinship to Kennedy. He was heartened by Germany's respect for the man; a new bridge of trust was building between Germany and the United States. In a word, what Fritz saw in Kennedy was hope. For decades, he had lived in the shadows of shame, in a world that his own negligence had darkened. Kennedy represented a new beginning—and, deep within Fritz, salve for his tortured soul.

But on November 22, 1963, he and Margret were on their post-dinner walk into town when someone they knew rushed to them with the news.

Kennedy had been assassinated. JFK's death reduced Fritz to tears. He could almost hear the gunshot all the way from Dallas. *Crack*. Just like that, JFK was gone, like Döring in the field at Weislingen.

Don

What saved Don Malarkey's life was family—Irene and the kids. In his desperate hours, driving through the snow near Mount Hood, it was the thought of them that convinced him not to fly off the road and kill himself. Convinced him to sober up and "fly right." Not that that was an overnight project—or one that would ever be complete.

But when the family moved from Portland to Salem in 1977, their lives took a turn for the better. Don had convinced Irene in a letter that he needed a smaller city, a slower pace. "I need to find peace," he wrote.

By then, the Malarkey family dynamic had changed. Only Marianne, thirteen, was still at home; Michael, twenty-eight, Martha, twenty-seven, and Sharon, twenty-four, had left to begin their own lives. Not that the three older kids had been troublemakers, but there was simply less potential for family fireworks. In essence, the three oldest had a different upbringing than did Marianne because Don's drinking was at its worst before the move to Salem.

Now living in the state capital, Don found a job with the state of Oregon's real estate division. The family moved into a 1938-built bungalow in southeast Salem. In the basement, Don carved out a precursor to the modern-day "man cave": shelves stacked high with Big Band albums, a touch of World War II memorabilia, his own black-and-white TV, and a comfortable couch on which to relax and watch it from.

The Cue Ball became Don's home away from home in Salem during the 1980s. Left to right: Stan Zeeb, Dale Shank, Henry Yoshiaki, Lenord Tong, and Don Malarkey. *Courtesy of the Malarkey Family Collection*

Don found a home away from home—the Cue Ball, an old-fashioned alcohol-free pool hall where the smoke was as thick as Astoria fog. The regulars were an eclectic bunch—"motley," Marianne would say—including Jim, the owner, who called himself "Don's babysitter"; Terry, a real estate salesman who doubled as a forest-fire crew cook; Leonard, a Chinese American computer geek; Henry, a Japanese American and lifelong Salem resident who had been sent to Japanese internment camps during the war; and Dale, a photographer and environmental consultant who was a Mennonite, married to a doctor, and had been a conscientious objector during the Vietnam War.

If what drew Easy Company together was a sense of patriotism and a fight against the Germans, what the Cue Ball boys shared was escapism, pool, and shooting the bull. Sarcasm was honored.

"Tree hugger!" Don would say to Dale Shank.

"Redneck!" Dale would fire back.

They seldom talked of war and politics. Malarkey would joke with Dale about Don's commanding officer, Dick Winters, being Mennonite—"and one helluva fighter." "Why bother to vote?" Don once said to Dale. "You and I are just going to cancel each other out on every candidate and every issue."

Years passed. If spending time at the Cue Ball was cathartic, if work was going better, if family friction had abated, the nightmares didn't stop for Don. December and January didn't get any less cold or dark. The faces were still there, in the bottom of his glass of scotch.

No turning back . . . keep drivin' . . . keep attacking.

In the mid-eighties, a few years before Don's retirement, he and Irene joined their second-youngest daughter, Sharon, and her husband, John Hill, at an oceanfront house at Cannon Beach, about half an hour south of Astoria. John's twin brother Tom and his wife Linda were also there for the weekend. As John would remember:

> There had been a lot of scotch poured and Don was jubilant and in his element, holding court and regaling the group with his many stories. . . . I can't remember exactly what Don had said, but the laughter was loud and long from us, including Don. Irene not so much; smiling, however, through yet

another recitation. Don then fell silent for a few minutes; his brow and demeanor becoming solemn and introspective.

He then began talking about the attack on Foy, Belgium, in January 1945. He told us how he was standing beside a building with another soldier and they were advancing toward the German position. Don was getting ready to advance across on open area as hostile enemy fire was striking around him. The soldier with him caught his arm and told him, "Don, let me go. I'm a corporal, you're a sergeant. It's my duty." The fellow soldier stepped out from the corner of the building and was immediately struck in the throat.

Don suddenly stopped talking and bowed his head and began sobbing uncontrollably and shaking. I remember my twin brother Tom putting his arm around Don's shoulder and comforting him for a few minutes as we looked on; helpless until the tears and sobbing had subsided and Irene and Sharon walked Don back to their bedroom and he took his troubled rest for the night.

For those who have never been in combat, it may be difficult to understand what Malarkey was going through. His wounds were not the kind an X-ray, MRI, or stethoscope could detect.

"Let me tell you what it's like," said a soldier quoted in Edward Tick's *War and the Soul*. "You can feel the connection between your body and your soul when it starts to break. It's like a thread that starts fraying. I tried so hard during the long nights, the earth shuddering, my hands over my ears. I concentrated to keep that thread from snapping. But I could feel it getting thinner and thinner."

When someone—a soldier, in this case—is in danger, the brain secretes stress-responsive substances that alter the functioning of the brainstem, the limbic system, and the frontal lobes. The brainstem and limbic system serve to mobilize the body to respond—fight, flight, or freeze—while the frontal lobes and other cortical areas evaluate the situation and determine the best response.

After the stressful event is over, some people are able to return to their normal state. Others can be so overwhelmed that it alters how they physically respond to trauma. It may manifest itself in a trip-wire temper or, as in Fritz's case, in quiet brooding and sorrow. The "threat-assessment" part of the brain becomes hypersensitive, and what others might deem a minor event can trigger massive stress, the kind of thing that happened to Malarkey when he was at Cannon Beach.

In Malarkey's case, this "stressful event"—war—comprised one traumatic situation layered over another—and another, and another. He served more days—177—on the front lines than anyone else in Easy Company. As a combat veteran quoted in *War and the Soul* said, "If you had seventy near-fatal car accidents in one year of your life between the ages of eighteen and nineteen, do you think that would mess you up all by itself? That's what it was like in [the war]."

When he was interviewed on camera for the HBO *Band of Brothers* series, Malarkey made reference to his post-war troubles: "You don't have a chance when friends go down to really take care of them as you might, especially when you're under attack, moving around. I withstood it well, but I had a lot of trouble in later life because those events"—at this point, he started choking up—"would come back . . . and you never forget 'em."

This is the seldom-told story of the aftermath of World War II. The war changed those who fought it. But after the decade-long Depression and a four-year involvement in a war that took the lives of 407,300 Americans, the last thing people wanted to do was wallow in yet another conflict, particularly one that could be hidden so well. They wanted to get on with their lives. But some couldn't.

"This comfortable assumption that 'the boys' returned home physically and emotionally unscathed, that no one drank too much, or abused his wife or children, could not be further from the truth," wrote Thomas Childers, author of *Soldier from the War Returning: The Greatest Generation's Troubled Homecoming from World War II.*

Although some men and women returned home without apparent emotional wounds, that wasn't the case for at least 1.3 million who not only suffered from some sort of psychological affliction but sought help through a Veterans Administration hospital because of it.

Some soldiers had been instructed not to tell anyone what happened, which only guaranteed that the ugly memories would be locked inside with nobody to bring a key.

The year 1946 saw the highest divorce rate in the recorded history of the United States, a record not exceeded until 1973, when women's liberation, the Vietnam War, and changing social norms put all-new stresses on marital relationships. One study showed that WWII combat vets were four times as likely as non-combat vets and non-vets to be heavy drinkers.

Though it would be more than two decades before the Vietnam War would lead to the diagnosis of PTSD, in 1947 more than half the beds in VA hospitals were occupied not by men with physical symptoms but by men with psychoneurotic symptoms: nightmares, outbursts of rage, survivor's guilt, and the like, symptoms that were most often expressed not in public but in the privacy of homes.

"We spend our childhoods being educated to behave with civilized restraint," wrote Tick. "Then war reawakens the primitive in us, and the conditions of battle necessitate it. We simply cannot take another's life without this reversion to the primitive, which leaves us feeling different and sullied. To feel qualified to return to society again, the first step we must take is to purify and cleanse."

Malarkey long believed that war had tainted him. In a letter to Bernice he had described his life as a soldier as "not an existence of a human being [but] the life of a madman."

"My dad was always tenderhearted," Marianne would say. "It was his weakness and his strength. My father was still tender in the war. That's why he struggled so much with his emotions for the rest of his life."

Malarkey's inability to forget the sixteen-year-old German soldier was classic PTSD. Experts say veterans suffering from combat stress are usually dealing with two things: the fear of someone trying to kill them, often day after day, or the guilt of having killed someone themselves. *Did I commit murder? Is God going to forgive me? What about that guy's family? Their pain is my fault.*

"I contend that every vet crying over his beer in some American Legion hall about something that happened sixty to seventy years ago is doing so not because of lost buddies, but because of lost honor, of shame," said Jeff Struecker, an author and former U.S. Army Ranger—part of the *Black Hawk Down* story—and a catalyst for *Saving My Enemy* being written.

A soldier's country might suggest he did good, as was the case with U.S. soldiers after World War II, but a soldier's conscience might contradict it, suggesting he did evil. For Malarkey, the inner struggle played out his entire life: "Not a day went by," he said at age eighty-five, "that I didn't think about killing that boy."

If Malarkey dared bring up the subject at the Cue Ball, his buddies would tell him he was shouldering blame that didn't belong to him. But as neat and clean and simple as that might sound, it didn't work for Don. A conversation Don had with a chaplain suggested that he was suffering what Edward Tick described in *War and the Soul*: "The soul freezes on this moral crisis point. It says . . . I killed whom I should not have killed and that is murder. I have become foul and cannot get clean again."

CHAPTER 12

First Steps

Fritz

When Fritz Engelbert first knelt at his friend Fritz Döring's grave in 1975, the finality of it overwhelmed him. Controlled and reserved in disposition, Engelbert was not easily overcome by emotion. But for more than thirty years he had harbored hope—albeit a slim hope—that Döring had not died at Weislingen in December 1944. After all, Fritz had only heard the crack of the rifle and seen his friend fall as the two sprinted across the farm field to the woods. He had not actually seen Döring die. Maybe he had only been hit in the calf. Perhaps the German reinforcements had arrived, diverting the Americans' attention, and Fritz had made it back to the German line after Engelbert's unit moved on.

But, no, here lay Döring. And now here knelt Engelbert, his wife Margret standing at his side. They had stopped en route to celebrating their twenty-fifth wedding anniversary in France. And Fritz wept. *Why him? Why not me?*

Fritz Engelbert unpacked the war gradually, carefully, thoughtfully, over three decades' time. Four years earlier, at age forty-six, he had talked his son Matthias, then fifteen, into taking a trip with him to see places where he had served. Matthias was game, partly because he had started learning French and this would give him a chance to test what he knew. Volker, four years older, was off "adventuring" with his girlfriend. And Margret was more than happy to stay home with Fritz's mother, Anna, then eighty-five.

The intricately laid-out plan was to visit more than a dozen cities and towns in France and Belgium over two weeks' time in July 1971. In Marvie, Fritz and Matthias found the spot near Lutrebois where Fritz had found the dead American soldier on Christmas Eve. In nearby Recogne, Fritz asked Matthias to take a photo of him next to the grave of Lieutenant Neupert, who, like Döring, had died right in front of him.

Fritz placed flowers on the headstone that Neupert shared with two other soldiers. His lips trembled, his face contorted ever so slightly, and his eyes glistened.

"Dieser Mann hat mir das Leben gerettet," Fritz said.

Matthias was stunned. How, he asked his father, had this man saved his life? Fritz told him the story of the battle at Marvie, where Neupert had ordered the half-track back to the woods rather than deeper into American resistance. Matthias may have been a typical teenager whose life was consumed by girls, sports, school, and Crosby, Stills, Nash & Young music, but he was astute enough to understand that neither his father nor he would be alive if the lieutenant had decided otherwise.

Fritz entered the chapel at the cemetery and wrote in the guest book, "With all my family, I thank Lt. Karl Neupert for his decision during the attack on Marvie on December 20, 1944." Matthias took a photo of it.

Until the visit to Neupert's grave, Matthias had only seen his father react to the war in anger. This was new. This was different. For the first time, Fritz had let someone inside his past. As the sentimental journey continued, Fritz shared what had happened at particular places, but little of how he felt about it. But Matthias read between the spoken lines.

"It intensified my understanding of what he'd gone through," he said. "For the first time, I began to understand what was behind his bitterness."

The two went to Laon, in France, where Fritz had been a prisoner; to Compiègne, to see the railway car where the German Reich had signed the capitulation to end World War I; and to Normandy, where father and son walked through the American cemetery at Colleville-sur-Mer above Omaha Beach. Nearly ten thousand white crosses and Stars of David stretched neatly across a sea of green grass.

"We were both moved to tears, and didn't talk much," said Matthias. "It still gives me the shivers, thinking of that visit."

In La Cambe they visited a cemetery with more than twice as many German soldiers: dark stones and endless lines of tomb slabs, each with the names of two German soldiers. "The whole impression lay heavy on us," said Matthias. "It felt very different from individually honoring and celebrating each liberator as at the American cemetery."

Upon their return home, Fritz mounted on the living room wall a photograph of himself standing beside Neupert's grave. Beside the photo he placed a poem by Wolfgang Borchert:

Und erzähl deinen Kindern nie vom heiligen Krieg:
Sag die Wahrheit, sag sie so rot, wie sie ist:
voll Blut und Mündungsfeuer und Geschrei.
[And never tell your children about the holy war:
Tell the truth, say it as red as it is:
full of blood and muzzle-fire and screaming.]

Below was a notecard on which he had typed, "Do unto others as you would have them do unto you," from the Gospel according to Matthew.

Life began to change for the Engelberts. In 1974, Fritz's mother, Anna, died at the age of eighty-eight. Soon Volker and Matthias were off on their own, both serving their mandatory fifteen months in the German army before going to the University of Bonn. For the first time in nearly three decades, Fritz and Margret were alone.

Naturally Fritz's response was to extend his hours at SIEMAG Transplan, his safe port. The timing was perfect. Ten years before, he had taken responsibility for the commercial management of the company; now he'd been elevated to the general management team. His usual pattern was to work ten-hour days during the week, five hours on Saturdays, then four more on Sundays at home—a fifty-nine-hour regimen that he relished.

In January 1977, Matthias filed for and was granted conscientious objector status with the Germany army. He had already fulfilled his obligatory post–high school military duty, finding the experience at best boring and at worst grating against all that he believed about how he should treat others, even the so-called enemies.

Matthias had been influenced by the German-Jewish pacifist Kurt Tucholsky, whose piece "Soldaten sind Mörder" [Soldiers Are Murderers] had been banned by the Third Reich, and Borchert, the poet who had defied Hitler and stripped away the glamor of war to "say it as red as it is."

But what clinched his decision was something he had heard his father say in a social gathering when the topic was war: "One has to keep in mind what war really means: World War II took seventy-five million lives; seventy-five million human lives wiped out for nothing; seventy-five million times unspeakable suffering and grief in countless families; seventy-five million times the fruits of years of upbringing in love and affection have been wiped out for an insane idea. What did my counterpart do to me that I just kill him?"

Matthias had decided then and there that his father was absolutely right. He could never kill another man—nor did he ever want to be in a position where he had to try.

His father, meanwhile, continued to spin further to the left in his politics. He had long been a supporter of Willy Brandt, the West German chancellor—and leader of the Social Democratic Party of Germany—who won the Nobel Peace Prize in 1971. Fritz had been driven to tears when Brandt knelt at the memorial for the victims of the Warsaw Ghetto in 1970. In late 1983, when twenty-seven-year-old Matthias was arrested for participating in a "die-in" in Bonn to protest nuclear arms, Fritz not only didn't scold his son, he applauded him. "If I were half my age, I would have been out there myself doing the same," he said.

Over three generations, an interesting family dynamic had evolved: Fritz Jr., who had once fought a cold war with his father over Hitler, had become much like his father in his political leanings. And Matthias and Volker had in turn become much like their father.

On May 8, 1985, on the fortieth anniversary of the end of World War II in Europe, Fritz was deeply affected by the courage of West Germany president Richard von Weizsäcker, who delivered a speech that echoed much of what Fritz believed, in particular regarding Germany's duty to own its World War II past.

"There is no such thing as the guilt or innocence of an entire nation," said Weizsäcker, the former president of the German Evangelical Church Assembly. "Guilt is, like innocence, not collective but personal. There is discovered or concealed individual guilt. There is guilt which people acknowledge or deny. All of us, whether guilty or not, whether young or old, must accept the past. We are all affected by the consequences and liable for it. We Germans must look truth straight in the eye—without embellishment and without distortion. There can be no reconciliation without remembrance."

He specifically called on Germany to own the crimes of Nazism. He dared to call May 8—the end of war in Europe—"a day of liberation." And he made a crystal-clear link between the Nazi takeover of Germany and the tragedies caused by the war. Finally, he boldly took issue with one of the most cherished defenses of older Germans against their guilt for the Holocaust.

"When the unspeakable truth of the Holocaust became known at the end of the war," he said, "all too many of us claimed they had not known anything about it or even suspected anything.

"We must not regard the end of the war as the cause of flight, expulsion, and deprivation of freedom. The cause goes back to the start of the tyranny that brought about war. We must not separate 8 May 1945 from 30 January 1933 [when Hitler came to power]."

Fritz Engelbert came into work the next day with an extra bounce in his step; the speech, and the praise it elicited at home and abroad, had made him feel, for the first time since the war, as though he were no longer a stranger in his own country.

In 1986, Fritz was named managing director of SIEMAG Transplan. In other words, he was CEO of the company. The promotion brought him to the apex of his professional life.

Two years later, his son Matthias married Beate. By then, Volker and his wife, Dorothee, had already added two grandchildren, Julia and Eva, to the family tree. Sunday gatherings were less apt to wind up in arguments about Hitler; Weizsäcker's speech had galvanized the country into an uneasy peace with the past and allowed Germans to move forward—something Fritz had already begun doing. His conscience demanded it.

"The first word that comes to mind when I think of him is integrity," his granddaughter Eva would say in 2020 at age thirty-three, looking back at the grandfather she remembered. "He was a man with high ethical values and lived by them."

But something happened in 1990 to remove the buffer zone that had afforded Fritz some protection from the past. At the mandatory German retirement age of sixty-five, he left SIEMAG after forty years. He had nowhere to go to distract him from the memories. He found ways to do contract work for the company and even kept a small office at the headquarters for five years. Still, his sons would remember, it was a long decade.

"The past was absolutely following him," Matthias would recall. "He could not forgive himself for being part of the Nazi machine that killed millions of Jews. He was sad, downbeat, pessimistic about virtually everything." Fritz had, in Weizsäcker's words, "looked truth in the eye," but he couldn't use that truth as leverage for anything good. Couldn't use the past to help create a new future. Instead, he just got stuck in it.

Despite the growing family, despite the freedom to relax, he returned to being, as Matthias called him, the "lost man." Quiet. Brooding. Distant.

"I remember a lot of 'don't do this' and 'don't do that' growing up," Elina, the third and final granddaughter, born in 1992, would remember. "Old-school manners. Never being unfair or loud, he definitely had my respect. But my grandma was the soft part of 'them.'"

Fritz was not alone among Germans, particularly of his generation, in being haunted by the past. While older people worldwide tend to have low levels of post-traumatic stress disorder, a 2008 University of Zurich study showed that older people in Germany—ages sixty to ninety-five—had PTSD levels three times higher than younger people.

In May 1998, after Fritz's fourteen-year-old granddaughter, Julia, was confirmed, the family returned to Volker's house to celebrate with coffee and cake. Fritz rose to honor her with a short speech. About twenty-five family members and friends were on hand. Julia looked toward Opa Fritz, anxious to hear what her grandfather would say.

In his short speech, he talked of how different it was to grow up in the 1980s and '90s, compared to when he was Julia's age.

"When I was fourteen," he told the well-wishers, "the year was 1939."

He paused. Swallowed. Remembered how that was the year that changed everything, the year Germany started World War II.

"I am thankful, Julia . . . that you have had the childhood . . . that I did not."

And with that he melted into uncontrollable tears.

Volker and Matthias quickly asked him questions to divert the subject from his time as a boy to his memories as a grandfather, but the guests were unsettled, embarrassed for both granddaughter and grandfather.

"Oh, my God, what did he do in the war?" someone whispered.

"Did he kill lots of people?"

"Was he a guard in a concentration camp?"

Volker would say that such moments were not uncommon; emotion would come over his father like an avalanche. "Once the box of his emotions was opened, he would lose total control."

Matthias and Volker tried to talk to their father. But what could they say? That he hadn't smelled the bloated bodies at Falaise? Hadn't heard his commanding officer gasp for breath at Marvie? Hadn't seen the face of the little girl at Lutrebois?

"Papa," said Volker. "You said it yourself: you never killed a single man yourself."

That didn't help. It wasn't the results that mattered, Fritz believed, but the Nazi process as a whole—which had killed millions of innocent people, and in which he had enthusiastically taken part.

"We tried to get him to forgive himself," said Volker, "but we could not help him find the absolution he sought."

It was Christmas 2000. Fritz Engelbert's arthritic hands were slowly opening a present from his sons.

Fritz was now seventy-five. His hair had thinned, started to recede, and turned nearly as white as the snow that winter would bring to Ferndorf.

The box he was unwrapping contained a Windows PC computer; Fritz's sons had thought their father might enjoy using it to write letters, send emails, and pursue his keen interest in politics. But the gift would prove to be far more than that. It would open up a new world to him that nobody could have imagined.

It was telling that when the computer was set up and Matthias showed his father how to navigate the internet, Fritz timidly placed the cursor in the search box and slowly typed: A-r-d-e-n-n-e-n-[the German spelling]-o-f-f-e-n-s-i-v-e. He wanted information on the Battle of the Bulge.

Volker cringed initially. He wanted to say: *Papa, the war is over. It is time to move on.* But each day Fritz learned more and more about the war in which he had taken part. He joined a World War II chat group. Started sharing a bit about his experiences. Printed out articles and filed them.

Fritz, seventy-one, in a rare upbeat moment at Matthias's fortieth birthday party on May 3, 1996. *Courtesy of the Engelbert Family Collection*

In late 2002, Fritz found an online ad for World War II books by Hans Wijers, a Dutch journalist who specialized in the Battle of the Bulge. He ordered two of the books and told the author in an email that he had fought in the Battle of the Bulge and would be willing to share his stories if they might help. Wijers took Fritz up on his offer and interviewed him online about his experiences.

In early 2004, another journalist, Belgian documentary-maker André Dartevelle, came across Fritz's story online and asked if he would be willing to be interviewed on camera in and around Bastogne, where the Battle of the Bulge had been fought.

"Nein," he told his sons without hesitation.

This documentary would feature survivors on all sides: German soldiers, American soldiers, Belgian civilians. To Fritz, telling his story in the safety of an email was one thing. To share it in the context of the very people he had once tried to kill, and amongst innocent bystanders whose families may have been killed, was quite another. How could he look those people in the eye? The Battle of the Bulge had cost the lives of nineteen thousand Americans, seventeen thousand Germans, and more than three thousand civilians. Their blood was on the hands of every German soldier who had picked up a rifle and done Hitler's bidding—Fritz included.

By now, Volker and Matthias had changed their tune: rather than running from the war, maybe what their father needed was to return to it and somehow make his peace. Again, Fritz resisted the idea of going to Bastogne.

"But Papa," said Volker, "you are stuck in a war that's been over for more than half a century. Your bitterness eats away at you every day. What is it the Americans say? *You can run, but you can't hide.*"

Like most German vets, Fritz had never spent a moment in counseling; just as in battle, veterans didn't sit around contemplating the losses, they just kept fighting. Fritz had done enough retreating in World War II.

"No," he told his sons. "People will say: 'Fritz, you were a Nazi. I won't talk to you. You and your comrades occupied my country and killed my people. I will never forgive you. Go home.'"

"But maybe something like this can help you move forward," said Matthias. "We want so badly to help you get over this, but we are stymied. Maybe this can help. And Papa, you need help in saving whatever life you have left. You're starting to live like a dead man."

Again, Fritz shook his head no.

Margret encouraged him to do the interview, too, though she preferred not to join him.

"We will take you," said Volker.

Finally, Fritz reluctantly agreed to go.

Once there, he was pleasantly surprised at how he was welcomed, particularly by Madame Esther Reyter, a Belgian woman roughly his age, and her family. She had been a seventeen-year-old girl in Marvie when American and German forces fought to control the village in December 1944.

Fritz, seventy-nine, paying his respects to Lieutenant Karl Neupert in Belgium, May 2004. *Courtesy of the Engelbert Family Collection*

Civilians had been caught in the crossfire. They fled to Lutrebois, two miles south, but the war would not leave them alone. American Thunderbolts pummeled the town on Christmas Day. People clustered in the church, but Esther found shelter elsewhere. The church, and everyone in it—civilians and German soldiers alike—died, but Esther survived.

Now, nearly sixty years later, she smiled and shook Fritz's hand, showing no animosity at all—this despite the war being of Germany's making and her father's having been killed when a grenade exploded near him in early 1945. Fritz was humbled by her willingness to forgive.

Beyond the Reyter family, Fritz met a U.S. soldier, Denis Parsons, who had been with one of the units that had done battle with the 901st at Marvie: the 101st Airborne Division, 327th Glider Infantry Regiment. If not warm, the American was at least respectful. The language barrier made communication all but impossible, but Fritz left the Bastogne experience feeling bolder about talking about the war; after nearly sixty years, someone had wanted to hear his story. It encouraged him, even if it did not completely quell the ghosts within.

As Fritz drove home with Volker and Matthias, he felt a lightness he had never felt. But as the months and years passed, the feeling did not last—and the nightmares did.

Don

When Don Malarkey first knelt in front of Skip Muck's headstone at the Luxembourg American Cemetery and Memorial in 1982, he didn't cry. Not one tear. He was closer to Skip, he once said, than to his own brothers. But he had steeled himself to stay in control. That's what soldiers did.

Don visiting Skip Muck's resting place in Luxembourg in 2005. *Courtesy of the Malarkey Family Collection*

Don later took another trip to the cemetery with historian Stephen Ambrose and two other Easy Company men, Dick Winters and Carwood Lipton. After decades as a self-described "hermit" when it came to revisiting the war, he now ventured forth like a man inching out on lake ice, fearing that it could break at any time and he would be swallowed by the cold. But venture forth he did.

In the late 1970s, Bill Guarnere talked Malarkey into driving with him to Missouri to see another Easy Company soldier, John Martin. It was a huge step for Malarkey.

Finally, in 1980—he was sixty-one—he decided to attend an Easy Company reunion in Nashville. It turned out to be both triumphant and tragic. Despite having bailed out of an airplane in the darkness of

Normandy at three hundred miles an hour, Malarkey hated to fly; in fact, this trip marked the first time that he had been on a jet. But he mustered the courage to do it. And he and Irene enjoyed making the connections and reconnections; Don hadn't seen his Easy Company pals in thirty-five years. They had dinner, then went to a club and drank and talked and reminisced. The experience was wonderful.

And then, suddenly, it wasn't. The deeper he got into the evening—and into the scotch—the more memories flooded back. It was as if he couldn't control the ghosts of the past. Unable to fight, he decided to flee. He bid a hasty farewell, told Irene he would meet her at the hotel, and started walking alone in a city he'd never been to before.

He got lost. Got scared. Panicked. Before long the rest of the group had enlisted the police to search for him. He made it back safely but felt sick at the worry he had caused.

Back in Salem, he sent apologies to a handful of people, then wrote to Winters. He told the Easy Company captain that he had found the experience "overwhelming"—and yet, at the same time, freeing.

> Back in 1944–45, a person had to discipline his emotions to such an extent, in order to keep your head screwed on, that you may not have properly demonstrated proper appreciation, compassion, sorrow, and the whole gamut of feelings that were rampant within you. I wanted you to know how grateful I was for your consideration of me throughout my entire time overseas. There was more than one instance when you very well may have saved my life—D-Day is one; ordering me in

from the outpost in Holland, at Hell's Corner, when I was caught in a heavy mortar attack; and pulling me off a combat patrol in Haguenau are a few. I am sure there are more.

There has hardly been an hour pass since I left France in November 1945 that I have not thought of you and the tremendous officers and men of our company and the 101st Airborne. . . . It was without question the proudest and most cherished period of my life, even though there are times when I succumb to depths of sadness that I am not strong enough to withstand, when I dwell too much on memories of the men we left behind. I am not ashamed of it—the Irish are known to have emotional weaknesses and I am no exception—except I did stay in control in combat.

Don with his three daughters in 2009. From left to right: Martha, Marianne, and Sharon. *Courtesy of Dale Shank*

Don and Irene became regulars at Easy Company reunions. Malarkey retired in 1987, traveled to Europe to see places where he had been in the war, and along the way got to know war historian Ambrose better. He corresponded with Easy Company men, becoming particularly close to Buck Compton, who had successfully prosecuted Sirhan Sirhan after the assassination of Senator Robert F. Kennedy in 1968. And he began to take being a father more seriously—though he was more successful with his daughters than with his son.

"My dad was always there when I needed him and he was good at calming me down," Martha, the oldest Malarkey daughter, would say. "My mom said he always knew what to say to me to help."

In 1990, when her son Tim was deployed to Saudi Arabia for the Gulf War with the 82nd Airborne, Martha called her mother. "I read the letter and Mom started crying and Mom put my dad on the phone and he was able to talk to me and calm me down. I still get teary-eyed thinking of that."

Michael had moved in with his folks after a divorce in 1987, and drinking—on the part of both father and son—only made the situation worse. Michael had developed multiple sclerosis in his forties. Don had bonded tightly with his Cue Ball buddies and his Band of Brothers pals; Michael always felt as if he were outside, looking in.

"My father's father never modeled how to be a dad," Marianne would say, "and, because of that, I'm afraid my father didn't know how."

Don's wife, Irene, with *Band of Brothers* executive co-producer
Tom Hanks at the HBO after-party for the 2002 Emmys. *Courtesy of the Malarkey Family Collection*

After Stephen Ambrose came to an Easy Company reunion and
decided to write a book about the unit, Malarkey was among the many
soldiers the historian interviewed. *Band of Brothers* came out in 1992
and quickly became a regular on the *New York Times* bestseller list. The
ten-part HBO miniseries produced by Tom Hanks and Steven Spielberg
was released almost a decade later.

Band of Brothers was the best thing to ever happen to Don Malarkey.
And the worst. On the one hand, when the series premiered in 2001 it
validated him and the men of Easy Company like nothing else could have.
When a superior officer pins a medal on a soldier's lapel, who's around

to notice? When the opening episode of *Band of Brothers* was shown on TV, ten million people watched.

Suddenly, forgotten soldiers were hailed as heroes, Malarkey among them. His usually happy-go-lucky character was played by actor Scott Grimes. At the world premiere party for *Band of Brothers* in France, Marianne turned to her mother, Irene.

"Mom, was Dad really that funny and silly as a young man?"

"Yes," she said. "Scott nailed it."

But three of the more memorable "Malarkey scenes" in *Band of Brothers* aren't funny: the death of Malarkey's best friend, Skip Muck, in Bastogne; Malarkey picking up laundry in England after the Normandy invasion—and realizing that many of the packages of clothes he's carrying are for guys now dead; and Malarkey talking with a captured German soldier in Normandy who, it turns out, had worked right across the street from Don at Schmitz Steel Company in Portland, Oregon.

Don's wife, Irene, and their son, Michael, at the Seattle premiere party for *Band of Brothers* in 2001. *Courtesy of the Malarkey Family Collection*

"*Band of Brothers* brought some light to a very dark subject for Dad," his daughter Marianne would say. "When Spielberg and Hanks bought the rights to the book, life changed for the veterans. Their stories came to life. My dad enjoyed every minute of the process. And Mom loved it, too. Suddenly, they were jumping into a limo in LA to go do sound editing in some studio—that kind of thing. It was new and exciting."

Seemingly overnight, a guy who favored jeans and Cue Ball windbreakers was gussying up in tuxedos for premieres at the Hollywood Bowl and on Utah Beach in France. Actor Scott Grimes was in Don and Irene's hotel room, singing "Danny Boy" for the family. People recognized Don in stores. Fan mail started pouring in. *Call of Duty*, a video game that came out in 2003, was based on the real experiences of the 506th Parachute Infantry Regiment, including Easy Company's Brécourt Manor assault on D-Day. The Cue Ball became a Malarkey shrine with billiard tables.

The book and miniseries helped people come to a deeper understanding of what these soldiers had faced in World War II. "When the book came out and I read it, I was pretty upset that my Dad had gone through so much hell," Don's daughter Martha would say. "So, I called him crying and told him that I had no idea that he had been through so much during WWII and I was sorry he had to go through all that."

Until the HBO series came out, Don's grandson Patrick, then twenty-one, had known virtually nothing about his grandfather as a soldier. Their relationship revolved around their shared love of jazz, Sinatra in particular—though Don conceded that Bobby Darin's version of "Mack the Knife" was better than Frank's. Now he was seeing his grandfather in an all-new light.

Once, when Patrick was playing *Call of Duty* online, another online player saw him signed in as "pmalarkey" and huffed something about "ripping off" the real *Band of Brothers* soldier Private Malarkey. Patrick just laughed.

Each week Don would get hundreds of requests to speak or sign autographs—many, he learned, to be sold for profit. He was given all-expenses-paid trips to fly to Europe and take part in World War II tours. He volunteered to take a USO trip to Afghanistan in support of the troops. But the best thing *Band of Brothers* did for him was give him validation. "It reminded me that we'd done a good thing—and over the years I'd forgotten that," he said.

Until that point, the standard modus operandi for World War II soldiers was to talk about their war experiences only with others who had been there. Now that began changing. Along with Tom Brokaw's book *The Greatest Generation* (1998) and the far more graphic movie *Saving Private Ryan* (1998)—based on the Niland brothers—*Band of Brothers* depicted World War II with a new realism. The publicity, talk, and spin-offs generated by these books and films gave World War II veterans a new-found permission to share their stories with others.

"My father found a new sense of peace," Marianne said. "Talking about it with his war buddies, going to events, schools, even sharing with folks one-on-one—it was good for him to get the war off his chest, open up and show his heart to everyone. He'd protected it forever, not wanting to appear weak."

Easy Company veterans at a dinner before the Emmy
Awards ceremony in 2002. From left to right: Background:
Frank Soboleski, Al Mampre. Foreground: Don Malarkey.
Background, facing the camera: Les Hashey. Foreground:
Shifty Powers, Don King, Roy Pickel. Background: Buck
Taylor. Foreground: Pat O'Keefe. Background: Rod Strohl.
Courtesy of the Malarkey Family Collection

It turned out to be a fragile peace; there was a flip side to this fame—
and Malarkey experienced it. *Band of Brothers* stamped the men of Easy
Company with approval as true American heroes. And heroes don't need
help. The result? The drama miniseries distracted the men from seeking
the help they might have needed—and that was now available. The affirmation that Don and the others got from *Band of Brothers* gave them a
false sense of security. Who needed to deal with PTSD when you were
busy signing autographs? Like most American vets, Don had never spent
a moment in counseling; the expectation had always been that you just
came home from the war and got on with your life.

"In 2001, my father was doing an interview with the BBC at the
world premiere party and he told the interviewer, 'I tried to drink the war

away,'" said Marianne. "I looked at my mom and said, 'Now I get it.'" It was the first time that Marianne had linked her father's drinking to his time in the war.

But *Band of Brothers* had another, less helpful effect. It led Don to go from one extreme to the other. "Decades before, it was as if he never talked about war, except maybe with his buddies and my brother Michael," Marianne would say. "After *Band of Brothers*, he couldn't talk about anything else. He could never find that happy medium."

For Malarkey, the past was insidious—and no respecter of fame or fortune. If facing it was therapeutic in some ways, it was painful in others. Once, he and family members were out to dinner with a couple of the *Band of Brothers* actors—Neal McDonough, who played Compton, and Richard Speight, who played Don's good friend Skip Muck—and the topic was war. Nearly as soon as the waitstaff took their orders, Don was already in tears.

Another time, Speight, hoping to understand Skip better for the part he would play, phoned Don to talk about his buddy. He was simply asking questions when he heard the line go dead; Malarkey, it turned out, had hung up on the actor.

"I just couldn't take it," Malarkey said.

Being reminded of Skip so vividly had begun as fun but ended in frustration. Malarkey melted into a pool of sobs. The kicker was not only his sense of survivor's guilt. It was his guilt for having let down the actor who would play Skip—which, of course, really meant letting down Skip himself. Don was right back in the endless loop of loss and regret and guilt again.

Malarkey called *Band of Brothers* a "roller coaster experience." It lifted his spirits. It created a diversion. But it didn't uproot the guilt; no amount of applause or autograph seekers could fix that. Celebrity buoyed the outward man but not the inner man, brightened Don's smile but didn't soothe his soul, and offered a temporary fix when he needed a solution that would last.

Just as sailors lost at sea may gorge themselves with food once they're rescued, Malarkey ate heartily when the *Band of Brothers* lifeboat arrived. But recognition, even fame, wasn't what he really needed. Thousands could sing his praises, but what he really needed—even if he didn't realize it—was forgiveness.

And not just from anyone, but from the enemy.

PART IV

ABSOLUTION

Remembering is not enough, if it simply hardens hate.

—Eric Lomax, *The Railway Man: A POW's Searing Account of War, Brutality and Forgiveness*[1]

CHAPTER 13

Incoming

Don

It was war that made Don Malarkey and Fritz Engelbert enemies—and war that helped make them friends. They fought in World War II, but it was an incident in the Iraq War sixty years later that served as the catalyst to bring them together.

On July 4, 2004, one week after control and sovereignty of Iraq had been handed over from the United States to an interim Iraqi government, Sergeant 1st Class Billy Maloney stood in the mouth of an aircraft hangar at a U.S. military outpost in Baghdad, his ear to a satellite phone. Around him: a dozen or so members of the 101st Airborne's 2nd Brigade, 1st Infantry Division.

On the other end of the line was Earl McClung, who had been a staff sergeant with Easy Company in World War II. Sergeant Maloney didn't know McClung, but when he'd phoned Denver-based Valor Studios to order a *Band of Brothers* illustration, he had asked if there was any chance of getting an Easy Company vet or two to offer some Independence Day encouragement to his weary soldiers. He knew that Valor, which specialized in paintings and other memorabilia honoring military personnel, had lots of connections. And by now his men and women desperately needed a boost for their morale; they had been in Iraq for more than sixteen months.

Adam Makos, who along with his brother Bryan co-founded Valor Studios, was so moved by Maloney's request—*Who reaches out from a combat zone on a satellite phone?*—that he made it happen. He rounded up six Easy Company vets and scheduled them all to make half-hour sat calls to the troops on July 4: Malarkey, Darrell "Shifty" Powers, Guarnere, Edward "Babe" Heffron, and Compton would all be calling with words of encouragement, in addition to McClung.

Maloney gathered a group of soldiers anxious to talk to the Easy Company vets on the satellite phone. Maloney made the first call, to McClung, eighty-two years old.

"Thanks so much, Earl, for taking time for us today," said Maloney, a forty-two-year-old "lifer" from the Bronx. The sound of helicopters taking off and landing was so loud that he had a finger plugged into his non–phone ear. "We got some folks who are anxious to hear from you. The first is—"

Boom!

"Incoming!" yelled Maloney as he dove for cover.

Through the satellite phone, McClung could hear the missile. *Whhhhhhhhhhhhhhh—pkkkkkkkkkkk!!!!!*

The blast sent Maloney flying. And at his home in Pueblo, Colorado, McClung recognized the sound on the line and instinctively did what he had done hundreds of times when shells were raining down six decades before. He dove for cover—in this case, beneath the living room table.

Surreally, McClung could hear what sounded on the phone like a bevy of exploding rockets. Shouts from Maloney and the others. More blasts. Groans. Chaos. My God, he thought, soldiers could be dying. In these frantic seconds, he wasn't in Colorado—he was in the Bois Jacques. It all came back, the panic, the fear, the feeling of being hunted with nowhere to hide.

"You OK, Billy?" he said into the phone. "Billy, you all right?"

No answer. A few minutes later the line went dead. When Maloney called McClung two days later, he said his unit had been attacked by 120mm rockets. A number of soldiers had been wounded, including Sergeant James Lathan, who would later die of his wounds. A woman from the Black Hawk unit—Maloney couldn't recall her name—had had most of the flesh torn from a leg.

McClung thought: *This is what these people are going through. Just like us. All these decades later.* He thought of the loneliness in the woods near Bastogne, the cold, the detachment from anything that made sense. Later, he thought: *These soldiers deserve more than a long-distance pep talk. They need to know this country is behind them.*

"Billy, what can we do to help?" asked McClung. "Beyond just a phone call?"

Maloney, who was based in Hanau, Germany, and married to a German woman, gave it some thought. He got back to Earl with the idea of bringing a group of Easy Company men to Germany for an event with active-duty soldiers. Have a dinner, share a few beers, offer them some encouragement. It could go a long way—even if it was just a few dozen soldiers, their new-found enthusiasm could "catch" to others.

McClung was all in. The more the two talked, the more enthused they became about the idea. Hell, they could peg it to the sixtieth anniversary of the Battle of the Bulge in December, providing Easy Company's men were willing to travel in the winter.

"And another thing," said Maloney, "how about if we invite some German World War II soldiers?"

There was a pause on the other end of the line.

"Earl," said Maloney. "You still there? Earl?"

Fritz

The Americans were coming. From a distance, across the pasture, Engelbert could see them through his field glasses. A run for the barn was his only hope.

"Schnell zur Scheune!" he said to the comrade at his side. The soldier did not respond.

"Schnell zur Scheune!" Engelbert barked.

Again, no response.

Fritz looked closer.

"Ahhhhhhhh!"

The soldier was frozen in place—literally. Glazed in ice. Fritz recoiled in fear.

The man, he realized, wasn't his comrade. He was the dead GI that Fritz had seen near Lutrebois on Christmas Eve of 1944. A corpse, eyes barely visible beneath eyelashes and eyebrows veiled in frost. Engelbert, his heart pounding, stared in horror at the agonized face.

The dead man's eyes suddenly blinked wide open. His right hand sprang forward like a striking rattlesnake and clutched Engelbert's throat. Engelbert gasped. The icy fingers squeezed. Tighter . . . tighter . . . tighter . . .

Fritz bolted upright in bed, panting, sweating, trying to catch his breath. By now, Margret had become so accustomed to the frequent nightmares that she didn't even wake up.

Why? Why? Why?

Why had Fritz said yes to this preposterous idea of gathering with American soldiers in Hammersbach? Why had he let Matthias and Volker change his mind? He had nothing to gain and everything to lose, foremost his pride.

An email had come from the Dutch journalist Hans Wijers, to whom Fritz had granted numerous interviews for his Battle of the Bulge book series. Wijers had heard from an active-duty American soldier, somebody "Maloney," about an event to commemorate the sixtieth anniversary of the Battle of the Bulge—and to inspire active-duty soldiers stationed in nearby Hanau. A handful of what the Americans called the "Band of Brothers" were coming to Germany. Apparently they were Hollywood movie stars. Would some German soldiers like to join them?

Nein! Nein! Nein!

He didn't even like socializing in comfortable settings with people
he knew and liked, much less in uncomfortable settings with people he
didn't know and might not like—and the prospect of meeting men he had
fought against in World War II was out of the question.

"But Papa," said Volker, "perhaps it will help the dark cloud of the
war go away."

"Why would I want to meet with American movie stars as they gloat
about their victory from long ago?"

"You did not want to go to Bastogne in May and look how much you
enjoyed that," Matthias reminded him. "I'm happy to drive you again. It
will be an adventure."

Fritz shook his head no.

"Other German soldiers have been invited," said Volker. "Your
comrades. You won't be alone."

"The war is over. Who needs comrades?"

Matthias, feeling particularly desperate, decided to play the history
card.

"Papa, do you remember how JFK came to Germany in '63 and gave
his famous 'Ich bin ein Berliner' speech?"

"Of course."

"I'm sure he was nervous, too. One American standing amid millions
of Germans. 'The enemy.'"

"I am not JFK, American president," he said. "I am Fritz Engelbert,
Hitler puppet."

"Papa, that is not you. And here is your chance to prove it."

Fritz sighed heavily. But he could see that his sons weren't going to relent.

"All right, all right," he said. "I will go."

CHAPTER 14

Face to Face with the Enemy

Don

The only way Don Malarkey could get through a flight, particularly a long one like this, was to order a scotch and tell the flight attendant to "keep 'em coming." In December 2004, en route to Europe for the sixtieth anniversary of the start of the Battle of the Bulge, he leaned back and closed his eyes.

By now, however, travel was as much a part of his life as brushing his teeth. He'd been to Europe more than a dozen times, schmoozed with Hollywood stars in LA, and signed more autographs than some sports heroes. The men of Easy Company had become rock stars—though some of them were rock stars with hearing aids, walkers, and wheelchairs.

Despite his fear of flying, Malarkey liked *Band of Brothers* events. Sometimes, his youngest daughter Marianne thought, perhaps a little bit too much. She had become Don's go-to travel companion and de facto manager.

"At times, I wondered if he was letting it go to his head a bit," she would say. Don enjoyed having meals and drinks bought for him. The family would go out for dinner and well-meaning folks would interrupt for autographs and photos with Don. It had started to make him act privileged. He could be ornery at home, but in the public's eye he could do no wrong.

Once, when Marianne and Dan took their children, Kyle and Erin, to buy shoes at a mall in Salem, she mentioned they were for a trip to Europe. When the salesman asked her about the trip, she mentioned that her father, Don Malarkey, was leading a *Band of Brothers* tour.

"Whoa! I know your dad!"

As he explained, back when he was in high school he and his mother had been in a Walmart parking lot when Malarkey backed into their car. Don got out of the car, apologized, and introduced himself while fishing for his driver's license.

"Hey, you're the World War II hero," the teenaged boy had said. "You came and spoke at my high school."

"Which one?"

"North Salem. Mom, this is the man I was telling you about, the war hero!"

The mother looked at her crumpled taillight, then at Don in his "Screaming Eagles" jacket.

"Oh, it's just a scratch," she said. "Don't worry about it."

Now, years later, the guy was thrilled to meet Don's family. "It was an honor to have your dad back into our car!" he said.

McClung had been taken aback when Billy Maloney suggested inviting Germans to the American base. He had never considered something like that. And, as the idea sank in, he was concerned that not all the Easy Company soldiers would be OK with it, even though he was. He shared his concerns with Maloney.

"Facing your enemy provides profound forgiveness," Maloney told McClung. "I saw Vietnam vets meet their enemies, and also read about it. The book *We Were Soldiers Once . . . and Young* and the follow-up to it, *We Are Soldiers Still*, best reflect that message."

"I'm game if you are," said McClung. "Just sayin' I'm not sure all our guys are going to go for it."

He was right. While neither Powers nor Malarkey had a problem with the Germans' coming, Compton was lukewarm on the "plus-Germans" idea, and Guarnere and Heffron voted "no krauts." Still, they agreed to come.

Guarnere's problems with Germans dated back to the night before the D-Day jump, when he had been informed that his brother had been killed in Italy.

"I was burning to get at those goddamn Germans," he would write in his memoir, *Brothers in Battle, Best of Friends*. "I would kill every one of them."

And he had killed plenty—losing a leg in Bastogne in the process. That's how Guarnere had gotten his nickname, because of his reckless attitude toward German soldiers. He was forthright, unpredictable, and unapologetic about it. And that's why the guys in Easy Company called him "Wild Bill."

Fritz

December 15, 2004, the evening of the gathering, arrived. Matthias Engelbert eased into a parking spot in front of Zur frischen Quelle, a quaint inn in Hammersbach, a small village east of Frankfurt. Fritz felt a tightening in his chest, a quickening of his pulse. He glanced furtively at Matthias in the driver's seat, then exhaled.

Why did I agree to come? What if the Americans treat me like they did the day they captured me? "And his cousin's Mickey Mouse!" *Why not retreat?* It wouldn't be the first time he had run from the Americans.

Matthias patted his father's left leg.

"Entspann dich. Es wird in Ordnung sein."

Relax, it will be fine? Sure, Fritz wanted to tell Matthias, *it will be fine—for you. You are a spectator. I am the German soldier whose country started this war, who slaughtered the Jews. And here I am, eating schnitzel with the men we were trying to kill—and who were trying to kill us.*

Father and son got out of the car and walked toward the inn, which dated back to the twelfth century. Fritz knew his history: Hanau had been home to the Brothers Grimm, and it had been virtually leveled by British air strikes in March 1945. The last of the Jews in Hanau had been loaded up and carted off to the death camps in May 1942—about the time Fritz had been trying to convince his pigheaded father to let him join Hitler's special Waffen-SS.

With his son guiding him by the arm, Fritz entered the inn's dining area, a typical half-timbered room welcoming guests with the warmth of a quaint house: massive wooden tables, lace curtains, Christmas lights and garland across the thick beams. And plenty of Binding, one of the most popular beers in the Frankfurt area.

The crowded room contained about a dozen active-service American soldiers, the six Easy Company vets, a few of their wives, and Fritz and Matthias.

Among the more animated Easy Company soldiers was Guarnere, he of the Philly accent and the take-no-prisoners attitude. Fritz noticed that Bill, as he sat down across from him, was missing a leg. An obvious war injury, he figured.

"Wo sind die anderen deutschen Soldaten?" Fritz whispered to Matthias.

Matthias, too, had thought other German veterans would be coming, but apparently none had shown up.

"Don't worry, Papa," he said.

The no-shows are smart, figured Fritz.

He was wearing slacks and a dark blue wool sweater; most of the Easy Company vets were in jeans, 101st Airborne hats, and either maroon jackets or bright yellow Easy Company jackets, which Tom Hanks and Steven Spielberg had given to them at the *Band of Brothers* premiere in Normandy.

The talk was of war. The young American soldiers had brought *Band of Brothers* memorabilia to be signed. Matthias had brought his new tin-box copy of the ten-part DVD set but didn't yet feel comfortable asking the Easy Company guys to sign it.

Fritz nodded some hellos—he spoke a little English—but couldn't hide the wish-I-were-anywhere-but-here look on his face. The beer was flowing, the conversations getting louder. World War II soldiers and active-duty American soldiers were all engaged in "soldier talk," while a sprinkling of wives enjoyed each other's company and waiters and waitresses tried to keep pace with the party of two dozen.

Some guests were perusing a paperback copy of *Band of Brothers*—the first time Fritz and Matthias had seen it. A videographer positioned a camera on a tripod. From time to time, young American soldiers timidly slipped over to get autographs from the *Band of Brothers* veterans. Fritz and Matthias had heard these men were popular, but until tonight they had had no idea of the extent of their celebrity. As the Easy Company men signed autographs, Fritz remembered his homecoming from the war, when he had felt like a ghost. Invisible. Just like he felt now.

Waiters arrived with the schnitzel for dinner. Empty beer glasses were filled up, the chatter rising with each refill. Fritz looked uncomfortable. In one photograph of the event, it appears as if everyone is in motion, but Fritz is frozen.

With Matthias interpreting, Fritz was introduced to Guarnere across the table.

"Or as we like to call him, 'Wild Bill Gonorrhea!'" Heffron, Guarnere's best friend, said with a hearty laugh.

Fritz shook Bill's hand, his grip as timid as Guarnere's was strong. Almost too strong, Fritz thought, as if Guarnere intended to send a little message. Billy Maloney watched with a touch of concern; inviting the Germans had been his idea, but he wasn't naïve. With a few beers under their belts, and telling their war stories—who knew how these Battle of the Bulge survivors would react to the German soldier at their table? As a precaution, Maloney had placed two MPs in the inn's guesthouse; he didn't need his "bury-the-hatchet" event to explode onto the front page of the *New York Times* with a report of a chair-throwing ruckus. He had purposely not invited the media: the event wasn't meant to be a photo op, but a morale boost for his soldiers, with a touch of "let bygones be bygones" thrown in for good measure.

Guarnere took another drag on his cigarette and blew the smoke toward Engelbert.

"Yo, it's 'Fritz,' huh?"

Engelbert nodded uncomfortably.

"Joyman, huh?" he said with his Philly accent. "A soyger?"

Over the din of noise, Matthias turned to his father. "Er fragt Dich, ob Du ein deutscher Soldat warst?"

"Ja," said Fritz, nodding. "Soldier." He swallowed hard.

Guarnere squinted and leaned across the table at Fritz. He began nodding his head slightly.

"Fritzy, m' boy, count y'self lucky that we did not meet sixty yiz ago," he said. "Utta wise, I'da kilt ya!"

For emphasis, he whipped his forefinger sideways across his throat in a violent slashing motion.

Fritz mentally recoiled. To a man seeking acceptance, it was like stepping on a landmine. It was the very thing he had feared.

Matthias began to interpret, but Fritz stopped him; he had understood "kilt" and there was no ambiguity in the throat-slashing gesture. Engelbert was not a lighthearted man by nature, and the stunned look on his face suggested that had not changed. Matthias was shocked;

perhaps his father had been right to be worried. A burst of nervous laughter ensued from others at the table.

As Fritz instinctively began shoving his chair back to leave, Matthias felt a pang of regret that he had encouraged his father to come in the first place. But also a pang of regret that neither of them had had a chance to get to know these *Bund der Brüder*. Matthias didn't want to leave. His father obviously did.

Then, just as Fritz was beginning to stand, Malarkey's tap-tap-tap of his beer glass with a knife brought the room to a hush. Fritz settled back in his seat, only to be polite. He would leave when the announcement ended. The room quieted.

"Mr. Engelbert, you'll have to excuse my friend 'Wild Bill,'" Malarkey said, looking Fritz in the eye. Matthias interpreted for his father. "Bill must have gotten some bad schnitzel or something."

Laughter warmed the room. Uncertainty creased Fritz's face. *Was this the second blow of some one-two punch to further humiliate "the Joyman"?*

And then, in a gesture that Fritz Engelbert would never forget, Malarkey lustily raised his beer into the air.

"Ladies and gentlemen," he said, nodding afar to his wife Irene, "and, uh, Wild Bill: a toast, to our new friend, Fritz Engelbert. Welcome to the Band of Brothers!"

For just a moment there was a pause, as if the people in the room were children being offered an undreamed-of privilege. *Can we do this?* Then two dozen glasses rose in Fritz's honor—none higher than the one belonging to Malarkey. Even the embarrassed Guarnere raised his glass.

Fritz looked right and left, not sure whether or not he could trust this sudden turnaround. *Was it real, or was it American humor, with him as the butt of the joke?*

Fritz toasted his new "adoption" into Easy Company with Earl McClung, left, at his side in Hammersbach, Germany, on December 15, 2004. *Courtesy of Matthias Engelbert*

Matthias saw Malarkey's eyes fix on his father's eyes in what seemed to be unmitigated soldier-to-soldier, man-to-man respect. When the toast segued to enthusiastic applause, Fritz finally gave in to the realization that Don was sincere. That Don was offering him the rarest of gifts: friendship, something Fritz had experienced little of in his years of quiet grieving. Not only friendship, but the friendship of a man who had once been his enemy.

All eyes were fixed on Fritz, whose son watched in quiet amazement as his father did something Matthias had rarely seen him do in nearly five decades. He smiled. It was, at first, a cautious smile, as if he felt himself undeserving of this honor. As if he were still at the mercy of a conscience that wanted him to believe forever that it was his fault Seligmann the Jew had been beaten by the Nazis. As if he doubted that the stain of war could ever be washed away. But with a slight nod of his head, Fritz raised his glass to affirm the toast and, for the first time in sixty years, to affirm himself.

The smile turned from medium to large, then from large to extra large.

CHAPTER 15

Comrades in Arms

Don and Fritz Together

The next day, when the group convoyed in two buses to see the Luxembourg American Cemetery and Memorial and Battle of the Bulge sites in Bastogne, Don's toast of respect had long since quelled Fritz's fears. It hadn't hurt that as the previous night's event was winding down Guarnere had come up to Fritz, shaken his hand, and given him a Binding beer coaster on which he had written, "Fritz Engelbert. Airborne love." Fritz carried it in his pocket as if it were precious gold.

When they arrived, Fritz was touched to see that his older son, Volker—who had been unable to make the previous night's event—had driven more than three hours to join his father and Matthias on this special day. Ludwig Lindemann, another German soldier whom Maloney had invited but who had been unable to attend the previous night's dinner, had also arrived.

When Fritz met Ludwig their greetings were polite but reserved. And it wasn't Fritz and Ludwig, the two Germans, who stayed together during the day. Instead, it was Fritz and Don, the German and the American. The two were all but inseparable, more like two school pals having a great time on a field trip than like two elderly veterans.

The American Cemetery and Memorial at Hamm, Luxembourg, December 16, 2004. Fritz stands behind as Don Malarkey and William Guarnere pay their respects to their fallen brethren. *Courtesy of the Engelbert Family Collection*

But when they visited the cemetery in Hamm, the mood changed. Beneath its frozen turf: 5,073 Allied soldiers. The white crosses and Stars of David were hardly discernible against the snow, which had lightly dusted the trees and grass overnight like baking powder. The tall pines in the forest beyond stood like white sentries, protecting the peace of this hallowed place. Amid a chilly fog, visibility was not much more than the length of a soccer field.

The six Easy Company soldiers made their way to the rows of graves. General Patton himself was buried here. But the vets made a beeline for the graves of Skip Muck and Alex Penkala, who had died together in the same Bois Jacques foxhole.

Fritz left the Easy Company men and stood off by himself. He watched, realizing this moment was not meant for him. In a navy blue beret and forest green winter jacket, he clasped his gloveless hands behind him— he was used to the cold—and watched respectfully as Malarkey, in his yellow "Screaming Eagles" 101st Airborne jacket, knelt at the grave of Skip Muck. Don's head fell forward in what his memoir would call "sixty years' worth of tears." Beyond were Heffron, Compton, and Guarnere—Bill clad in a beige camo jacket and leaning on his braces, his missing leg a sad legacy of war.

Bois Jacques, Bastogne, December 16, 2004. Fritz and Don were overwhelmed by the Belgian children who came to honor them. *Courtesy of Matthias Engelbert*

Matthias slipped quietly backward to take a photo of his father watching the Americans honor their fallen brothers. When he returned, he heard sniffles. And saw his father's eyes blinking back tears.

After the group huddled beneath a large canopy for steaming-hot soup, they were taken to the Bois Jacques forest in Belgium, where foxholes were still visible sixty years after the Battle of the Bulge. The experience was emotional—every one of the vets had tears in his eyes—but the mood lightened when they were surprised by Belgian schoolchildren who had come to honor the men. The kids were all stocking caps and rosy cheeks and runny noses. They had each brought a homemade card, written in French: "Tous ensemble!" ("All together!") and "Thanks for liberating us!" and "No more war!" Some drawings showed the Belgian and German flags next to each other. Some said "peace," *paix* (French) and *Frieden* (German).

"My father couldn't believe this, and his tears flowed," said Volker. "He expected to be ignored by the Belgian kids—or worse."

Instead, the children smiled, giggled, and splashed the afternoon with a lightness that belied the mournful woods beyond. The soldiers had had no idea they were coming, and they relished the moment. (Only later would Fritz learn that an effort to have Belgian veterans meet with the Easy Company men had been dropped because a vets' group had heard Germans might be with them; they wanted nothing to do with the "men who had supported and fought for a criminal regime." As Volker would say, "It was ironic that the children could forgive, but not the adults.")

The children leaned into the men, asking for autographs, showing off their drawings, and posing with them for photos.

A local television camera crew joined the throng, which was approaching a hundred people. At six feet, Fritz was a couple inches taller than Don, but with the same thinning white hair, the same glasses, the same smiles, and the same solid, slim builds, the two could have passed for brothers.

As the cameras clicked, Fritz wrapped an arm around Don. In one photo the two men are arm in arm, Fritz's hand on the shoulder of a child in front of him. The two men appear locked in a commonality of purpose that belies their past as enemy soldiers. The image suggests protection, safety, affirmation for all people. It stands in contradiction to the time sixty years before when the grandparents and great-grandparents of these Belgian children were caught in the crossfire of war.

When the TV reporter asked Don and Fritz about their new friendship, they laughed, struggled with language, and kept their arms around each other. Their relationship was just getting started. Already Matthias had noticed an air about his father that he had never seen before. It was smiles. It was energy. It was peacefulness. Fritz had affixed himself to two things in life that were important to him—SIEMAG and his family—but it was the war that had defined him. And now, for the first time, he felt a sense of belonging in connection with that.

Everywhere the two went, people asked for autographs. Don had signed thousands in his life. Fritz hadn't signed one until now. He signed the drawings the kids had done, he gave autographs to the U.S. soldiers, and he signed a piece of parachute from World War II brought to him by a high school history teacher in Bastogne. In the Bois Jacques, where foxholes from the 101st could still be recognized, he accepted a warm handshake from Easy Company's Earl McClung, answered questions from the active-duty American soldiers, and tried to make small talk with Easy Company member Babe Heffron.

"Hey, Malark," Heffron would say later, "we wuz wrong about the Joyman. Good man, Fritz!"

At a grocery store in Bastogne, a woman looked at Fritz as if she knew him.

"Monsieur, je vous ai vu à la télévision hier soir! Vous avez serré la main d'un soldat américain!"

Matthias translated her French. "Papa, she says, 'Sir, I saw you on the TV news last night! You shook hands with an American!'"

"Ja, er heißt Don Malarkey. Wir waren Feinde im Krieg. Aber jetzt ist er mein Freund!"

"He says, 'Yes, his name is Don Malarkey. We were enemies in the war. But now he is my friend.'"

The woman touched Fritz on the arm and smiled.

That night, father and son went—how else can it be said?—bar-hopping in Bastogne with Easy Company members, though Malarkey wasn't among them. It was like nothing Fritz Engelbert had ever done before. But he was enjoying every moment—as if a lifetime of repression was being released in a spree of pizza, beer, and *Bund der Brüder* fans.

"We were stunned at the attention the *Band of Brothers* guys got," said Matthias. "I don't think they bought a drink of their own all night."

When the two returned to the Hotel Melba, Fritz noticed Malarkey and a few other Easy Company men in the lobby, having drinks. Just as he had at the cemetery, Fritz stayed back, not wanting to intrude. Malarkey, after taking a sip of his scotch, saw Fritz and Matthias standing by themselves.

Don and Fritz at the Hotel Melba in Bastogne, December 16, 2004, moments before they bared their souls to each other over beers. *Courtesy of Frederic Dubois*

"What the hell?" he said. "Get over here, Fritz, and let me buy you a beer!"

He beckoned Engelbert with a nod and a flip of his hand. Fritz approached cautiously, Matthias trailing behind. Malarkey pointed to a table, nodded at the bartender, and held up two fingers for beers. Don sat in one chair in a brown and plaid shirt; Fritz across the table in a navy blue sweater; and Matthias, translating for them, to the side. Two men, sitting across from each other on the sixty-year anniversary of the start of a battle in which, given the opportunity, they would have killed each other—not necessarily because they wanted to but because, as soldiers, they were required to.

The two men looked similar, but they were markedly different in many ways—and not just because one was American and the other German. Malarkey had grown up like Huckleberry Finn, free to seek and find adventure. He was brash, cocky, and a legitimate war hero. He had killed plenty of German soldiers and then returned to a country awash in optimism.

In some ways, he had gotten more in life than he deserved. He had improbably survived his foolhardy attempt to snag what he thought was a Luger. He and his badly outnumbered Easy Company boys had knocked out four 105mm howitzers the Germans were using to pound soldiers coming ashore at Utah Beach. Despite being a kid from a hardscrabble background, he'd married a country-club girl. Despite being a guy in a windbreaker who hung out at the Cue Ball, he had wound up dining out with Hollywood stars.

Engelbert, on the other hand, had grown up as a pawn of a militaristic despot who controlled him like a puppet. He was reserved and humble and—as Matthias said—"never a hero like Don but his experience as a soldier also made him special, a convinced democrat and pacifist longing for reconciliation." Not only had Fritz not shot a single American soldier, but he had spent much of his war in retreat and was ultimately taken as a prisoner of war. And then he returned to a country awash in misery.

In some ways, he had gotten less in life than he deserved. He'd shown the courage and humility to give up the set of beliefs inculcated in him throughout his youth for a better set, in the name of human dignity. He had taken care of his mother, provided for his family, and let his sons be who they wanted to be. He had maintained close friendships with two fellow POWs for most of his life. And he had quietly climbed the ladder at work, earning a reputation for "respect," "integrity," and "honesty," the words bandied at his retirement party.

Malarkey could take over a room, Engelbert was reserved. Malarkey hopped from job to job, Engelbert worked at SIEMAG for forty-five years. Malarkey spoke about his service around the world, Engelbert divulged his memories with great reluctance. Politically, Don leaned way right, Fritz way left. But ultimately none of these differences mattered as much as the secret that drew them together. Deep down, they were bound by an ache of war that simply would not go away, an ache etched in shame for Fritz and guilt for Don. Both halves of Erich Maria Remarque's description of World War I soldiers fit them: "a generation of men who, even though they may have escaped shells, were destroyed by the war."

Outside, snow had begun falling. The two men began talking, a touch awkwardly. Of their wives. Of war. As the staccato exchanges were translated by Matthias, the two got to know each other better. It was the first time in the two days that they had been able to really talk.

The drinks kept coming. The snow kept falling. The subject turned from Fritz's time in Hitler Youth to the Battle of the Bulge. It turned out that in a war fought in more than a dozen countries and on two continents, the two had been fighting within five miles of each other, Don a couple miles north of where they sat now, Fritz a couple miles southeast.

Don talked of Easy Company's foxholes in the ghostly Bois Jacques, Fritz of his unit huddled in cellars in Marvie and Lutrebois. Don of losing his best friend, Skip Muck; Fritz of losing his, Fritz Döring.

They drank and shared, peeling away the layers of machismo that so often keep men from ever really knowing each other. The beer and stories of death softened whatever barriers had separated them. At one point Malarkey's gaze was through the window, to the snow. He sniffed, cleared his throat. His mind was sixty years away.

"At Foy, I had to—we were advancing and there was a soldier I killed," he said. "When I pulled out the record from his pocket, I realized that he was only a boy. Just sixteen."

Fritz told of seeing the frozen U.S. soldier in the snow on Christmas Eve. Suddenly his face reddened. He slowly ran a hand over his mouth, his eyes turning glassy.

"Das Blut dieses amerikanischen Soldaten klebt an meinen Händen," Fritz said.

Don looked to Matthias, who translated. "He said, 'That American soldier's blood is on my hands. I did the bidding of a madman, Hitler.'"

Malarkey shook his head, but Fritz kept talking.

"Und das Blut der Juden klebt auch an meinen Händen!"

"And the blood of the Jews is on my hands, too."

Again, Malarkey shook his head.

"Fritz, you had no choice. You were forced into Hitler Youth. You were given a weapon and sent to war."

Fritz bowed his head and wiped his eyes with two hands.

"Don't you understand?" Malarkey said. "It's not your fault, Fritz. Let it go. Nobody's holding that against you. You've done well. You're a good man. You raised good sons."

At that, the levy broke and the tears Fritz had been holding back since 1945 flowed. His sons had known a father whose emotions were as unchanging as the Rock of Gibraltar. Now, in this moment, Matthias was stunned: He had seen his father seethe quietly in anger. He'd seen him sad—at Neupert's grave near Marvie. But this was different. This was a man who had been relieved of a burden, freed from a prison, forgiven a debt.

"Danke, mein Freund," said Fritz, taking a deep pull on his beer.

"Hey, I know that one, I know that one!" said Malarkey. "You said 'thank you.' But what was that other part at the end—the 'my fruit' stuff?"

Fritz nearly spat out his beer. He burst into uninhibited laughter, triggering the same in Don and Matthias, who had never seen such spontaneous levity in his father—not even on the recent beer-and-pizza spree. *Never.*

"He said, 'Thank you, my friend,'" said Matthias.

"Oh, got it," said Malarkey. "Mein fried."

Fritz laughed hardily. He was enjoying this *Bund der Brüder* Malarkey.

"'Freund,' not 'fried,'" said Fritz.

Malarkey returned Fritz's laughter with his own—not the laugh of an eighty-three-year-old man but the laugh of a college kid who might have been at the College Side Inn with his fraternity brothers.

Then it happened: Malarkey's laughter segued into tears, and the tears into sobs. The mood quieted. Matthias lightly patted Don's shoulder. In this moment, it was as if Don and Fritz were trading roles. Don wiped his eyes and blew his nose. He then looked Fritz dead in the eye.

"You are not alone in your shame," he said. "Hell, I still see the eyes of the kid I killed at Foy. Every. Single. Day. And more in December and January. God, is it just me or does it seem extra dark and cold in those months?"

Fritz nodded after Matthias's interpreting.

"Just like Bastogne," said Don.

"Die Erde war so gefroren, dass wir Probleme hatten, unsere Toten zu begraben."

"Fritz says, 'The earth was so frozen, we had trouble burying our dead.'"

Malarkey nodded, his eyes still wet. The brief quiet suggested that neither man was here now. They were both shivering outside in the winter of 1944–1945.

"Was du zu mir gesagt hast, mein Freund, musst du dir selbst sagen," said Fritz.

Matthias turned to Don.

"Fritz said, 'What you said to me, my friend, you must say to yourself.'"

Don mulled the suggestion. Fritz continued his thought.

"Musst es nicht nur sagen, sondern auch glauben. Es ist nicht deine Schuld, Don. Dein Land hat Dir eine Waffe in die Hand gegeben und Dich in den Krieg geschickt. Du hattest keine Wahl."

"'Must not only say, but *believe*,'" said Matthias. "'It's not your fault, Don. Your country put a weapon in your hand and sent you to war. You had no choice.'"

Fritz reached across the table, placed his hand on Malarkey's, and widened his eyes.

"Ja?"

Malarkey was a firm handshake guy. But, in this moment, Fritz's gentle hand on his felt good, as if the touch were not to his hand but to his very soul.

"Ja!" he said.

And he put his other hand atop Fritz's.

PART V

LEGACY

Let my spear lie idle for spiders to weave their web around it.
May I live in peace in white old age . . .

—Euripides, *Ion*[1]

CHAPTER 16

New Connections

Don was eighty-three, Fritz seventy-nine. With the men in their twilight years and more than five thousand miles between them, the friendship was never destined to last long or to be sustained by frequent get-togethers. But last it did, its strength rooted not in physical proximity but in conscience. Both men came home from Bastogne having unloaded baggage that needed unloading. Their relationship was fueled less by words spoken than by affirmation offered.

"It seemed to me that embracing the former enemy and realizing that Don forgave him helped Opa Fritz to forgive himself," Fritz's granddaughter, Julia, who was twenty at the time of her grandfather's trip to Bastogne, would say. "Afterward, for the first time he could talk about the war without crying."

Fritz put a collage of photos of himself with Malarkey and the Belgian children up on his wall. He watched all ten parts of the HBO *Band of Brothers* series, and so did Matthias and Volker. Fritz was deeply impressed with the realism of the series, believing it showed the horror and cruelty of war without prejudice. "Not every German was evil," he said, "and not every American was good."

He said to Volker, "Dieser Bund der Brüder Malarkey ist ein feiner Kerl," suggesting Don was a "fine guy."

Matthias and Volker noticed that their father seemed more *entspannt*—relaxed. And more enthusiastic about life. On Easter Sunday 2005, Fritz said to Matthias and his wife, Beate: "What do you think? I feel so close to my friends in Marvie. Wouldn't it be a good idea to celebrate my eightieth birthday with them?"

Matthias and Volker were stunned. This from a man who didn't like social gatherings in the least.

"Well, Papa, if that's what you want, then that's what we should do," said Volker.

Among the invitees were the Dutch journalist Hans Wijers; Madame Esther Reyter, who had survived the battle for Marvie; and André Dartevelle, the renowned Belgian documentary filmmaker who had interviewed Fritz in 2004. Esther's daughter, Monique Nicolas, was happy to help coordinate the event. Catering was arranged for a community hall in Marvie. And Esther and Monique insisted that the ten Engelbert family members stay in the holiday home of Monique's brother, Roger.

The event came off as planned. Nearly three dozen people attended. Before the dinner, Madame Reyter showed the family the stable in which she and others had hidden during the first attack on Marvie on December 20, 1944. She also took Fritz and the family to visit the headstone of her husband, Jean, who had recently died.

A devout Christian, she said, "I can't wait to meet with Jean. I am so happy to tell him that I met Fritz!"

The Engelberts blinked back tears.

For the event that evening, Fritz's Marvie friends had created a cake with "Fritz 80," a dove of peace, and both Belgian and German flags on it. After dinner, Matthias read greetings and congratulations from the Malarkeys in America and from former West German president Richard von Weizsäcker—all arranged by Matthias—in honor of Fritz.

Documentary filmmaker Dartevelle offered impromptu remarks, saying how impressed he had been by Fritz's ability to remember the details of his war story; by the facts, names, and places he still had in his mind; how deeply these events had been engraved in Fritz's memory. Dartevelle honored Fritz for daring to return to this place, face his fears, and move forward in peace.

Then it was time for Fritz to speak, with Matthias translating his words into French. Fritz offered an overview of his life. He honored one of the guests in attendance, "Monsieur Guy Maquet, who was ten years old during the Ardennes offensive in December 1944, and was able to see both sides and recognized that among German soldiers there were 'decent and honest' men, too, as he wrote in his memoirs." He honored Madame Esther Reyter, whose family's house had been set on fire and destroyed by U.S. troops in the quest to liberate Marvie.

"She told me that three of our armored vehicles had reached their garden, where they were destroyed by the American defenders. On this memorable day, December 20, 1944, we were not far from each other, without knowing it."

Fritz did not break into tears, as he had been known to do when talking of war at other events. Instead, midway through his talk, he shifted the focus from his life to the idea of reconciliation between people of different countries. He told how, on December 22, 1944, from this very village, he had written to his parents: "Since December 16 we are back in enemy territory."

"I am all the happier that I can say today, 'I am in friends' territory.'" The Belgians smiled and nodded in appreciation.

It was as if, for the first time, Fritz had been able to return to the past and not get stuck there. As if he'd finally found a way to turn the past into perspective for the future, the way a dam harnesses water power and turns it into electricity. As if his time with Don in Bastogne six months before had been a catalyst for him to stop pitying himself and move forward. He had even channeled a bit of his hero, President Weizsäcker, whose speech on the forty-year anniversary of the war's end had been about the need to take responsibility for the past so as not to repeat it, and then move forward.

"I consider it a sign of reconciliation after long periods of enmity," said Fritz. "Let's leave the past behind and focus on the present. But remember: reconciliation is not possible without remembrance."

Peace, he said, was something that should never be taken for granted. "Since the end of the Second World War—sixty years now—we are allowed to live peacefully here in Europe, and it is unthinkable that we will ever kill each other again. We cannot be thankful enough for that."

In conclusion, Fritz said: "I hope that we will all understand each other—even if we speak different languages." Applause and smiles warmed the community hall, the perfect ending to the perfect day.

On the drive home Volker could only shake his head about all that had happened. His father the hermit had come out of his shell.

Back in Ferndorf, Fritz traded letters with Don Malarkey. He smiled more. He hugged more. He took more risks with people.

In September 2006, he accepted an invitation to go to Berlin and be interviewed for a segment on the History Channel TV series *The Lost Evidence*. He insisted that Matthias join him so that they could pay their respects at the memorial for Stauffenberg and the others who had tried to assassinate Hitler and been executed for it. Fritz cried.

"It was like the events in 2004—the first trip to Marvie and meeting Don and the Band of Brothers—had restored life in our father," Matthias would say. "Before, he walked with his head down, ashamed of having been a soldier; afterward, he kept his head up. It was like he had become 'Fritz 2.0.' It was like someone turning on the light in a dark room. It was that sudden. Our father was never the same after the day he met Don Malarkey."

If dehumanization is a necessary part of war, if making the enemy "them" can help one side more easily justify killing the other side, if keeping them at a distance decreases their worth in the eyes of "the other side," Fritz had now learned the opposite: sitting across a table from a man and getting to know him and listening to him could make him amazingly human—make him friend, not foe.

PTSD expert Edward Tick says that soldiers must face the pain to "refill the soul." They need to feel a sense of "cleansing"—an acknowledgment of that pain, a release from having done something wrong. But history suggests that nations are far better at sending soldiers off to war than at helping them readjust upon their return.

In a perfect world, says Tick, a country sending a soldier to war would say: "You did this in our name and because you were subject to our orders. We lift the burden of your actions from you and take it onto our shoulders. We are responsible for you, for what you did, and for the consequences."[1]

Instead, soldiers usually shoulder the burden alone. But Don and Fritz no longer had to. They had each other. On that night in Bastogne, they had taken each other's emotional burdens, lightened each other's loads, and released each other from the guilt and shame.

Their friendship was built on a foundation of courage. Billy Maloney had had the far-reaching vision to invite German soldiers to the 2004 gatherings, Fritz had had the guts to come, and Don had had the boldness to offer a toast. That same friendship had been fueled by the consciences of two men who wouldn't let their wartime experiences go unresolved. Their bond was sustained by their compassion, which inspired them to make things right for each other.

Volker and Matthias had always been quietly ashamed of their father because, in Volker's words, "he would moan and cry" over the war. Now both had a new respect for the man who had owned his past and emerged as a peacemaker, making his birthday celebration not about himself but about drawing together people who had been enemies.

At one family gathering, Fritz found himself on the patio with just Volker and Matthias. "As a father, I am too old to give you advice," he said. "But let me make an exception. Be peacemakers. Carry on whatever little I have done to that end."

After Don and Fritz met, the Malarkey family began seeing changes in Don, too. He started to notice and appreciate those around him more. He laughed more often. And he seemed freer with his thoughts and emotions—something that would both help and hinder him in some hard times ahead.

Irene, seventy-nine, died in April 2006 after a struggle with breast cancer. Don was in California, speaking, when he heard that she had collapsed and was on life support. He and his son Michael headed back on the first available flight. Empathy had never been a strength of Don's, but when he arrived in Salem at the hospital, he realized the emotional tornado that his oldest daughter, Martha, who had been staying with her mother when she collapsed, had experienced.

"My God," he said, "you've been through hell."

Martha was stunned; it wasn't like her father to notice something like that. Then, when she was leaving that night to return to Portland, he told her, "I love you."

Later she would say: "That was the only time I ever remember him saying he loved me, so it's a moment I treasure."

A similar incident took place four months later. In August 2006, Michael, fifty-six at the time, broke his pelvis in an all-terrain vehicle accident. Don arrived at Oregon Health & Science University in Portland with some buddies, including his Easy Company pal Buck Compton.

Sarah, Michael's thirty-three-year-old daughter, was already there. She had long lamented the disconnect between her father and her grandfather; in her eyes, Don's notoriety as a soldier had cast a wide shadow in which Michael had gotten lost, feeling that he could never live up to Don's high expectations, that he had been a disappointment. But Sarah watched a moment unfold that she had never expected.

"My grandpa instantly began to cry and told my dad that he loved him," she would say. "That moment, that feeling for me was a gift. It was a moment that my heart will always remember. I had never heard my grandfather tell anyone he loved them. I'd never seen him cry.

"It was a lesson. It was an explanation. It explained my grandpa and explained my dad. Two men of extreme pride. Two men with true hearts of gold. Two men who had high expectations of life—and yet their drinking, high pride, and low self-esteem took them down. Neither was a bad person. They were amazing to many. They were loved—yet had no idea how to love their own families."

Don had risen to the occasion in the face of Irene's collapse and death and of Michael's accident, two events in a four-month stretch that had wrenched him deeply. In December 2006 he hit rock bottom. At Christmas, he got horribly drunk in front of Marianne's husband's entire family. It was an ugly scene. Marianne worried that he might do something rash. It had been more than three decades since Don, now eighty-six, had almost taken his life near Mount Hood, but he desperately needed something to focus him on the future.

"Dad," Marianne said a few days later, "would you want to go see Fritz Engelbert again?"

Malarkey's spirits rose like a hot-air balloon. And Fritz was thrilled to hear of plans for Don to come to Europe in May for another event that Billy Maloney was organizing, this time in Illesheim, Germany, near where his unit was based.

Fritz was adept at the computer, but Don was not; he would dictate letters and Marianne would type them. In the process she got to know Matthias and Volker, who were helping Fritz do the planning. She was eight years younger than Matthias and twelve years younger than Volker.

As the days before the Illesheim trip passed, Don spent much of the winter doing interviews with this author, who was helping him write his memoir, *Easy Company Soldier: The Legendary Battles of a Sergeant from WWII's "Band of Brothers."* Talking about the war had never been difficult for Don. In fact, as Marianne McNally would say, "it ended up being very therapeutic for him."

In late May 2007, Don and Fritz met for an event at Sergeant Billy Maloney's house and garden in Illesheim. They were joined by five other Easy Company men—Compton, Guarnere, Heffron, Perconte, and Rod Bain—and three actors from the *Band of Brothers* series: Jimmy Madio (Frank Perconte), Michael Cudlitz (Denver "Bull" Randleman), and Richard Speight (Skip Muck). Volker and Matthias joined the gathering, along with Matthias's wife, Beate. Fritz's wife, Margret, chose not to come; though she was glad to see Fritz involved in these meetings, she was, according to Volker, "very sensitive and emotional about anything that had to do with the war. But she didn't want to stand in the way of Fritz having the experience."

Fritz proudly wearing the autographed Easy Company hat presented to him on May 24, 2007, in Illesheim, Germany. *Courtesy of Matthias Engelbert*

Fritz and Don greeted each other with a firm handshake. Don then greeted Volker, Matthias, and Beate, to whom he took a particular shine. He mentioned his wife's passing, and the trio offered their condolences.

In the afternoon, active-service soldiers from Maloney's 2nd Brigade, 1st Infantry Division, mingled with the veterans and the actors at a barbecue accented with music. Wives and significant others sipped drinks and chatted. The veterans autographed hats, posters, and DVD box sets of the HBO *Band of Brothers* miniseries.

Fritz posed for a photo with Guarnere, the two of them clasping hands. Some of the vets presented Fritz with an autographed Easy Company hat. Volker and Matthias couldn't remember the last time they had seen their father wearing a hat, but he did that day—with great pride and a smile to match.

It was a three-generation, two-nation gathering, with much mixing and mingling between veterans, active-duty soldiers, and civilians. "But only one person was just completely interested in us, and that was Don," said Matthias. "Everywhere we went, he went. He enjoyed us. And we enjoyed him."

In the evening, one of the two *Band of Brothers* episodes set at Bastogne—"Breaking Point"—was shown in the basement of Maloney's house for just the six veterans, the three actors, the four Germans, and Maloney. "Don and Fritz were just so happy to be with each other," Volker would say. "I've seldom seen my dad so lighthearted."

The Engelberts were wowed. Who gets to watch a realistic depiction of the Battle of the Bulge not only with the men who fought it, but also with the actors featured in the world-famous miniseries about it? "It was surreal," according to Matthias Engelbert. "An incredible moment."

It all deepened Fritz Engelbert's sense of pride. As a soldier, he had at times been made to feel worthless, "treated like a dog," as he said of his time in his first assignment near Paris in 1943. Now he was being treated like a king, even if he felt unworthy of such honor. When Fritz told that to Malarkey, Don dismissed the idea.

"Hell, Fritz, you're as worthy as any other man who served," he told him.

"Du bist zu freundlich," said Fritz.

"He says, 'You are too kind,'" said Matthias.

Though Don was eighty-six and Beate had just turned fifty, they soon were arm in arm, Matthias's wife charming the Easy Company veteran with wink-wink whimsy. In photos from the event you can see his arm wrapped around her waist. In the evening Don really turned on the charm, serenading Beate with Sinatra's "Night and Day."

"Like the beat, beat, beat of the tom-tom, when the jungle shadows fall, like the tick, tick, tick of the stately clock, as it stands against the wall . . ."

"That's quite a daughter-in-law you've got there, Fritz," he said, winking.

Fritz nodded. "Ja!"

When it was time to go, Don turned to his friend, asking Matthias to interpret for him.

"I might be coming again, Fritz, to Bastogne, on a tour, in August. Maybe we can meet again."

Fritz nodded his head and then, for the first time, reached for some English. "I would like that! We would love to see you again."

They shook hands goodbye.

Back home, Don was soon talking with his daughter Marianne about family members' joining him in Europe for a World War II tour that he'd been asked to help lead in August.

"I was thinking of inviting Fritz and his family to meet us in Bastogne."

Marianne knew it would mean lots of moving parts, coordinating a meeting between two families that didn't even know each other. They might not even like each other. But it had been a long time since her father had been this excited about anything; Marianne dared not douse the fire.

"Let's try to make it happen," she said. And she went to work on the logistics.

In early July, Don pulled out a pen and some "Don Malarkey" stationery that a Frenchwoman had sent him to thank him for helping liberate her country. He wrote the Engelberts, asking them to meet him in August back in Bastogne; he would like to meet the rest of Fritz's family—his wife and granddaughters. Could they come?

He thanked Matthias for the photos he had sent, said he hoped he would see the Engelbert family soon, and ended his letter with, "Best wishes and love to you—and I am proud to not be one who hated Germans."

Soon Marianne received an email from Matthias. The Engelbert family, including two of Fritz's granddaughters, would be honored to join Don's family in Bastogne! Don rejoiced.

In the weeks before the trip, Marianne saw a sparkle in her father's eyes that she had not seen in a long time. It had been a rough couple of years. He had lost his wife and was now living with the regret that he had not been the husband he might have been. He had almost lost a son.

"What's on your mind?" she asked.

"Fritz," he said. "Can't wait for you and the family to meet him. Like nobody I've ever met."

"How so?"

"Hell, we can't even speak each other's language—well, him a little of mine—but I feel as close to him as I do to my own brother. In some ways, closer."

"Because?"

"Because we both saw guys blown from here to hell's half-acre in the war. Both lived with regret. And—I don't know—I guess we both needed someone to tell us it wasn't our fault."

"What did you think was your fault, Dad, and what did Fritz think was his fault?"

"I dunno, I had a lot of guilt, killing all those guys, especially the boy—and then getting to come home when Skip and the others didn't get to. And turns out Fritz felt a lot of shame, feeling like he did the bidding of Hitler."

"So, you forgave each other."

Don's eyes were misty.

"I guess we did, yeah. And it doesn't matter that we wore different uniforms. In fact, maybe that's the best part. That we were once on opposite sides. Now, he's my friend."

"I can't wait to meet him—and his sons. They seem nice."

Marianne smiled to herself. What made her father happy made her happy. And Fritz Engelbert did just that.

Later, she would liken her father's recovery from the war to a puzzle: Easy Company reunions, *Band of Brothers*, and Don's telling his own story in *Easy Company Soldier* were all significant pieces. "But Fritz was the final piece in the puzzle," she would explain. "And probably the most necessary. He was just the right medicine at just the right time for my father."

And vice versa.

"Don and Fritz had never had the chance to meet in peace and find out what they had in common," Matthias would say. "When they met sixty years after the war, they just felt they had survived the same horrors and were just happy to leave the hostility and hatred behind and focus on the wonderful feeling of forgiveness."

If Hilchenbach would always be Fritz's *Heimat*, the place where his roots were deepest, he had found a kind of second home—in Bastogne, of all places. As if this place of horror and defeat in the war were now the place of a new beginning. And victory.

The event on August 7, 2007, introduced a new twist to the Don–Fritz relationship: the two men's families would meet for the first time. After a tour of World War II sites in Normandy and the Netherlands, three generations of the Malarkey family were on a bus tour that was stopping at the Bastogne Historical Centre and the Mardasson Memorial. And three generations of Engelberts would be there to meet them. Volker and Matthias had also invited Esther Reyter and her daughter, Monique, as well as the French photographer, Frederic Dubois.

When Don and Fritz met in Bastogne in 2007, they hugged each other immediately. *Courtesy of Marianne Malarkey McNally*

Of the forty-seven people on board the bus, nearly a quarter had
Malarkey connections: Don, who was among the tour guides; his daughter Marianne, her husband Dan, and their children Kyle and Erin; his
daughter Sharon, her husband John, and their son Nathan; and Nathan's
wife-to-be Stacey, and her grandfather, Bill. Awaiting them, after a three-
hour drive from Ferndorf, were the Engelberts—Fritz; Volker; Matthias;
Beate; two granddaughters, Elina and Julia; and Julia's boyfriend, Arne.

When the Malarkeys arrived, Don, in a plaid shirt and white Easy
Company jacket, was the first off the bus. Fritz was waiting, the beer coaster
autographed by Bill Guarnere in the shirt pocket of his light blue dress shirt.
Neither man was a hugger by nature; in Illesheim they had greeted each
other and said goodbye with handshakes. Today was different. They flew
into each other's arms. At their age it was a slow flight, but fly they did.
And as the others watched, both Fritz and Don seemed reluctant to end the
embrace, which triggered tears in both men and their families.

First came introductions, which spawned laughter because they involved no fewer than twenty-one people. Then came the tour. Don and Fritz emerged as the leaders of it; the others would have it no other way. Beneath the sculpted eagle commemorating the 101st Airborne, the party read these words: "May this eagle always symbolize the sacrifices and heroism of the 101st Airborne Division and all its attached units. December 1944–January 1945. The city and the citizens of Bastogne."

On a series of large metal maps, Don and Fritz pointed out where each had been during the Battle of the Bulge. In the grotto beneath the monument, the American group, led by Don, began to sing "America the Beautiful." Members of the Engelbert family were taken aback and touched; since World War II, Germans had not known that kind of patriotism.

In Bastogne, Don and Fritz were inseparable. At the Mardasson Memorial, Bastogne, August 7, 2007. *Courtesy of Frederic Dubois*

"Watching Dad and Fritz walk to the memorial was so emotional," according to Marianne. "Here were two enemies who years earlier would never have walked side by side, now showing a unified front."

Meanwhile, despite the language barrier, living far apart, and having known each other for less than an hour, the families began melding. It felt like instant friendship. Genuine friendship.

"The Engelberts were just so sweet to us," Marianne would say, "and we had so much in common. We both were dealing with fathers dealing with nightmares from the war, survivor's guilt, and plain sadness. We didn't know it at the time that this would link us together in a way that most people would never understand."

Don with granddaughter Erin on her tenth birthday, walking in the same woods he had fought in during the Battle of the Bulge. *Courtesy of the Malarkey Family Collection*

Matthias and Marianne's husband, Dan, found themselves bonding over their quest for photographs to capture what was unfolding. "We were smiling, talking, joking because it was clear we were totally on the same wavelength," said Matthias. "We were both thinking: Let's freeze these moments so we can remember them for a lifetime."

Don's grandson, Nate, found common ground with Matthias; they both worked in the tech industry. Volker and Don's son-in-law, John Hill, discovered a mutual love of classic rock; Volker, who speaks reasonable English, told John about his collection of Fender Stratocasters.

"I was touched by how easy it was to talk to Matthias and Volker," John would say. "The friendship and goodwill that emanated from Don and Fritz quickly spread between the two families. With help from a translator, there was laughter and tears between Don and Fritz. It was evident that Don held Fritz in a special place in his heart. Don and Fritz captivated the small crowd that now encircled them."

As the man's son-in-law for thirty-two years, John Hill knew Malarkey well. "He hated 'phonies,' having perhaps one of the world's greatest bullshit detectors. Don had a special hatred for Lyndon Johnson, two-letter Scrabble words, and anyone who tried to come across as someone they weren't. Fritz was no phony—and it was evident by the affection that Don showed for him."

Don and Fritz stayed close to each other. The members of their families enjoyed just sitting back and watching them—like a movie dance scene where everyone stops dancing and watches one particular couple because they dance so well.

When Don wasn't with Fritz, he gravitated to Matthias's wife, Beate, whom he had met at Illesheim. The two continued their flirtatious relationship, holding hands, Beate rubbing Don's back. The others enjoyed such lighthearted touches; it blunted the pain of more serious moments when the focus was on war and death.

Don's daughter Marianne watched her children—Kyle, fourteen, and Erin, ten on this very day—as they listened to Fritz telling his Battle of the Bulge story. "It all made such an impact on them, the guys pointing to the map and hearing about them, in essence, shooting at each other, and now here they are, embracing each other and sharing their families with each other. It was a huge learning opportunity— forgiveness at the highest level."

When it was time to leave, Marianne was stunned at how attached she had already become to the Engelberts in just four hours together. "Matthias and Volker felt like brothers to me," she said.

The time had gone far too fast. The group formed a half-circle around Fritz and Don, who hugged once again. Both men's eyes were wet with tears. Nobody said it, but it was as if they knew: the two men—once enemies, now the closest of friends—would probably never see each other again.

"Thank . . . you . . . my friend," said Fritz in perfect English.

Malarkey accepted the challenge. "*Danke . . . mein*, uh . . ."

"*Freund*," Fritz said, laughing. "Don't worry, someday . . ."

"Someday, I will get it right—for you!" said Don.

And they hugged one last time.

As Beate watched, the last goodbye for Don and Fritz; they would never
see each other again. *Courtesy of the Engelbert Family Collection*

At eighty-six, Don bought a computer so it would be easier to communicate with Fritz. Matthias was so inspired by the Malarkey–Engelbert
meeting that he used the photographs he had taken of it to create a
"peace calendar" that he sent to members of both families, to Easy
Company vets, and to friends who had learned of the story of the two
families' "merger."

When Billy Maloney received his copy, he was so touched that he
took his eighteen-year-old son, Raffael, from Illesheim to Bonn to visit
with Fritz and the rest of the Engelbert family. They called Don Malarkey
and wished him a happy New Year 2008. Don told them that his new
book, *Easy Company Soldier*, would be out in the spring. Matthias
ordered an advance copy on the spot.

Meanwhile, Marianne arrived home incredulous about how close she already felt to the Engelbert family, particularly Matthias and Volker. "It's like when you're a kid and you meet someone new at school and, instantly, they're your best friend," she would say. "There is kindness and love between us. It just seemed like, instantly, our family expanded. We felt as though they were truly part of our family—just an ocean apart. We understand each other, we like the same things, and we understand what each other went through with our parents having been to war."

Volker and Matthias were on the same page.

"After waving goodbye to Don and his family, everybody was on cloud nine," Matthias would say. "We couldn't stop talking about all that we'd just experienced with these strangers who were now almost family. Honestly, an observer at the memorial would have assumed we were lifetime friends. It's hard to explain, but it's as if the Malarkeys and Engelbert families instantly connected, our common bond being fathers who, weirdly, had fought against each other in the biggest war in history."

Then tragedy struck the Malarkeys. On October 3, 2007, Don's son Michael died unexpectedly of a heart attack. He was fifty-seven. And in 2009, Don's daughter Marianne was diagnosed with Stage 3 breast cancer, a unique type. She went through a bilateral mastectomy, months of chemo, and then weeks of radiation.

But the silver lining was that it drew father and daughter closer than ever before. Until now their relationship had focused on Don and his Easy Company connections; with most of the men gone, Marianne had been among the adult children who breathed new life into the annual reunions. But now she was the one who needed help, rides, and encouragement.

"And he was there for me, every step of the way," Marianne would explain. "It was like a side of him that had been missing earlier, a softer, more caring side. And I wasn't the only one who'd seen it. It was as if war had taken this piece away from my father and only Fritz could replace it."

Across the pond, the Engelberts continued to see in Fritz a "changed man."

"Above all, he was at peace," Volker would say of his father. "Like he'd been lifted to a new level. And that brought an all-new peace and serenity to our family. All because of 'that American soldier'—*Bund der Brüder* Malarkey!"

"It's impossible to compare his friendship with Don to any other he ever had," Matthias would say. "The friendship with Don changed him deep within. They did not have to talk much—couldn't talk much—to know what each had been through. They just *knew*. You could tell they had a deep respect for each other, as much as there can be for men of their generation. Our father had no other relationship even close to the intense feeling he had about Don."

CHAPTER 17

Farewell

Fritz was the first to go—on December 12, 2015. His death was preceded by many painful years; in some ways, it could be said that his last truly happy moment was his hug with Don Malarkey at the memorial in Bastogne in 2007. Although their meeting helped him find a new peace about the war, it couldn't wash away all the memories.

On November 9, 2008, the seventy-year anniversary of Kristallnacht, Matthias and Beate were having dinner with Fritz; Margret was elsewhere helping with a Red Cross blood drive. Just months before, twelve *Stolpersteines*—stumbling stones—had been placed in Hilchenbach's town square, each representing a Jewish person from the town who had died in the Holocaust. They were created by a German artist named Gunter Demnig. Among those remembered was Fritz's classmate, Arthur Holländer.

"I wonder," asked Fritz, eyes misty, "if anyone from Jewish families in Hilchenbach was able to survive and now has offspring somewhere in the world."

The next day Matthias began searching for an answer. In a German newspaper he found a 2008 online article about Alice, the granddaughter of Seligmann Hony, revisiting Hilchenbach in 1983 with her husband, Tom Lewinsohn. After more sleuthing he discovered an address. Why not? He wrote Alice a letter, ending it like this:

> Four years ago, we were able to get in contact with American veterans who, like my dad, fought and survived the Battle of the Bulge. We have had the chance to meet them and their families in Belgium several times and are also in contact with families in Belgium who suffered losses during the fights in December 1944.
>
> These meetings have changed so much in my dad's and in our family's life: To see them shake hands and meet friends sixty years later is always touching and heart-warming for everyone lucky enough to be there. It makes me dream of maybe someday being able to shake hands with you and your family.

Thirteen months later, it happened. After hearing back from Alice, Matthias and Beate flew to Kansas in January 2010. Alice, who had been four years old when she left Hilchenbach, was now seventy-five. En route to America, Matthias thought back to 1930s Germany and remembered how indoctrination in the Hitler Youth had almost convinced his father to report Fritz Sr. and Anna for helping Alice's grandfather.

Then came a reassuring thought. *His father couldn't do it.* Despite the Nazi pressure, despite the peer pressure, his father's conscience prevented him from being the whistleblower.

The plane landed. "When Alice and Tom recognized us at the airport, we hugged and it was like meeting family after a long, long time," said Matthias.

As director of personnel for Kansas City, Missouri, Tom decreed Matthias "an honorary citizen" of the city.

At Alice and Tom's house in Overland Park, Kansas, Matthias told them about his grandparents' helping out her grandfather, Seligmann Hony, and about his father's dilemma as a member of Hitler Youth: to turn in his parents or not? He and Beate also listened to the Lewinsohns' fascinating story: in 1938, sensing a shadow of doom creeping toward Jewish people, Alice's parents—Seligmann's son and daughter-in-law—had emigrated to the U.S. with Alice.

Tom, three years older than his wife and also Jewish, had been born in Berlin and escaped in 1941 on the Trans-Siberian Railway to Shanghai, where he survived in a ghetto. He caught a ship to America in 1948 at age seventeen, became a U.S. citizen, and later served in the Korean War. He met Alice at the Orchid Room jazz bar in Kansas City.

Soon after arriving for the 2010 visit to Kansas, Matthias called his father, as was his habit when he travelled, to tell him he and Beate had arrived safely. Then he put Alice on speakerphone. In German, Alice told Fritz that she and Tom were happy to have his son and daughter-in-law visiting. "We've left the past behind," she said, "and are now enjoying being together as friends."

"I'm happy to hear that you are doing fine," Fritz said. "I, I—"

His voice broke. He began to sob.

"Don't worry, Papa," said Matthias. "All is well. We are going to see the graves of Alice's parents, Kurt and Hilde Hony. All is well."

When the visit with Alice and Tom was over and Matthias and Beate were flying home, it dawned on Matthias: *None of this would have happened without Don Malarkey.* "Without the experience of forgiveness with Don and the salvation it meant for Fritz," he later said, "I would never have tried to find Alice Hony from Hilchenbach. Never."

The night after celebrating her eighty-fifth birthday, Fritz's wife Margret had a stroke. She would never be the same. For a vivacious woman who had still been skiing into her eighties, it was tragic. After the stroke, she could recite poems and songs she had learned by heart in her childhood, but she had a hard time remembering what had happened that morning.

"Looking back," Matthias would recall, "I think our best time together as a family was from 2004 to 2009—from the moment we experienced our father's change when he found forgiveness in Bastogne until right before our mother had her stroke in 2009. Our father's search for forgiveness and reconciliation, thanks to Don, finally came to an end."

Margret's stroke shook Fritz to his core. The woman who had taken care of him for fifty-nine years was essentially gone—there in body, but not in spirit. A series of caretakers began coming to take care of Margret and, to some degree, Fritz.

Matthias and Beate lived in Bonn, and the now-divorced Volker lived in Bornheim, just west of Bonn. Fritz and Margret wanted to live in their house as long as possible. To that end, Matthias and Beate took turns with Volker visiting their parents in Ferndorf every weekend.

Fritz grew depressed, seldom leaving the house. Then he became delusional and started referring to Margret as his mother. In September 2010, he was diagnosed with cancer of the stomach. In an attempt to cheer up his father, Matthias created a "World of Friendship" calendar, relying heavily on photos of Fritz and Don from 2004 and 2007.

Radiation and other treatments for his stomach cancer prolonged his life, but in 2013 Fritz learned that he had aggressive prostate cancer. On the two-hour drive home from the hospital, he turned to Matthias, who was driving the car.

"I am alive today because, in the field at Weislingen, I zig-zagged and Döring did not."

Matthias was incredulous. The man had just learned he was dying, and a memory from nearly seven decades ago was the thing on his mind. The ghosts, Matthias realized, were even stronger than he'd believed.

Fritz hung on much longer than any of the doctors expected. But mentally he soon dropped off the edge. In September 2015, when Beate entered his room at the family house in Ferndorf, he appeared busy at work. He told her that he was in contact with the harbor of Stockholm, Sweden. There was cargo on a ship that his company, SIEMAG, was waiting for. It could not be unloaded and sent to Germany because they needed a telex first. Fritz was in charge, but there had been a power blackout.

Slowly, Beate guided him back to reality. In November, after a series of other bizarre encounters, Fritz told Matthias and Beate, "Yesterday I thought I was going to die. Everything turned dark."

"And, Fritz, how did that feel?" Beate asked.

"Actually, quite pleasant—and I want it, too."

He asked, "When I close my eyes now, is everything well taken care of?"

"Yes, Dad, no worries, everything is well taken care of."

He died two weeks later, on December 12, 2015. He was ninety years old.

Matthias and Volker would learn that their first thoughts had been identical: *Thank God he never has to have even one more nightmare about war.*

At the funeral in Ferndorf, there was no official representation by the Malarkeys. That didn't surprise Matthias and Volker. It had been more than eight years since Fritz and Don had last seen each other in Bastogne. Marianne and Matthias had traded an occasional email and followed each other on Facebook. In 2008 the Engelberts had read Don's memoir, *Easy Company Soldier.* And there had been talk of an Engelbert visit to Oregon someday. But with both veterans failing in health, and with Marianne's cancer, there hadn't been a lot of time to spare for nurturing the long-distance relationship.

Fritz Engelbert's friend Fritz Koppenhagen had passed away, but his other POW pal, Armin Meisel, eighty-nine, spent six hours on a train by himself to attend the service. For nearly seventy years Armin and Fritz had talked every week. Volker and Matthias were godfathers to Armin's grandchildren.

Fritz's Marvie and Bastogne friends could not come. But they had a stone made for Fritz's grave that said: "Thank you Fritz, for weaving this bond of friendship between our families. You will forever be a symbol of peace, love and reconciliation. Esther Reyter, her family and your friends from Bastogne."

Armin Meisel, Fritz's friend dating back to their POW days, with Matthias and Volker after Fritz's funeral, December 19, 2015. *Courtesy of Beate Engelbert*

At the funeral, Pastor Volker Bäumer spoke of how reliable Fritz had been, how he never quit. He worked for one company, SIEMAG, his entire life. He had one wife, Margret, in a marriage that lasted sixty-five years. He was, as his granddaughter Eva said, "a man of integrity." Late in his life, Pastor Bäumer told the mourners, Fritz had befriended an American soldier who helped restore his soul.

A song written by Dietrich Bonhoeffer, the pastor who died in defiance of Hitler, was played: "Von guten Mächten wunderbar geborgen"

("By Gracious Powers So Wonderfully Sheltered"). Bonhoeffer had written it in prison and sent it to his mother just before year's end 1944, about the time that Fritz, serving as a soldier, was listening to Hitler's empty promises on the radio.

Most in attendance at the memorial service were familiar with that song, but not with the music played after the service. It was beautiful. Haunting. But unfamiliar.

It was the theme song from the HBO series *Band of Brothers*.

CHAPTER 18

An End, and a New Beginning

D on passed a little less than two years later, on September 30, 2017. His final years, like Fritz's, were marked by mental discombobulation. He suffered dementia for more than five years, beginning about the time a bleeding bowel threatened to kill him. He was in pain, and not particularly upbeat. Eventually he was placed in a residential care home in Salem, the dementia helping him leave the war behind—or so it seemed.

Marianne didn't tell him when Easy Company men died. "Why?" she would say later. "He'd only forget it the next day and be sad in the meantime. He'd protected me my whole life. It was my turn to protect him."

Then, in 2012, came a day she would never forget. Marianne was visiting with Don when the chaplain from hospice came to see him. It was a woman.

"My first thought was—what's my father going to think of this?" Marianne would say. "In his world, only men hold such positions."

She pulled up a chair for what Marianne would describe as "the most amazing ninety minutes I ever spent with my dad." The chaplain was a cut-to-the-chase type who had worked at the VA hospital in Portland; she knew vets. And she wanted to talk to Don about heaven.

"I'm not . . . going to . . . heaven," said Don, his speech slow.

"Why not?"

"Because of . . . all the bad things . . . I did in the war."

"Like what?"

"Killed . . . a lot . . . of Germans."

"Seems to me you did what your country asked you to do, in the name of taking down Hitler and freeing Europe. Is that a bad thing?"

Don didn't answer her question.

"I am afraid," he said, "to die."

Marianne knew this was her father at his absolute realest; normally his Archie Bunker disposition wouldn't have allowed him to be so vulnerable with a grizzled foxhole pal, much less with a woman he had never met before.

"I'm . . . going . . . to hell."

"Don, what is it you feel you need to do to get to heaven?"

He looked away. The chaplain wasn't making this easy for him—or perhaps that's exactly what she was doing.

"I think I'd need . . . to apologize . . . to all the parents . . . of the German boys . . . that didn't get to come home . . . because I killed them."

Marianne wondered if her father's dementia was getting the better of him.

"OK, let's write a letter," said the chaplain. "Marianne, will you do it? And then, Don, we'll make copies and send them to the families of the German soldiers you killed."

Never mind the impracticality of fulfilling that promise. If this would help bring her father peace, Marianne was all in. She grabbed the yellow notepad and Sharpie that her father used to communicate when he wasn't able to speak.

"OK, Don, what is it you need to say?" asked the chaplain.

He swallowed, eyes far away.

"Dear . . . parents," he said, his hands trembling, his face grim, his words slow. "I'm sorry—so sorry . . . for your loss. A friend of mine . . . like no other friend . . . I've ever had . . . a German soldier whose name I forget . . . told me . . . 'You only did . . . what you had to do . . . because your country . . . told you to do it.'"

He paused. Swallowed. Marianne reached in her purse for Kleenex.

"And your son . . . did the same . . . for his country."

Marianne dabbed her eyes.

"It isn't fair. But maybe ... part of your son ... lives on ... in those of you ... who loved him."

The chaplain's eyes glistened. She waited to make sure he was finished. He wasn't.

"Please forgive me. Then sign my name."

"Beautiful, Don," said the chaplain, sniffling a bit. "Well done."

He looked off to the distance.

Marianne turned to the chaplain. "There was a German soldier, Fritz, who—geez, nearly ten years ago—Dad met in Bastogne. They'd fought within a few miles of each other in the Battle of the Bulge. And they absolutely did have that conversation. They forgave each other. Dad helped Fritz heal. And Fritz helped Dad heal—but, of course, the memories of what he did in the war will never go away. Even with the dementia. He can't remember what he had for breakfast, but he can remember killing a sixteen-year-old German boy."

"It's the PTSD talking," said the chaplain. "I've heard it a thousand times. So sad."

Marianne was getting ready to leave when Don turned to the chaplain.

"One . . . last thing," he said. "I'm worried . . . that my stories . . . will be forgotten."

She nodded her head to reassure him that she understood.

"So, Don, who do you think could carry your stories forward?"

He looked at Marianne. "She knows . . . them all. She can tell them . . . so people don't forget."

Marianne walked into another room and came back with *Easy Company Soldier*, Don's memoir. The chaplain had no idea that he'd written a book. She asked for it, then handed it to Don.

"So, let's have a little ceremony. Don, you hand the book to Marianne to symbolize the passing on of this story—all that happened to you to the point this one was written—and all that's happened since. The story that Marianne will help tell, going forward from your memoir."

Don's gnarled, trembling hands—hands that had once fired mortars—passed the book to Marianne to signify that the story would be told.

"And don't forget," he said, "to talk . . . about that . . . German guy."

"Fritz?"

"Yes, Fritz."

"I promise, Dad."

Her father was still alive five years later when Marianne McNally took a risk. As head of the 2017 Easy Company reunion—to be held in nearby Portland, Oregon—she decided to do something unprecedented in the sixty-year history of the gatherings: invite the family members of a German soldier to be special guests.

The Malarkeys and Engelberts—preoccupied with taking care of, respectively, Don, Fritz, and Margret—had not seen each other in ten years. But something whispered to Marianne: *invite them to America.*

She was excited about showing Don's "stomping grounds" to Matthias and Volker, but she was also afraid of repercussions at the reunion. It's not as if Marianne thought that inviting the sons of a German soldier would trigger mass protests from the sixty people or so expected to come, mainly sons and daughters and nieces and nephews of Easy Company soldiers. But she worried that if even a few people grumbled about "Nazis" being invited, it could sour everything. After all, some of these folks were representing their loved ones who had been killed by German soldiers like Matthias's and Volker's father.

"I confess, we were all a little nervous," she said. "How would the others act toward them? Would they accept them? Would they be mad at me? And, of course, what would the fallout be for the Engelberts? We loved these guys. They were family. But what if the others were put off by their presence?"

She didn't go to the board to seek permission. She simply reasoned that she was in charge and this was a good thing to do. So she made the invitation to her "brothers" in Germany, who wasted little time saying that they would be honored to come. Beate, Matthias's wife, wanted to come too, as did Volker's second wife, Irene.

Marianne whooped and hollered. It would be wonderful to have them visit—as long as no reunion attendees objected to the Germans' presence. She imagined saying to skeptics, *If anyone has a problem with this, you're just going to have to put on your big-girl and big-boy pants and understand that it does nobody any good to stay mad at the people from a country we fought more than seventy years ago.*

She was more diplomatic on the group's Facebook page, mentioning changing times, changing cultures, changing governments. "It's not often that you have an opportunity to forgive," she wrote. "This is ours."

In a letter to the Engelberts, Marianne wrote: "I wanted to extend the invitation to you because of our history and our story. I wanted you and your brother to be our special attendees! This, in my opinion, is a very healing relationship. There is a part in the *Band of Brothers* miniseries in which Shifty Powers talks about how, if an American and German soldier met under different circumstances, they might have been good friends. 'We might have had a lot in common,' he said. 'He might've liked to fish, you know, he might've liked to hunt.' I love that thought! I love that he said that! It is so true; we all want the same things in life!"

She also mentioned that the "war memories" had returned to haunt her father; he was no longer the happy-go-lucky guy they had seen in Bastogne in 2007.

Matthias replied:

We can't tell you how overwhelmed we were, and still are, about your invitation. It was very touching to read your mail. I remember very well how impressing it was to hear Shifty Powers talking about American and German soldiers meeting under different circumstances. His thoughts and words were so honest, respectful, upright, and true.

And when our father Fritz had the privilege to meet your father and some of the "Brothers" it proved to be right. They really had very much in common and created a relationship that was in fact healing—not only to them, but to everybody who was lucky to witness it. Healing, forgiveness, and peace: that's what our dad and our family have found by meeting and shaking hands with Don and the other veterans.

It hurts and breaks our hearts to know that—to this day— Don is being haunted by his memories and experiences. Your dad is such a loveable, empathetic, and compassionate man. It would be our greatest desire to give back a little of the for- giveness he brought to our family. We were thrilled to read: "I am keeping my promise to bring our Dad to one last reunion!" The thought of being able to see your dad again really brought tears to our eyes.

When Marianne posted the news on Facebook that the Engelberts were coming, the response was all positive. But that didn't mean that some people weren't grumbling behind the scenes, she thought, and they might let it be known at the reunion. As the August 25, 2017, event approached, even Matthias and Volker expressed some concerns. As Germans, Volker and Matthias had felt cold shoulders in a number of countries.

In Denmark in the 1980s, Volker and his father, on holiday with their families, were standing by their respective cars—with German plates—when a Danish man spat at their feet.

"I was angry, but my father was shocked," said Volker. "I told him, 'Maybe he's jealous of our cars or that we dominate them in football.' But my father was agitated. He believed it was because of him. Maybe they saw him as a former German soldier who'd ravaged their country."

"I never feel 'proud to be a German' in the way that, say, an American feels proud to be an American," Volker would explain. "You see the Olympics and the American winners are crying during the national anthem, I was always jealous."

And then along came the McNallys, who not only didn't give the Engelberts a cold shoulder but offered them room and board. Friendship. Oregon craft beers. And an invitation to a reunion celebrating the soldiers against whom their father had fought.

After Don moved into a residential care home in 2011, Marianne and Dan moved into his old house, the one that Marianne remembered from her childhood. The house came with what Don's granddaughter, Sarah, called her grandfather's "war room" in the basement. Since the *Band of Brothers* series had come out, Don had plastered it with posters and plaques and pictures related to World War II in general and Easy Company in particular. Much of the stuff was still on the walls. Marianne worried: "Would the Engelbert family feel like we were rubbing it in their faces?"

But it was a moot point, because it would take a solid week to hide the World War II memorabilia, and the visitors were arriving soon. And when the German guests showed up, they had no problem with the décor.

The families exchanged hugs and kisses—condolences, too; Matthias's and Volker's mother, Margret, had died the previous month at age ninety-three, eight years after having her stroke.

The guests were anxious to visit with Don, whom they hadn't seen in a decade. Marianne warned them that he wasn't the same Don Malarkey he had been in 2007 in Bastogne. He had just turned ninety-six, he was in a wheelchair, and he was suffering from dementia. When they arrived at the care home, Don's face was blank, his hair thin, his mouth slightly open.

"Don't take this the wrong way," Marianne said to her guests, "but I'll need to signal you when Dad's had enough socializing. He usually starts getting agitated with guests in about ten or fifteen minutes. So, don't get too comfortable."

"Dad," said Marianne, turning to her father, "do you remember meeting Fritz, the German soldier, in Bastogne?" asked Marianne. "The man who became your friend? These are his sons—remember Matthias and Volker?"

His eyes widened just a bit and the slightest smile warmed his face. He nodded.

"And remember Beate, Matthias's wife?"

His eyes widened more. Way more, in fact. Beate said something to him in German. Matthias interpreted.

"She said, 'Remember in Illesheim, you sang me 'Day and Night'? It was beautiful.'"

Don's brow furrowed. He began shaking his head sideways, the most animated he'd been since his guests' arrival.

"No," he said. "No, no, no!"

Marianne's heart lurched.

"What's wrong, Dad?" she asked. Had he misinterpreted what she'd said? Was he angry? Marianne glanced at her watch, thinking maybe it was time to leave lest Don do or say something embarrassing.

"It . . . wasn't 'Day and Night' . . . I . . . sang . . . you. It . . . was . . . 'Night . . . and . . . Day.'"

Everyone broke into laughter, amazed at his recall. He smiled large. Somewhere deep down, the memories were still there.

The Engelberts stayed all afternoon. Marianne was astounded. "He never once acted as if he was tired of the guests." They posed for photos with Don. They gave him a pillow they'd had made for him, featuring a photo of Don and Fritz together in Bastogne. They gave him a book they'd created of letters that Don had written Fritz after their first meeting in 2004 and of photos of that get-together and the two gatherings that followed.

"It was amazing to watch his face when he looked at this book," Marianne would say. "It was almost like the memories were coming back to him. And when Beate sat beside him you'd have thought he was going to break out in Sinatra's 'Fly Me to the Moon.' Ever since he'd met her in 2007, he'd flirted with her. He'd sing for her, hold her hand. She'd rub his back. Now, as he smiled, it was clear he still remembered her after ten years."

This was the fruition of the moment in 2004 when Don and Fritz had first met, the power of reconciliation so strong it could awaken a man who for years had little passion to live. On that night in Bastogne, Malarkey and Engelbert had done something profound, and totally unplanned: given each other a second chance. New life.

In Don's eyes, Fritz was the manifestation of the sixteen-year-old German soldier he'd killed come back to say, *It's OK.* And in Fritz's eyes, Don was the manifestation of Seligmann Hony and the little girl at Lutrebois, come back to say, *You're forgiven.* Absolution for the sins that both men had carried for sixty years. They had been two drowning men treading water—until they miraculously rescued each other.

The day of the reunion arrived. Ever since learning that Portland had landed the 2017 event, Marianne had been praying for two things: *Please, God, may my Dad be alive to enjoy one last reunion right here in his home state.* And: *May our German guests be warmly welcomed by our Easy Company friends.*

"When we arrived in Oregon," said Volker, "we were nervous. We knew what it was like to be shunned."

Matthias hoped for acceptance, but he was worried. "For the first time, I understood why my father was on edge that night we met the Americans in Hammersbach," he would say. "It's not easy being an outsider—especially when the context is war, where people's loved ones have died, and lives have been changed."

One of the reunion's events—the one Don would attend—was at the Evergreen Air & Space Museum in McMinnville, southwest of Portland, on Saturday afternoon August 26, before a dinner in Beaverton that evening.

Marianne took the handles of her father's wheelchair and began rolling Don to the private dining area that had been reserved for lunch. As soon as people started recognizing her father and Bill Wingett—the only two veterans in attendance—her tears broke loose.

"I wanted everybody to see my father one last time," she said, "and I wanted him to see everybody one last time. I was overcome by emotion." When Tracy Compton, Buck's daughter, saw Marianne, she, too, started crying. It was as if everyone knew this would be the final farewell for the Easy Company soldiers.

Don's spirits rose with the sight of each familiar face. He posed for photos. Shook hands. And, at lunch, stole half of son-in-law Dan McNally's sandwich, ate it, and laughed when he got caught.

"Dad's mind was clear, his smile bright," said Marianne. "This day was one beautiful gift. I think my father understood how important the reunion in Oregon was. He hung on for one last hurrah. His mind was so clear that day that it was as if he could take it all in and report back to all our Easy Company families in heaven—and, of course, to Fritz—that we were continuing to honor the promise we had made to the men before they passed. They'd never be forgotten."

2017 *Band of Brothers* reunion, "Continuing to Honor," at the Evergreen Aviation and Space Museum. Don's last reunion. Behind Don, from left to right: Sharon, Marianne, Sarah, Erin, and Martha. Back row left to right: John, Dan, and Kyle. Photograph by Matthias Engelbert. *Courtesy of the Malarkey Family Collection*

Don's arrival eased the tension for the Engelberts, taking the focus off Volker and Matthias. They had gotten to know some of the Easy Company people on tours to Mount Hood, Multnomah Falls, and Willamette Valley wineries in previous days, but this was one of two "everybody-together" gatherings. If cold shoulders were going to be turned on them, this would be the time and place.

But that did not happen. The Engelberts met nothing but open arms. Hugs. Handshakes. Not one person objected to their presence.

"Thank you for traveling to America to attend our Easy Co. reunion," wrote Ann Winegarden, daughter of Rod Bain, in a card that was circulated for the German guests. "It is a special day when history has a chance to heal old wounds. We are grateful for your willingness to come and meet us and join our family."

"A pleasure to meet the Engelbert boys," wrote Kenny Gunther, nephew of Walter Gunther, who'd been killed on D-Day at Sainte-Mère-Église. "Looking forward to a long friendship."

"Fantastic that y'all were able to visit!" wrote Chris Langlois, whose grandfather, medic Eugene Roe, had broken the news of Skip Muck's death to Don. "A pleasure to meet your family."

They laughed, shared photos, told stories. Don watched from his wheelchair as Marianne introduced Volker and Matthias to friends. *Who would have imagined that sons of a German soldier would be part of an Easy Company reunion?*

At that night's banquet in Beaverton, Matthias and Volker were formally introduced to wide applause that brought them both to tears. They told their story of Don and Fritz's meeting in Bastogne and how the friendship between the two veterans had inspired a wider friendship between the two extended families. The crescendo came when Tracy Compton said, in front of everyone, "Welcome to the family!"

"Unbelievable," Volker would later say. "I could never have imagined such a thing. It is like we have been welcomed into a new family. And it makes us feel proud, and unashamed, as if we belong."

Don Malarkey and Fritz Engelbert's friendship may have had the life span of a butterfly—they saw each other only three times—but it was a friendship greater than the sum of its parts. It gave each man something he couldn't find anywhere else: forgiveness. Found not in conquering an enemy, but in welcoming that enemy. Not in force, but in friendship. Not in annihilation, but in absolution.

When the Engelberts had come to visit Don in his care home, his memory had been clearer than Marianne could have imagined. Now, as he watched his daughter and Fritz's sons together, the sparkle in his eyes suggested that he had once again found at least a wisp of clarity. It was as if he were on a jet flying through thick clouds that every so often afforded just a glimpse of the earth below, and in one of those clearings there it was: Bastogne.

Fritz across the table. The words "It wasn't your fault . . ." The feel of Fritz's hand atop his and of a burden lifted. And, finally, the one thing Don had never been quite able to say: "Danke, mein Freund."

Outside, where tens of thousands of German and American soldiers had died in battle sixty years ago, the snow fell softly. It covered the fox-holes of the Bois Jacques and the farmhouses of Marvie and the Ardennes Forest beyond, as if the past had finally been forgiven. As if the war guilt had finally been put to rest. As if each man had finally found his peace.

Epilogue

Don Malarkey died on September 30, 2017, five weeks after the Easy Company reunion. Just as Fritz's death had given Matthias and Volker a sense of relief—no more nightmares of war—so did Don's death bring solace to Marianne: no more dark Decembers and Januarys. Marianne and her two sisters, Sharon and Martha, chose to have a simple service for their father. There was no mention of war.

As of January 2021, it was believed that only 1 of the 148 Easy Company men to jump on D-Day was still living: Brad Freeman, 96, of Caledonia, Mississippi, who fought alongside Don at Brécourt Manor.

In 2015, Marianne McNally learned that her cancer had metastasized. Now fifty-five, she continues to be treated with both radiation and chemo pills. She heads up a "Breast Friends" support group in Salem and serves as vice president of the Residential Real Estate Council's Region 12. Of her illness, she says, "With my cancer, I really don't know how this will play out, so I just keep moving forward and try not to think about that."

Dan McNally, fifty-four, is in his thirty-second year working for the state of Oregon. He is an assistant basketball coach for South Salem High, which won the conference title in 2020 and was among the favorites to capture the state title when the coronavirus put an end to the season.

Volker, sixty-seven, is head of ELGEMA, a company that sells appliances, and lives in Bornheim with Irene. He has three daughters and two grandchildren.

Matthias, sixty-three, is a software engineer for ProUnix GmbH, a company that develops applications for Oracle databases. He and his wife Beate, a schoolteacher, live in Bonn.

After their initial meeting in 2007, Marianne, Dan, Volker, and Matthias wanted to see each other again. But the failing health of three of their four parents and Marianne's cancer meant putting overseas travel on hold.

But since Don's death in 2017—the last of the four parents to die—Marianne and Dan's relationship with the Engelberts has only deepened. They have gathered five times:

- At a *Band of Brothers* Switzerland reenactment event, where they were guests, in 2018

- For Easy Company reunions in Philadelphia that same year, and in New Orleans in 2019
- For the seventy-fifth anniversary of D-Day in Normandy, in June 2019, after which Marianne, Dan, and their son Kyle stayed a week at Volker's and Matthias's homes in the Bonn region and visited Berlin
- To give interviews for this book, in Eugene and Salem, Oregon, in 2019

"It started with our meeting them in 2007 in Bastogne—instant connection," said Marianne. "But when they came to Portland in 2017 for the reunion it really bloomed. It's as if they needed the friendship as much as we did. We have fun together, we never lack to find something to talk about, or we can just be silent. I think all of us see a bigger picture. It's not just about us, it's about our dads, our countries, a war, and the future."

Before the New Orleans trip, Marianne's husband, Dan, met Volker and Irene in Memphis. En route from there to New Orleans, Dan and Volker visited clubs, museums, Elvis's Graceland, and Civil War battlefields, and, as Marianne says, "basically acted like college boys on a post-graduation trip, drinking and listening to music into the wee hours."

It was at the *Band of Brothers* reenactment event in Switzerland in 2018 that Marianne, Dan, Matthias, and Volker met Jeff Struecker, a former U.S. Army Ranger, author, and part of the *Black Hawk Down* story.

In Switzerland for a *Band of Brothers* reenactment event in 2018. In front of a photo of Don Malarkey, from left to right: Matthias, Volker, emcee Christoph Scheidegger, Marianne, her husband Dan McNally, and Samuel Kullmann, interpreter. *Courtesy of Birgit Lehmann*

After the Engelbert–Malarkey story was shared in front of the hundred people in attendance, Struecker told them, "I was gripped by this story. You need to write a book."

Afterword

When I (Bob Welch) asked the two sons of Fritz Engelbert and the youngest daughter of Don Malarkey what their fathers' friendship has taught them, they pointed to three things: peace, family, and forgiveness. Since they are the ones charged with carrying on their fathers' legacies, I asked them to offer readers some parting words on the subjects.

Peace

We (Marianne, Volker, and I) enjoy a privilege that our fathers Don and Fritz did not have. We were born in times of peace—seven, eleven, and nineteen years, respectively, after the end of World War II. At least, peace in the places where the three of us grew up: North America and Europe.

Our dads showed us the value of peace. Don fought for peace and saw many of his comrades sacrifice their lives for it. Fritz was indoctrinated to go to war against peaceful neighboring countries, but toward the end he wished for nothing more than peace.

After World War II, our fathers weren't able to find peace within. The horrors of war haunted them all their lives. We, on the other hand, enjoyed being raised in times of love, peace, friends, music, sports, hobbies, and opportunities to do (almost) whatever we wanted. We could go to school without fearing for our lives, we were entitled to learn whatever we wanted. We were allowed to learn foreign languages, travel to foreign countries, discover other cultures, and make friends abroad.

Of four generations of our family, Volker and I were the first to travel to neighboring countries such as Belgium, Denmark, France, Luxembourg, and the Netherlands without entering "enemy territory" in times of war. Our great-grandfather had fought against France in 1870–1871, our grandfather Fritz Sr. fought in France during World War I, and our father, Fritz, fought in France, Belgium, and Germany in World War II.

As Fritz's sons, we were presented with the gift of peace without even asking for it. We took it for granted. But by watching our fathers suffer and crave for what we already had, we came to see peace in a new light. We came to cherish the peace of our times.

Though we could not undo what Fritz and Don had gone through during the war, we could ease their minds and help them on their quests for peace. In the end, we virtually reversed the relationship between parents and their children: our fathers let us take their hands and guide them to places they would not have dared to go alone. But Don and Fritz were the ones with the courage to actually build this relationship with each other, a relationship that has taught us so much.

Matthias , Marianne, and Volker at the bridge at Remagen, Germany, in 2019. *Courtesy of Beate Engelbert*

Our helping them was a wonderful way of giving back the love we have savored since our childhood days. In the process, they helped us, broadened our perspectives, and inspired us to carry on their example.

I offer my deepest thanks to Don and Fritz. Seeing them embrace and find their "peace at last" has enriched our lives in so many ways. With Marianne, her family, and the extended Easy Company family, we will continue to honor our fathers by celebrating—and promoting—the precious peace that our fathers taught us never to take for granted.

—*Matthias Engelbert*

Family

When I was growing up in the fifties and sixties, the fathers of my two closest friends had fought for Germany in Russia. I grew up hearing that the Eastern Front, not the Western Front where my father had fought, was where the "real war" had taken place. In some ways, I felt as if my father, Fritz, had experienced "war lite." He wasn't cool like my friends' fathers.

But I no longer believe that the measure of a man is his fighting experiences—and that's the perspective of someone who has served in the German army and would fight for my country if my country were attacked. Don and Fritz taught me the more significant value not only of peace, but of family.

Of individual families, yes, but also of the universal family. What nationality we are and what color uniform we wear and what kind of leaders our country has are less significant than how we treat each other as human beings.

I'm not sure I would have understood this without the lessons of Don and Fritz. When I first heard of my father being invited to the gathering with Easy Company soldiers, I never dreamed it would turn into the positive thing it did: healing for these two vets and a whole "new family" for Matthias and me.

It's amazing what can happen when people are simply nice to each other. Dan and Marianne inviting us to Portland for the Easy Company reunion in 2017 was like nothing I could have ever imagined. You must understand that Germany has never had the sense of "family" that the United States has. While visiting countries that Germany fought against in World War II, I've had people look at my German license plate and spit at my feet.

With that in my past, can you imagine what it felt like to be in a roomful of relatives of Easy Company soldiers applauding my brother and me when we were introduced in 2017?

These people became our third "new family." First, we watched Don and Fritz create a sort of two-person family. Second, Matthias, Beate, and my family were so warmly accepted by Marianne and Dan and their families. And, finally, we were welcomed into the Easy Company family—by people whose fathers fought against our father.

I must admit I had an uncertain feeling when we were on the way to the room where all the Americans were celebrating. How would they react? Did they like the idea of Germans being around? Would we disturb the celebration? But we had such a warmhearted and welcoming reception. It was overwhelming. All was good.

In Germany we say that Americans are uncomplicated, friendly, and hospitable. And that's exactly what we found. We had such a wonderful time. And in the end, when Buck Compton's daughter, Tracy Compton, said, "Welcome to the family," I was touched and proud.

Meanwhile, Marianne is like the little sister Matthias and I never had—and, Dan, her husband, like another brother. We love them both.

And it all began with our fathers, Fritz and Don, who taught us that the power of family transcends all sorts of barriers, making us stronger as individuals and as countries. I only hope that I can show the same kind of love to others that these Americans have shown to us.

—*Volker Engelbert*

Forgiveness

Psychologists define forgiveness as a conscious, deliberate decision to release feelings of resentment or vengeance toward a person or group—someone who has harmed you, regardless of whether they actually deserve your forgiveness or not. Forgiveness does not mean forgetting, nor does it mean condoning or excusing offenses.

Forgiveness is used every day of our lives. And though you would think it would be almost impossible to forgive a nation for killing our sons and daughters, *Saving My Enemy* speaks to just that: Americans forgiving Germans and Germans forgiving Americans.

Some find forgiveness quickly, some take decades, some never do. But carrying resentment for a lifetime is hard work; it takes a toll on your body.

I don't believe Don and Fritz carried resentment toward each other's nations for long after World War II ended. Instead, they were searching for forgiveness—whether in a glass of scotch, in an obsession with work, or in just checking out of life now and then.

When our country calls on us to protect it, fight for it, and kill others in the process, we do it. We don't think, *How will this make me feel?*

Don and Fritz served their countries. And they didn't ask that question. Nobody did—perhaps because nobody wanted to hear the truth. No one was prepared to handle the effects of war. Men of that generation didn't believe in talking about their feelings.

No matter how forgiveness starts for us, all that matters is that we start the process. Don and Fritz did so in their own way and own time. For them, the beginning was their first meeting in 2004 and their offering each other forgiveness on that second night. Not only did they offer it, but they accepted each other's forgiveness.

That's the other step to the process, acceptance. That doesn't mean forgetting or condoning what you did or what happened. World War II happened; it's *there*. But that doesn't mean we let what we did hold us prisoner our entire lives. In Bastogne in 2004, with only a few words, with a toast, these men forgave each other.

At the end, these men embraced each other in hugs that you don't typically see from men of their generation. This was everything to them, to us, their children. We knew this was forgiveness at its deepest level. They understood each other. We witnessed it, and our smiles told the story—and, I hope, continue to tell the story.

Volker, Matthias, and I will carry this forward. If our fathers can forgive, so can we—not just for this moment in our history, but in everyday life. We have vowed never to take forgiveness for granted, to accept it, cherish it, and practice it by being kind to others—in honor of our fathers, who showed us how.

—*Marianne McNally*

Acknowledgments

Bob Welch

I owe many debts of gratitude, including to:

Sally Welch, whose patience and encouragement helped me make my usual "Mad Hatter" sprint to the finish line on this one. And who did an incredible job playing host to Matthias, Beate, Volker, Marianne, and Dan in August 2019. How cool to have Volker—a guy who grew up in a seventeenth-century inn and knows *real history!*—ask permission to photograph her antiques and quilts!

Jeff Struecker, author and former U.S. Army Ranger, who spent time with the Engelberts and McNallys in Switzerland and convinced me that this was an amazing story that needed telling.

Ron Palmer, whose expertise on the Battle of the Bulge—and five-pound books about it—answered questions for me time and again.

Ann Petersen, whose deft editing once again saved me from myself—and who taught me the proper use of the word "imbue." And who laughed when I tried to justify my writing "serve serve" instead of "serve" by telling her it was simply the tennis equivalent of a double fault. That said, I take responsibility for any errors.

Clarice Wilsey, who, as I was working on her book *Letters from Dachau: A Father's Witness of War, a Daughter's Dream of Peace*, was understanding of my need to also work on *Saving My Enemy*. And who prayed for our success.

My grandfather, Ben Schumacher—whose father was born in Heidelberg, Germany—and his wife, Gayle, for their generosity in passing down an Oregon coast beach cabin, where much of this book was written.

Dale Shank, a buddy of Don's from the Cue Ball, for insights about a man who was different from him but with whom he shared a special friendship.

Greg Johnson, my agent with WordServe Literary, for believing in the story and finding a buyer for the manuscript. And Regnery Publishing, for being that buyer.

St. Martin's Press and editor Marc Resnick, who published and edited my original book on Don Malarkey, *Easy Company Soldier*, and gave me the opportunity to know and understand Don at a deep level.

Easy Company historian Joe Muccia, for his meticulous read of the manuscript and for having a better understanding of this group of men than perhaps anyone else on earth.

Fritz's granddaughters—Julia, Eva, and Elina—who, within twenty-four hours of my request, had offered me great insight on a man whom they loved deeply but could also see objectively.

Members of the Malarkey extended family, who answered a seemingly unending list of questions from me: Don's daughters, Sharon Hill and Martha Serean; son-in-law, John Hill; granddaughters, Sarah Malarkey Johnson, Haley Hill, and Erin McNally; and grandsons, Tim Serean, Matthew Malarkey, Patrick Malarkey, Kyle McNally, Nathan Hill, Carson Hill, and Tom Serean.

To the memory of Michael Malarkey, a man whom I met only briefly before his passing but who, as a victim of "friendly fire," reminds us that the victims of war stretch far and wide. And that they, too, should never be forgotten.

Finally, to Matthias Engelbert, Volker Engelbert, Marianne McNally, and Dan McNally, who helped create what was one of the richest journalistic experiences of my life. Without complaint—and with much-needed humor—they answered literally hundreds of questions about their fathers; dug up photos, letters, and miscellaneous info from the past time and again; trusted me; encouraged me; and simply could not have been better partners in a story that became so close to all of our hearts.

In Germany, Matthias and Volker became my informational tooth fairies; I would email them a ton of questions just before going to bed—about the time they were waking up—and in the morning, presto, I'd awaken to find the answers. Marianne and Dan had the vision to see this story's potential, the patience not to "write me off" when I didn't fall immediately in love with it; and the trust in me to lead the project.

Finally, all four of these "Don-and-Fritz-kids" had the courage to let me—a flawed author—paint their fathers as the flawed men they were in real life, which, I believe, only made their own lives all the more honorable, their friendship all the more genuine, and their story all the more compelling.

All of these people deserve, and have, my deepest thanks.

Marianne

Dan, thank you for going on this journey with me, standing beside me, challenging me to be better, and calming me during the storm. You are my Christopher Robin: "You're braver than you believe, stronger than you seem, and smarter than you think." Thank you for loving us and giving us your all. I love you!

Kyle and Erin, thank you for your understanding why I missed activities and times with you because of caring for Grandpa. You have taught me about living life to the fullest, doing what makes you happy, and unconditional love. I continue to grow into a better person because of you. Grandpa and Grandma loved you and were so proud of you. Carry on the stories when I am gone; pass them on to your children. Never let them be forgotten. I love you to the moon and back!

Dennis Trune, if, at a Normandy museum, you had not stopped to talk to the reenactors who were dressed as American World War II 101st Airborne Soldiers but were speaking Swiss German, this book would not have happened. I am forever grateful to you.

Andreas Reinhard and the Swiss Band of Brothers, I am grateful that I was the one who could speak to your Band of Brothers Switzerland reenactors. Our time with you, your family, and all the men in your company was life-changing for Dan and me. I was so proud and honored to be with your group on the seventy-fifth anniversary of D-Day. It was a powerful moment in my life. We love you!

Jeff Struecker, thank you for planting the seed, in Switzerland, to write a book. Now here we are in full bloom. Thank you for your service to our country; we are honored to know you!

Martha, Sharon, John, and all my nieces and nephews, thank you for encouraging me to do this and letting me share more family stories. I hope this book makes you proud. Looking back at pictures, thinking back about family stories, does prove that we had—and have—a rich life. Family is everything. I love you!

Michael and Mom, thank you for being our angels, for watching over us from heaven. You are the wind beneath my wings. We are deep in a dream of you. Love you always.

Ellen and family, my exchange student–Dutch sister, your parents' love and respect for my dad was one of my first experiences of understanding exactly what my dad did during the war. *Ik hou van jou!*

Christelle Zuccolotto and Charles de Vallavieille, your passion for World War II history is unmatched. Thank you, Christelle, for teaching the stories of the men in your classroom. Charles, Brécourt Manor—where you once lived—will always be a memorable place for us. Thanks for keeping history alive at the Utah Beach Museum. Thank you both for your love and friendship. *Je t'aime.*

Makos family, thank you for everything Valor Studios has done for my dad over the years. He admired your passion for World War II. You are an "A" Class family.

McNally family, you knew my dad when he was just "my dad." You have helped me through some tough times with him and I appreciate your tenderness, attention, and guidance. Love to you all!

The Cue Ball crew (Jim, Dale, Henry, Leonard, and Terry), thank you for giving my dad your love, making him laugh, and listening to his stories. Jim, I know I still need to pay you your babysitting wages. Dale, thank you for continuing to check in on me. Your friendship is priceless.

Joe Muccia, thank you for being our Easy Company historian. Your input was invaluable. Hang tough!

Easy Company family, thank you for your years of friendship with our family. We will continue to honor Easy Company. Our reunions are the highlight of the year for me. Thank you for making the Portland reunion one for the books! *Currahee!*

Bob and Sally Welch, thank you for making our story come to life. Thank you Sally, a.k.a. "She Who Puts Up with Bob," for opening your house to us all, decorating it with German and American flags, supplying endless nutrients to keep us going, and creating a cozy space outside on a beautiful summer day for us to work. Love you both!

Dad and Fritz, thank you for showing us how to forgive. We will continue your legacy and work towards a world with no more wars. Thank you for zig-zagging, for giving us life, and for your perseverance. Love you!

Finally, my German brothers—when I think about us, the vision of the *Wizard of Oz* comes to mind. Matthias is the Scarecrow: positive nature, a happy-go-lucky personality, someone that you can't help but love and adore. Volker is the Cowardly Lion: larger than life, courageous, and protective. I am, of course, Dorothy. I have asked you to follow me on the yellow brick road. It's 2021, and we are arriving at the emerald gates. We are together, arm in arm! *Ich liebe euch!*

A postscript: I am sure I have forgotten to thank some people. There are people from around the world who have made a difference in my dad's life. You know who you are. Thank you from the bottom of my heart. I am humbled by all who loved my dad.

Matthias

Thank you to my wife, Beate, my dearest friend of forty-two years, for always being there when I need her, never letting me down when coping with the challenges of our family life and with Fritz's wartime experiences. I feel blessed to have you by my side—and proud to see how far we have come together!

Volker

Thank you to my wife, Irene, for listening to all the stories and sharing them and being with me at the reunions.

And to my kids, Julia, Eva, and Elina, for listening so many times to all the stories and offering their feedback.

Matthias and Volker

Our deepest thanks to:

Waltraud Menn from Hilchenbach, Germany, for contributing many details about Fritz and Hilchenbach in former times.

Armin Meisel from Leipzig, Germany, for contributing information about the times of imprisonment in Laon, France, and for his life-long friendship with Fritz.

Pastor Volker Bäumer from Kredenbach, Germany, for his empathetic and affecting funeral speech that deeply touched our family and helped us cope with our loss by celebrating Fritz's life.

Esther Reyter and her family (especially her kids Monique and Joseph Nicolas) and friends from Marvie, Belgium, for reaching out their hands and reconciling with Fritz and our family.

Alice and Tom Lewinsohn from Overland Park, Kansas, for their forgiveness and the friendship between our families.

Billy Maloney from Illesheim, Germany, for all his efforts to bring together American and German veterans; without him, Don and Fritz never would have met, and this story could not have been written.

Hans Wijers from Brummen, Netherlands, for all his research and writing about the Ardennes Offensive and for interviewing and bringing together surviving witnesses of the fights, such as Don and Fritz.

The Makos family (Adam, Bryan, Bob, and Erica) from Denver, Colorado, for their support and sponsorship and promotion of trips of veterans and reunions between former enemies.

Thank you, Bob and Sally Welch, for receiving us in your beautiful home as if we were your German ancestors! Bob, it was an incredible journey you've taken us on, often connected by common soundtrack in our heads: on "The Long and Winding Road," humming "Carry On,"

"Teach Your Children," and "Imagine." Thank you for believing in the story of our dads, Don and Fritz, and for writing this wonderful, compelling book.

From the bottom of our hearts: Thank you, Marianne and Dan, for your friendship and for making this book possible. Marianne, your energy and motivation were the motor to get this book project running. You, your dad, and your family have presented us with so many unforgettable, wonderful moments that have changed our lives forever. We love you!

Source Notes

Saving My Enemy was written after Don Malarkey and Fritz Engelbert had died. However, each man had shared extensively about his life, particularly his time in World War II, in his later years. Just as significantly, each was blessed with adult children who not only knew their father's stories but became part of those stories. Who witnessed Don and Fritz's friendship bloom and grow. Who took photographs, asked questions, and jotted notes.

Having grown up with the men, they had also witnessed the fallout from their fathers' war-related PTSD. Don's three daughters remember their father's drinking episodes. Fritz's two sons remember their father's breakdowns at family gatherings. Thus, the bulk of the information for Don and Fritz's story came from spoken and written accounts by the two men themselves and their families.

Don Malarkey shared the nuances of war with Stephen Ambrose for the historian's 1992 book *Band of Brothers*. He dug far deeper into his foibles and fears as a human being in his 2008 memoir, *Easy Company Soldier*. As his coauthor, I interviewed him more than a dozen times over a three-month period—resulting in 320 pages of single-spaced typed notes—so I came to understand him at a fairly deep level.

Before I began writing this book, one of my concerns was that Fritz might get lost in Don's shadow because I knew so much about Malarkey—because everybody knew so much about Malarkey. But that was before Matthias and Volker Engelbert started translating dozens of Fritz's letters from German to English and writing down the stories he had told, including his "I'd-rather-hang-myself" moment. Before they interviewed Waltraud Menn, ninety-six, a childhood friend of their father's. Before they spoke to Armin Meisel, who was a fellow POW with Fritz in Laon. And before Matthias interviewed Sergeant 1st Class Billy Maloney about the attack in Iraq while he was on the phone with Earl McClung and about Maloney's orchestrating the event in Hammersbach at which Don and Fritz met.

Matthias dug out more than a hundred photos of his father, maps of where he'd been in the war, poems he had hung on the wall—a treasure trove of information that helped me, as the writer, really understand the man. He culled through 302 letters that Fritz had written home to his parents between 1943 and 1947 and transcribed 80, from about half of which we gleaned valuable information.

In addition, between Matthias, Volker, Marianne, and me, we went through more than five hundred photos to find information that might help us tell their fathers' stories.

Beyond that, it helped immensely that Fritz had done numerous interviews with Dutch journalist Hans Wijers, had been interviewed by the History Channel for the 2006 program *The Lost Evidence*, and had written of his experiences himself, including a detailed chronology of his war service that he shared at his eightieth birthday party in Marvie.

This book is actually weighted a bit toward Fritz in terms of "pages devoted to." That's appropriate, I believe, because most readers will understand lots about the American part in the war, but little about the German part. And, of course, Fritz's childhood will help readers understand not only him but the country that—for better or worse—molded him.

At its core, *Saving My Enemy* is about seeing, and accepting, people different from us, and Matthias and Volker did a herculean job of helping me understand the evolution of their father in that regard. I also thought sprinkling the German language in the book would give it authenticity, which the two brothers helped with immensely. Both speak German and English.

As I began writing *Saving My Enemy*, I was finishing up another World War II book, *Letters from Dachau*, about an army doctor who served heroically in the war but suffered terrible PTSD. So I had already deeply immersed myself in the subject of war and its emotional effects on those who fight it. I'm particularly indebted to Edward Tick, whose *War and the Soul: Healing Our Nation's Veterans from Post-traumatic Stress Disorder* shines light on a subject left far too long in the dark.

While Don and Fritz's childhoods and times at war are critical to the story, I believe the strength of their story is the battle they returned to at home: with themselves. Their struggles to leave the memories behind. And their friendship that finally helped them make peace with those painful memories. The fact that more than half the book covers the postwar years of their lives underscores the theme of this book, which is less about conflict than about compassion.

Being a native Oregonian—and knowing a bit about Don's childhood home of Astoria—helped me understand the context in which he grew up. (Even though I never found a fitting place in the book for a favorite fun fact: Don's Sigma Nu fraternity house would later be used in the filming of the 1978 comedy *Animal House*.) However, I didn't know Germany. I needed Volker and Matthias to help me understand the cultural context in which their father grew up. And they did. In fourteen months of working on the book, I received 757 emails from the two brothers.

When they and Matthias's wife, Beate, came to Oregon in August 2019, I peppered them and Marianne with more than a hundred questions, in addition to the nearly two hundred I had already sent to the three of them and other family members. Little did I know that I was only beginning to understand Don and Fritz.

Don and Fritz became who they were in part because of their childhoods. Most of the information on Don's growing up came directly from him; he had told me about his childhood of individual freedom and adventure in 2007. Much of the information about Fritz's childhood of institutional coercion is based on written accounts of Hitler Youth.

Susan Campbell Bartoletti's *Hitler Youth: Growing Up in Hitler's Shadow* was a particularly good source on this subject because her "storytellers" were peers of Fritz Engelbert, people who were roughly his same age and served in Hitler Youth at the same time he did. Conversations that Fritz had with Matthias and Volker confirmed that his experience was similar.

The cold war between father and son was as icy as I describe. And his blind acceptance that "Seligmann the Jew" was suspicious and a deterrent for Germany becoming great again was straight from the Hitler Youth culture in which Fritz was immersed.

Part of what made this story so appealing to me was the willingness of Matthias, Volker, and Marianne not to sugarcoat it. Their fathers were imperfect men caught up in the cultural milieus of their respective countries. Both men were flawed. But that's what made their bond so powerful and beautiful—the unlikeliness of its happening in the first place.

After the *Band of Brothers* HBO series was released in 2001, Marianne served as Don's manager. She set up his travel, flew to Europe with him, arranged for him to give speeches, took him to TV interviews, helped him answer mail, the works. She has heard just about every question that could possibly be asked about Don Malarkey. And when she heard one she didn't know the answer to, she would ask her father and find another piece of the puzzle.

Marianne has attended more than twenty Easy Company reunions and come to know the men with whom her father had shared foxholes. She was with him in the spotlight when the *Band of Brothers* miniseries premiered, and she was with him in the shadows when, as a dementia-wracked man, he told a chaplain that he thought he deserved to go to hell for all the German soldiers he'd killed. Nobody knew Don Malarkey better than Marianne McNally.

What these amazing sources of information have allowed me to do is tell a story that breaks new ground and asks questions that are rarely asked: What can war teach us about peace? Why do nations devote so much time, money, and energy to prepare soldiers for war and so little to help them heal once the war is over? And when will we begin to respect a power even greater than physical force: the power of forgiveness?

—*Bob Welch*

Notes

Epigraph

1. Dietrich Bonhoeffer, *The Cost of Discipleship* (New York: Touchstone, 1995), 147.

Chapter 2: Dueling Loyalties

1. Susan Campbell Bartoletti, *Hitler Youth: Growing Up in Hitler's Shadow* (New York: Scholastic Focus, 2005), 145.
2. Anne Kratzer, "Harsh Nazi Parenting Guidelines May Still Affect German Children of Today," *Scientific American Mind*, January 4, 2019, https://www.scientificamerican.com/article/harsh-nazi-parenting-guidelines-may-still-affect-german-children-of-today1/.

Chapter 4: Into Battle

1. S. Hart, R. Hart, and M. Hughes, *The German Soldier in World War II* (London: Amber Books, 2000), 8.

2. Nearly fifty years later, Winters would confirm in a letter that it was Malarkey's telling this story to *Band of Brothers* author Stephen Ambrose in a 1991 interview that led to the movie *Saving Private Ryan*. Ed Niland, it turned out, had not been killed. Instead, he was imprisoned in a Japanese POW camp in Burma for a year. He was released on May 4, 1945.

Part III: Home
1. Erich Maria Remarque, *All Quiet on the Western Front* (New York: Ballantine, 1958), 87.

Chapter 9: Reckoning Up the Damage
1. Edgar Taylor, "Karl Katz: A Mystery Solved," regarding a story from *German Popular Stories and Fairy Tales*, https://bit.ly/3iGP9ZJ.

Part IV: Absolution
1. Eric Lomax, *The Railway Man: A POW's Searing Account of War, Brutality and Forgiveness* (New York: W. W. Norton & Company, 1995), 286.

Part V: Legacy
1. *Ion*, trans. Robert Potter, in *Euripides, The Complete Greek Drama*, 2 vols., ed. Whitney J. Oates and Eugene O'Neill (New York: Random House, 1938), 136.

Chapter 16: New Connections
1. Edward Tick, *War and the Soul: Healing Our Nation's Veterans from Post-Traumatic Stress Disorder* (Wheaton, Illinois: Quest Books, 2005), 237.

Bibliography

Ambrose, Stephen E. *Band of Brothers*. New York: Simon & Schuster, 1992.

Barris, Ted. *Rush to Danger: Medics in the Line of Fire*. Toronto: HarperCollins Publisher Ltd., 2019.

Bartoletti, Susan Campbell. *Hitler Youth: Growing Up in Hitler's Shadow*. New York: Scholastic Inc., 2005.

Childers, Thomas. *Soldier from the War Returning: The Greatest Generation's Troubled Homecoming from World War II*. New York: Houghton Mifflin Harcourt, 2009.

Collins, Michael and Martin King. *Voices of the Bulge: Untold Stories from Veterans of the Battle of the Bulge*. Minneapolis, Minnesota: Zenith Press, 2011.

Cowdrey, Albert E. *Fighting for Life: American Military Medicine in World War II*. New York: The Free Press, 1994.

Engelmann, Bert. *In Hitler's Germany: Everyday Life in the Third Reich*. New York: Schocken Books, 1986.

Fritz, Stephen G. *Frontsoldaten: The German Soldier in World War II*. Lexington, Kentucky: The University Press of Kentucky, 1995.

Guarnere, William "Wild Bill" and Edward "Babe" Heffron with Robyn Post. *Brothers in Battle, Best of Friends*. New York: Caliber, 2007.

Hart, S., R. Hart, and M. Hughes. *The German Soldier in World War II*. London: Amber Books, 2000.

Hedges, Chris. *War Is a Force That Gives Us Meaning*. New York: Anchor Books, 2003.

Hoyt, Edwin P. *The GI's War: American Soldiers in Europe During World War II*. New York: Cooper Square Press, 2000.

Krug, Nora. *Belonging: A German Reckons with History and Home*. New York: Scribner, 2018.

Linderman, Gerald F. *The World within War: America's Combat Experience in World War II*. New York: The Free Press, 1997.

Malarkey, Don with Bob Welch. *Easy Company Soldier: The Legendary Battles of a Sergeant from World War II's "Band of Brothers."* New York: St. Martin's Press, 2008.

Marshall, Samuel Lyman Atwood. *Bastogne—The First Eight Days*. Washington, D.C.: Infantry Journal Press, 1946.

Murphy, Audie. *To Hell and Back*. New York, Picador, 1949.

Obmascik, Mark. *The Storm on Our Shores: One Island, Two Soldiers, and the Forgotten Battle of World War II.* New York: Atria Books, 2019.

Patton, George S. *War as I Knew It.* New York: Houghton Mifflin Company, 1947.

Remarque, Erich Maria. *All Quiet on the Western Front.* New York: Little Brown and Company, 1929. New York: Fawcett Crest, 1958.

Rempel, Gerhard. *Hitler's Children: The Hitler Youth and the SS.* Chapel Hill, North Carolina: The University of North Carolina Press, 1989.

Schrijvers, Peter. *Those Who Hold Bastogne: The True Story of the Soldiers and Civilians Who Fought in the Biggest Battle of the Bulge.* New Haven, Connecticut: Yale University Press, 2014.

Spielvogel, Jackson. *Hitler and Nazi. Germany: A History.* Upper Saddle River, New Jersey: Prentice Hall, 1996.

Tick, Edward. *War and the Soul: Healing Our Nation's Veterans from Post-Traumatic Stress Disorder.* Wheaton, Illinois: Quest Books, 2005.

Time Capsule 1932. New York: Time-Life Books, 1968.

Welch, Bob. *American Nightingale: The Story of Frances Slanger, Forgotten Heroine of Normandy.* New York: Atria Books, 2004.

Wijers, Hans. *Battle of the Bulge Volume 1: The Losheim Gap/Holding the Line.* Mechanicsburg, Pennsylvania: Stackpole Books, 2009.

Wilt, Alan F. *The Atlantic Wall: Hitler's Defenses for D-Day.* New York: Enigma Books, 2004.

Index